Introduction to Generative Syntax

Introduction to Generative Syntax

By

Muteb A. Alqarni

BRILL

LEIDEN | BOSTON

Library of Congress Cataloging-in-Publication Data

Names: Qarnī, Mutʿab, author.
Title: Introduction to generative syntax / Muteb A. Alqarni.
Description: Leiden ; Boston : Brill, 2020. | Includes bibliographical references and index.
Identifiers: LCCN 2020027158 | ISBN 9789004427150 (paperback)
Subjects: LCSH: Grammar, Comparative and general–Syntax. | Generative grammar.
Classification: LCC P291 .Q37 2020 | DDC 425.01/822–dc23
LC record available at https://lccn.loc.gov/2020027158

Typeface for the Latin, Greek, and Cyrillic scripts: "Brill". See and download: brill.com/brill-typeface.

ISBN 978-90-04-42715-0 (paperback)

Copyright 2020 by Koninklijke Brill NV, Leiden, The Netherlands.
Koninklijke Brill NV incorporates the imprints Brill, Brill Hes & De Graaf, Brill Nijhoff, Brill Rodopi, Brill Sense, Hotei Publishing, mentis Verlag, Verlag Ferdinand Schöningh and Wilhelm Fink Verlag.
All rights reserved. No part of this publication may be reproduced, translated, stored in a retrieval system, or transmitted in any form or by any means, electronic, mechanical, photocopying, recording or otherwise, without prior written permission from the publisher. Requests for re-use and/or translations must be addressed to Koninklijke Brill NV via brill.com or copyright.com.

This book is printed on acid-free paper and produced in a sustainable manner.

Contents

Acknowledgements XIII
To the Teacher XIV

SECTION 1
Lexicon

Unit 1   Language I   3
Unit 2   Language II   4
Unit 3   Grammaticality I   5
Unit 4   Grammaticality II   6
Unit 5   Lexical vs. Functional Categories   7
Unit 6   Lexical Categories   8
Unit 7   Functional Categories   9
Unit 8   Categorization I   10
Unit 9   Categorization II   11
Unit 10   Categorization III   12
Unit 11   Categorization IV   13
Unit 12   Categorization V   14
Unit 13   Categorization VI   15
Unit 14   Categorization VII   16
Unit 15   Categorization VIII   17

SECTION 2
Phrase Structure

Unit 16   Heads   21
Unit 17   Specifiers   22
Unit 18   Complements   23
Unit 19   Complement Selection I   24
Unit 20   Complement Selection II   25
Unit 21   Adjunct I   26
Unit 22   Adjunct II   27
Unit 23   Summary   28
Unit 24   Constituency   29
Unit 25   Stand-Alone Test   30
Unit 26   Substitution Test   31
Unit 27   Displacement Test   32
Unit 28   Coordination Test   33

SECTION 3
Phrase Structure Rules

Unit 29   Basics I   37
Unit 30   Basics II   38
Unit 31   Noun Phrase I   39

Unit 32	Noun Phrase II	40
Unit 33	Random Phrases	41
Unit 34	Verb Phrase I	42
Unit 35	Verb Phrase II	43
Unit 36	Sentence I	44
Unit 37	Sentence II	45
Unit 38	Complementizer	46
Unit 39	Conjunction	47
Unit 40	Adjunction	48
Unit 41	Summary I	49
Unit 42	Summary II	50

SECTION 4
Tree Structure

Unit 43	Representation	53
Unit 44	Nodes and Branches	54
Unit 45	Dominance	55
Unit 46	Precedence	56
Unit 47	Noun Phrases	57
Unit 48	Random Phrases	58
Unit 49	Verb Phrases	59
Unit 50	Sentences	60
Unit 51	Complementizer Phrases	61
Unit 52	Conjunction Phrases	62
Unit 53	Adjoined Phrases	63
Unit 54	Tree Drawing I	64
Unit 55	Tree Drawing II	65
Unit 56	Tree Drawing III	66
Unit 57	Ambiguity	67

SECTION 5
X-Bar Theory

Unit 58	Motivation I	71
Unit 59	Motivation II	72
Unit 60	Motivation III	73
Unit 61	Motivation IV	74
Unit 62	Motivation V	75
Unit 63	Motivation VI	76
Unit 64	Motivation VII	77
Unit 65	Motivation VIII	78
Unit 66	Motivation IX	79
Unit 67	Representation I	80
Unit 68	Representation II	81
Unit 69	Representation III	82
Unit 70	NP, AP, PP, AdvP, VP	83
Unit 71	TP and CP	84
Unit 72	Adjunction Rules I	85

Unit 73	Adjunction Rules II	86
Unit 74	Determiner Phrase I	87
Unit 75	Determiner Phrase II	88
Unit 76	Determiner Phrase III	89
Unit 77	Determiner Phrase IV	90
Unit 78	Determiner Phrase V	91
Unit 79	Determiner Phrase VI	92
Unit 80	Determiner Phrase VII	93
Unit 81	Complementizer Phrase I	94
Unit 82	Complementizer Phrase II	95
Unit 83	Complementizer Phrase III	96
Unit 84	Auxiliaries and Modals I	97
Unit 85	Auxiliaries and Modals II	98

SECTION 6
Transformations

Unit 86	Yes/No Questions I	101
Unit 87	Yes/No Questions II	102
Unit 88	Yes/No Questions III	103
Unit 89	Yes/No Questions IV	104
Unit 90	Yes/No Questions V	105
Unit 91	Yes/No Questions VI	106
Unit 92	Principles I	107
Unit 93	Principles II	108
Unit 94	Principles III	109
Unit 95	Principles IV	110
Unit 96	Principles V	111
Unit 97	Principles VI	112
Unit 98	Negation Movement I	113
Unit 99	Negation Movement II	114
Unit 100	Verb Movement I	115
Unit 101	Verb Movement II	116
Unit 102	Tense Markers I	117
Unit 103	Tense Markers II	118
Unit 104	Affix Hopping I	119
Unit 105	Affix Hopping II	120
Unit 106	Wh-Questions I	121
Unit 107	Wh-Questions II	122
Unit 108	Wh-Questions III	123
Unit 109	Wh-Questions IV	124
Unit 110	Wh-Questions V	125
Unit 111	Wh-Questions VI	126
Unit 112	Wh-Questions VII	127
Unit 113	Adjunction Revisited I	128
Unit 114	Adjunction Revisited II	129
Unit 115	Topicalization I	130
Unit 116	Topicalization II	131

SECTION 7
Theta Theory

Unit 117	Thematic Roles I	135
Unit 118	Thematic Roles II	136
Unit 119	Thematic Roles III	137
Unit 120	Thematic Roles IV	138
Unit 121	Thematic Roles V	139
Unit 122	Thematic Roles VI	140
Unit 123	Thematic Roles VII	141
Unit 124	Thematic Roles VIII	142
Unit 125	Subject Condition I	143
Unit 126	Subject Condition II	144
Unit 127	Subject Condition III	145
Unit 128	Subject Condition IV	146
Unit 129	Subject Condition V	147
Unit 130	Subject Condition VI	148
Unit 131	Subject Condition VII	149
Unit 132	Passive I	150
Unit 133	Passive II	151
Unit 134	Passive III	152
Unit 135	A- and A'-movement I	153
Unit 136	A- and A'-movement II	154
Unit 137	Summary	155

SECTION 8
Constraints on Movements

Unit 138	PBC I	159
Unit 139	PBC II	160
Unit 140	PBC III	161
Unit 141	Locality I	162
Unit 142	Locality II	163
Unit 143	Subjacency I	164
Unit 144	Subjacency II	165
Unit 145	Islands I	166
Unit 146	Islands II	167
Unit 147	Islands III	168
Unit 148	Islands IV	169
Unit 149	Islands V	170
Unit 150	Islands VI	171
Unit 151	Summary	172

SECTION 9
Government and Binding Theory

Unit 152	Case Markers I	175
Unit 153	Case Markers II	176
Unit 154	Case Markers III	177

Unit 155	Case Assignment I	178
Unit 156	Case Assignment II	179
Unit 157	Case Assignment III	180
Unit 158	Case Assignment IV	181
Unit 159	Case Checking I	182
Unit 160	Case Checking II	183
Unit 161	Exceptional Case Marking I	184
Unit 162	Exceptional Case Marking II	185
Unit 163	Exceptional Case Marking III	186
Unit 164	Exceptional Case Marking IV	187
Unit 165	Exceptional Case Marking V	188
Unit 166	Exceptional Case Marking VI	189
Unit 167	Exceptional Case Marking VII	190
Unit 168	Unaccusative I	191
Unit 169	Unaccusative II	192
Unit 170	Unaccusative III	193
Unit 171	Binding Theory I	194
Unit 172	Binding Theory II	195
Unit 173	Binding Theory III	196
Unit 174	Binding Theory IV	197
Unit 175	Binding Theory V	198
Unit 176	Binding Theory VI	199

SECTION 10
Advanced Topics

Unit 177	Raising I	203
Unit 178	Raising II	204
Unit 179	Raising III	205
Unit 180	Raising IV	206
Unit 181	Raising V	207
Unit 182	Raising VI	208
Unit 183	Control Theory I	209
Unit 184	Control Theory II	210
Unit 185	Control Theory III	211
Unit 186	Control Theory IV	212
Unit 187	Control Theory V	213
Unit 188	Control Theory VI	214
Unit 189	Control Theory VII	215
Unit 190	Control Theory VIII	216
Unit 191	Control Theory IX	217
Unit 192	Control Theory X	218
Unit 193	Control Theory XI	219
Unit 194	Control Theory XII	220
Unit 195	Control Theory XIII	221
Unit 196	Raising vs. Control I	222
Unit 197	Raising vs. Control II	223
Unit 198	ECM vs. Control I	224
Unit 199	ECM vs. Control II	225

SECTION 11
Split Projections

Unit 200	Split DP Hypothesis I	229
Unit 201	Split DP Hypothesis II	230
Unit 202	Split DP Hypothesis III	231
Unit 203	Split DP Hypothesis IV	232
Unit 204	Split VP Hypothesis I	233
Unit 205	Split VP Hypothesis II	234
Unit 206	Split VP Hypothesis III	235
Unit 207	Split VP Hypothesis IV	236
Unit 208	Split VP Hypothesis V	237
Unit 209	Split VP Hypothesis VI	238
Unit 210	Split TP Hypothesis I	239
Unit 211	Split TP Hypothesis II	240
Unit 212	Split TP Hypothesis III	241
Unit 213	Split CP Hypothesis I	242
Unit 214	Split CP Hypothesis II	243
Unit 215	Split CP Hypothesis III	244

SECTION 12
Minimalist Program

Unit 216	Introduction	247
Unit 217	Feature Checking I	248
Unit 218	Feature Checking II	249
Unit 219	Feature Checking III	250
Unit 220	Feature Checking IV	251
Unit 221	Feature Checking V	252
Unit 222	Feature Checking VI	253
Unit 223	Category Features	254
Unit 224	Subcategorization Features I	255
Unit 225	Subcategorization Features II	256
Unit 226	Subcategorization Features III	257
Unit 227	Subcategorization Features IV	258
Unit 228	Feature-Driven Movements I	259
Unit 229	Feature-Driven Movements II	260
Unit 230	Feature-Driven Movements III	261
Unit 231	Feature-Driven Movements IV	262
Unit 232	Feature-Driven Movements V	263
Unit 233	Feature-Driven Movements VI	264
Unit 234	Feature-Driven Movements VII	265
Unit 235	Feature-Driven Movements VIII	266
Unit 236	Feature-Driven Movements IX	267
Unit 237	Agreement and Case I	268
Unit 238	Agreement and Case II	269
Unit 239	Agreement and Case III	270
Unit 240	Agreement and Case IV	271
Unit 241	Agreement and Case V	272
Unit 242	Phases I	273

Unit 243	Phases II	274
Unit 244	Phases III	275
Unit 245	Copy Theory I	276
Unit 246	Copy Theory II	277
Unit 247	Bare Phrase Structure I	278
Unit 248	Bare Phrase Structure II	279
Unit 249	Bare Phrase Structure III	280
Unit 250	Bare Phrase Structure IV	281

Exercises 283
Glossary 294
References 296
Index 299

Acknowledgements

This book would not have been written if I had not had the chance to study under Eric Potsdam, Professor of Syntax at the University of Florida (UF). Prof. Potsdam taught me two courses (Syntax and Issues in Syntax) during my PhD studies at UF and I learned a lot from his lectures, slides, handouts and assignments, as well as his direct supervision of my dissertation titled "The Morphosyntax of Numeral-Noun Constructions in Modern Standard Arabic". I am thankful for every minute he shared his expertise with me, whether in class or in his office. I benefited from his clear argumentation and professional presentation, and that aided me in producing this textbook. Prof. Potsdam is not responsible for any errors in this book as he did not have the opportunity to view or review it. I am also grateful to Erich Beer for proofreading and editing this manuscript. As a typical disclaimer, all errors are my own.

To the Teacher

"Introduction to Generative Syntax" is an introductory textbook that aims to address the topics commonly encountered in the study of syntax in a more engaging, problem-solving manner. The textbook consists of 12 broad topics, broken down into 250 units. These topics include Lexicon, Phrase Structure Rules, X'-Theory, Transformational Grammar, Theta Theory, Government and Binding Theory, Raising and Control, Movement Constraints, Split Projections and the Minimalist Program. The topics progress from simple through complex to advanced.

The textbook begins with an introduction to the field of linguistics, and stresses the need for developing a syntactic theory for a given language. It introduces students to the different types of sentences, such as grammatical, ungrammatical, standard, non-standard, ambiguous, anomalous etc. Given that language consists of lexicon and grammar, the first section (units 1–15) familiarizes students with the basic components of the lexicon, such as the words' parts of speech. These units provide students with three diagnostic tests from semantics, morphology and syntax to help them determine a word's lexical category.

After students become acquainted with words and their lexical or functional categories, they move on to Section 2 (units 16–28) to learn about the other component of language, namely grammar. In these units, students learn how phrases are constructed out of words, and they explore the syntactic view that phrases consist of obligatory heads, optional specifiers, and obligatory or optional complements. In units 19–25, complement selection is discussed, and four tests are proposed to differentiate between complements and adjuncts. In units 24–28, the most important grammatical concept in syntax, namely constituency, is introduced. These units familiarize students with four diagnostic tests (stand-alone, substitution, displacement or coordination) to determine whether a phrase is a constituent or not.

The third section (units 29–42) deals with the structure of phrases. This section provides an introduction to the various kinds of phrases, such as noun phrases, verb phrases, adjective phrases, tense phrases (i.e. sentences) etc. It develops a rule-based system (syntax) that generates an infinite number of phrases and sentences. Section 4 (units 43–57) aims at teaching students how to represent the information discussed in the earlier three sections in graphic formats, such as brackets or trees. In these units, basic concepts in syntax—such as dominance, precedence and structural ambiguity—are discussed in detail.

In the fifth section (58–85), X'-Theory is motivated, and all the information learned in the former sections are re-projected according to the X'-theory scheme. In these units, noun phrases are redefined as determiner phrases, and problems associated with complementizer phrases are further discussed. Additionally, the position of modals and auxiliaries in the sentence structures is discussed and identified to prepare students for the next section on transformational grammar. Section 6 (units 86–116) on transformational grammar is devoted to the Principles and Parameters framework, and seeks to familiarize students with the apparatus that transposes elements from one position to another, as in yes/no questions, wh-questions, verb movement, affix hopping and topicalization. During the discussion of these topics, syntactic principles such as Deep Structure, Surface Structure, the Structure Preservation Principle, Projection Principle, Recoverability Principle, Inclusiveness Principle etc. are discussed and motivated.

The seventh section (units 117–137) presents Theta Theory, and teaches students the thematic roles that the arguments in the structure may play. Students are familiarized with the principles of theta role assignment, and the issues that arise from the violation of the Extended Projection Principle (EPP). They learn more about the Subject Condition, Expletive Insertion, Passive Structure and A- and A'-movements. Section 8 (units 138–151) deals with the constraints imposed on syntactic movements, such as Head Movement Constraint, Proper Binding Condition, No Extraction Constraint, Subjacency etc. These units acquaint students with the structural islands from which elements cannot be extracted, such as Left Branch Island, Coordinate Structure Island, Complex Noun Phrase Island etc.

The ninth section (units 152–176) is dedicated to the Government and Binding Theory framework, which consists of two parts: (i) government and (ii) binding. In the first part (units 152–170), students learn about the principles of government, c-command and m-command. They are familiarized with Case and Exceptional Case Marking, as well as the two approaches to license case on arguments, namely case assignment and checking. The other part of this section (units 171–174) is devoted to the three principles of Binding Theory.

In the tenth section (units 177–199), the differences between raising and control constructions are discussed at great length. Section 11 (units 200–215) deals with issues that arise from languages other than English, and motivates split analyses, where determiner phrases, tense phrases, and complementizer phrases etc. are expanded into different layers.

The final section (units 216–250) focuses on the Minimalist Program. This section aims to keep students up to date with the most recent developments in syntactic theory, such as the types of features (interpretable and uninterpretable), and the Agree approach that manipulates feature checking. In units 224–236 of this section, students learn how to cast subcategorization, movement and agreement in a feature-based model. Phase Theory, Copy Theory and Bare Phrase Structure are introduced in units 242–250. In these final units, students are familiarized with the two most basic operations for structure derivation: Merge and Move.

The body of the text is followed by exercises for further practice. These exercises are meant to consolidate what has been learned in the previous units, and are best attempted as the units they are based on are completed.

SECTION 1

Lexicon

∵

UNIT 1

Language I

Language

Language is a means of communication that delivers and receives spoken, written or sign messages. The scientific study of human language is called **LINGUISTICS**. Linguistics has three branches aiming to analyze the properties of (i) sounds, (ii) meanings and (iii) grammars in all the languages of the world.

I. *Sounds in Language*
   – **PHONETICS** studies the articulatory, auditory and acoustic properties of sounds.
   – **PHONOLOGY** focuses on the patterns and systematic organization of sounds.
II. *Meanings in Language*
   – **SEMANTICS** examines the denotations of words, phrases and sentences.
   – **PRAGMATICS** is concerned with the correlation between meaning and context.
III. *Grammars in Language*
   – **MORPHOLOGY** is the study of words and their constituent parts (i.e. morphemes).
   – **SYNTAX** is concerned with the structure of phrases and sentences.

Properties of Human Language

Human language differs from non-human languages in two main respects: (i) **PRODUCTIVITY** and (ii) **DISPLACEMENT**. As for productivity, humans can use a finite number of rules to produce an infinite number of words, phrases and sentences. For instance, words such as *Khalid, Ahmed, hit(s), and,* and *Ali* can produce six possible sentences, all of which are different in meaning.

1. *Ahmed hits Ali and Khalid*
2. *Khalid hits Ali and Ahmed*
3. *Ali hits Khalid and Ahmed*
4. *Ahmed and Khalid hit Ali*
5. *Ali and Ahmed hit Khalid*
6. *Khalid and Ali hit Ahmed*

Other creatures' languages are not productive in the above sense since animals have a fixed set of expressions for communication. Concerning the property of displacement, humans can discuss matters at any time and in any place. In other words, they can communicate about issues happening now, issues that happened in the past, and issues that will happen in the future. They can discuss concrete or abstract things, such as *tables* or *love*, and things that are close at hand or farther removed, such as *this book in front of me* or *other books in the library*. As for animal communication, it "seems to be designed exclusively for this moment, here and now. It cannot effectively be used to relate events that are far removed in time and place" (Yule, 2010:12).

UNIT 2

Language II

Morphology vs. Syntax

To develop a linguistic theory, we should bear in mind that every human language consists of two components: (i) **LEXICON** (a language's inventory or dictionary that contains morphemes and words) and (ii) **GRAMMAR** (a rule-based system that creates phrases and sentences).

While **MORPHOLOGY** (i.e. the study of morphemes/words) draws on the lexicon, **SYNTAX** (i.e. the study of phrases/sentences) is concerned with grammar. Thus, both morphology and syntax have rules: (i) **MORPHOLOGICAL RULES** that construct words out of morphemes and (ii) **SYNTACTIC RULES** that construct sentences out of phrases.

Morphology

In morphology, a fixed set of rules constructs words from smaller units called **MORPHEMES**. Morphemes are meaningful units of language that cannot be further divided, such as *-ing, come, un-* etc. The lexicon may contain random morphemes such as those in (1).

1. ive, ion, de, ate, act *(random morphemes)*

Using certain morphological rules, these random morphemes in (1) can be arranged and organized into a well-formed word such as the one in (2).

2. de+act+ive+at(e)+ion *(a well-formed word)*

Syntax

Syntax is the study of phrases and sentences (statements or questions). A set of syntactic rules is used to build phrases and sentences out of the words already constructed by using the morphological rules mentioned above. The lexicon may contain random built-up words as in (3).

3. the, early, sleep, kids. *(random words)*

The words in (3) belong to different parts of speech: *early* (adverb), *sleep* (verb), *kids* (noun), and *the* (determiner). Syntax uses rules to arrange these random words in (3) to generate a statement as follows: it puts the determiner *the* before the noun *kids*, and the newly formed phrase *the kids* is positioned before the verb *sleep*. The adverb *early* is added at the end. This process generates (4) out of (3).

4. The kids sleep early. *(a well-formed statement)*

UNIT 3

Grammaticality 1

Grammatical vs. Ungrammatical Sentences

The current book aims to develop a syntax (a rule-based system) that generates grammatical sentences and at the same time does not generate ungrammatical sentences, but how can we determine whether a sentence is grammatical or not? In English, as in any other languages, sentences can be either **GRAMMATICAL** or **UNGRAMMATICAL**. If a sentence is grammatical in English, it means that it is legitimate and acceptable to a native English speaker as in (1). If a sentence is ungrammatical, it is unacceptable to a native English speaker as in (2). Ungrammatical sentences like (2) are conventionally marked with an asterisk (*).

1. John drove his car.
2. *Her husband are serving a three-year sentence in jail.

Under certain circumstances, it is not easy to determine the grammaticality of a sentence. For example, native English speakers may not agree on whether sentence (3) below is grammatical or not. Such disputable sentences are written with a preceding question mark (?).

3. ?To succeed, the guy plans.

Standard vs. Non-standard Sentences

Grammatical sentences can be **STANDARD** or **NON-STANDARD**. Standard sentences are ideal and correct to all English speakers as in (1) above. In contrast, non-standard sentences are correct only to a group of English speakers who share a unique variety of English, such as African American Vernacular English. Sentence (4), for instance, is a non-standard yet grammatical sentence.

4. I been bought it. (cf. African American Vernacular English)

Given that English varieties and vernaculars are rule-governed versions of English, their sentences can be non-standard but still grammatical. Therefore, in our development of a syntactic theory, we need an inclusive and encompassing system capable of generating non-standard sentences as well.

Anomalous Sentences

Among the grammatical sentences that our syntax should generate are **ANOMALOUS** sentences, which are grammatically correct but semantically strange. Due to their semantic peculiarities, anomalous sentences as in (5) are conventionally written with an exclamation mark (!).

5. !This fish drove its car.

UNIT 4

Grammaticality II

Ambiguous Sentences

Our syntax should also generate grammatical sentences that are **AMBIGUOUS**. Ambiguous sentences have two or more possible meanings, and they can be (i) **LEXICALLY AMBIGUOUS** sentences or (ii) **STRUCTURALLY AMBIGUOUS** sentences.

Lexically Ambiguous Sentences

Lexically ambiguous sentences are sentences involving polysemous words. In such sentences, ambiguity resides in the words of the sentence as in (1).

1.   We decided to meet at the bank.

In (1), the word *the bank* is ambiguous because it may mean (i) the financial institution where people deposit or withdraw money, or (ii) the river's side. Syntax should generate lexically ambiguous sentences easily because it handles ambiguous words as units irrespective of their meanings. More lexically ambiguous sentences from headlines are given below.

2.   Iraqi heads seek arms.
3.   Stolen paintings found by tree.

Structurally Ambiguous Sentences

A structurally ambiguous sentence appears when the structure of a sentence (i.e. the rearrangement of its phrases) leads to different meanings as in (4) below.

4.   Fatima saw the man with the binoculars.

Sentence (4) has two meanings. By the reordering of the phrase *with the binoculars*, we can illustrate the two meanings in (5) and (6).

5.   Fatima [saw with the binoculars] the man.
6.   Fatima saw [the man with the binoculars].

In (5), Fatima used the binoculars and saw the man. In (6), Fatima saw the man who was carrying the binoculars with him. In the following units, we will learn how our syntax generates structurally ambiguous sentences, and represents their meanings in different structural positions. More structurally ambiguous sentences from headlines are given below.

7.   Two sisters reunited after 18 years in checkout counter.
8.   New housing for elderly not yet dead.

UNIT 5

Lexical vs. Functional Categories

Lexicon

To summarize, the goal of this book is to develop a syntax that generates only grammatical sentences, be they standard, non-standard, anomalous, or ambiguous. Given that sentences are made up of words, let us first consider the properties of words. For the purposes of syntax, it is crucial to establish whether a word is a noun, verb or determiner etc. You will recall that the first component of human language is **LEXICON**. The lexicon is the language's inventory of **LEXEMES** or **LEXICAL ITEMS** (i.e. words). Because there are many words in any given language, we need to group or categorize them into different **SYNTACTIC CATEGORIES**. 'Syntactic categories' is another term for 'parts of speech'. Thus, English syntactic categories may include nouns (N), verbs (V), adjectives (A), adverbs (Adv), determiners (D), auxiliaries (Aux), conjunctions (Conj) etc. These syntactic categories can be subdivided into two types: (i) **LEXICAL CATEGORIES** and (ii) **FUNCTIONAL CATEGORIES**. The distinction between lexical and functional categories depends on two criteria: (i) *semantics* (whether a word in a given category bears meaningful content or not) and (ii) *neologism* (whether we can add a new word to a given category or not).

1. Semantics (Meaning vs. Function)
    i. If a syntactic category expresses essential and indispensable content in a sentence, it is deemed to be a lexical category. Nouns, adjectives and verbs are said to be lexical categories because *man* (N), *smart* (A) and *believe* (V) have clear and important meanings in the sentence. Without lexical categories, sentences would be meaningless.
    ii. If a syntactic category, on the other hand, has a grammatical function, and its meaning is less important, it is considered to be a functional category. Determiners, auxiliaries and conjunctions are said to be functional categories because *an* (D), *would* (Aux) and *or* (Conj) are less meaningful. They only appear to express grammatical functions.
2. Neologism (Open vs. Closed)
    i. If a syntactic category is an open class, i.e. if we can add a neologism (i.e. a newly coined word) to it, it is a lexical category. Thus, we say that nouns, adjectives and adverbs are lexical categories because we can add newly invented words to these categories: *facebook* (N), *snapchatty* (A) and *googled* (V).
    ii. If a syntactic category is a closed class, i.e. if we cannot add a newly coined word to it, it is a functional category. Thus, we say that determiners, auxiliaries and conjunctions are functional categories because we cannot add new words to the sets of determiners, auxiliaries and conjunctions. There is a fixed number of determiners, auxiliaries and conjunctions in English.

UNIT 6

Lexical Categories

Lexicon

In light of the two criteria (semantics and neologism) discussed earlier, it is now easy to determine whether a word belongs to a lexical or functional category. Given that **LEXICAL CATEGORIES** are meaningful, and we can add new words to them, we can conclude that the lexical categories in English are **NOUNS** (N), **VERBS** (V), **ADJECTIVES** (A), **ADVERBS** (Adv), **PRONOUNS** (Pron) and **PREPOSITIONS** (P). All these parts of speech bear important meaningful messages in sentences, and most of them are open classes. You may have noticed that pronouns and prepositions are closed classes because we have a fixed number of them. Does this mean that they are truly functional categories? This is debatable. Although pronouns and prepositions are closed classes, syntacticians classify them as lexical categories because pronouns are as meaningful as nouns (*man = he, women = she, cat = it* etc.) and prepositions are as meaningful as adverbs (*highly = up, closely = near,* etc.). Consider the lexical categories with their examples in the table below.

Lexical categories	Examples
Nouns (N)	
common nouns	*Man, woman, pen, book, city, country etc.*
proper nouns	*Ahmed, Fatima, John, Jennifer, Jack etc.*
abstract nouns	*Truth, danger, time, love, humor, fun, etc.*
Verbs (V)	
intransitive (no object)	*Come, sleep, leave, arrive, go, lie, etc.*
transitive (one object)	*Hit (it), put (it), find (it), grab (it), etc.*
ditransitive (two objects)	*Give (him a pen), pass (him the ball), mail (him letters)*
Adjectives (A)	*Smart, big, red, circular, afraid, etc.*
Adverbs (Adv)	*Quickly, rapidly, silently, differently, etc.*
Pronouns (Pron)	*I, he, she, it, they, you, we, us, him, them, etc.*
Prepositions (Prep)	*In, at, above, below, around, near, by, etc.*

UNIT 7

Functional Categories

Functional Categories

FUNCTIONAL CATEGORIES are characterized as functional because they have grammatical functions rather than lexical contents. Thus, they are also known as **NON-LEXICAL CATEGORIES** (i.e. the opposite of lexical categories). They include **DETERMINERS** (D), **TENSE WORDS** (T), **COMPLEMENTIZERS** (C), **AUXILIARIES** (Aux), **CONJUNCTIONS** (Conj), **DEGREE WORDS** (Deg) and **NEGATION WORDS** (Neg). Although the meaning of lexical categories is easy to capture, it is harder for a speaker to apprehend the meaning of functional categories. For instance, the meaning of lexical categories such as *man* (N) and *eat* (V) is much more conceivable than the meaning of the functional categories *the* (D) and *would* (Aux). Consider the closed functional categories with their examples in the table below.

Functional categories	Examples
Determiner (D)	Determiners usually precede nouns.
Articles	*a, an, the*
Demonstratives	*this, that, these, those*
Quantifiers	*some, many, most, few, every, all, each*
Numerals	*one, two, three, four, five, etc.*
Possessive Pron	*my, your, his, her, its, their, our*
Wh-words	*what, which, whose, e.g. what question*
Tense words (T)	Tense-related words usually precede verbs.
Auxiliaries	*is, am, are, was, were, has, have, had, do, did, does*
Modals	*can, shall, will, may, could, should, would, might*
Infinitival *to*	*to, e.g. I want to read.*
Complementizers (C)	Complementizers precede sentences.
Complementizer	*that, if, whether, for*
	e.g. *I believed that someone would come.*
Degree words (Deg)	*so, too, more, very, quite, rather etc.*
Conjunctions (Conj)	*and, or, but, nor*
Negation words (Neg)	*not*

UNIT 8

Categorization 1

Lexical Category Identification

Because functional categories are closed classes, we can easily memorize them and determine their categories: whether they are D, T, C, Deg, Conj or Neg. However, lexical categories are open classes. We continually come across new words; these new words need to be categorized, i.e. they need to be identified as N, V, A, P or Adv. Sometimes, a word belongs to more than one lexical category. Consider the examples in (1) and (2) below.

1. a. Business is going **well**. [adverb]
   b. All is **well** with us. [adjective]
   c. The **well** was drilled fifty meters deep. [noun]
   d. Tears **well** up in my eyes. [verb]

2. a. Give me a **round** figure. [adjective]
   b. Shall we play another **round** of cards? [noun]
   c. He had a look **round**. [adverb]
   d. They walked **round** the tree. [preposition]
   e. The floor function **rounds** down. [verb]

In (1), the word *well* can be categorized as Adv, A, N, or V. In (2), the word *round* fits five possible lexical categories: A, N, Adv, P, or V. Because of these difficulties, syntacticians have proposed tests that help in determining whether a word is N, V, A or Adv. In (1) and (2), the lexical categories of *well* and *round* are determined by many factors, two of which are 'what morphemes (i.e. morphological inflections) do they bear?' and 'what words precede and follow them?' (i.e. syntactic distribution). The determination of the lexical category of a given word is known as **CATEGORIZATION**. In the coming units, we will learn a step-by-step mechanism that helps in word categorization.

Criteria of Categorization

Each word carries (i) phonological, (ii) semantic, (iii) morphological and (iv) syntactic information. When we learn a word, we are concerned with the way it is pronounced (phonology), interpreted (semantics), and inflected (morphology), and the way it is distributed in phrases and sentences (syntax). Each category has a special set of phonological, semantic, morphological and syntactic properties, so there are correspondingly four possible criteria in determining the lexical category of a given word. Phonology (how a word sounds) alone does not reveal to speakers whether a word is N, V, A, P or Adv. For example, the pronunciation of *hound* as /haʊnd/ does not provide conclusive evidence that the word *hound* is a noun. The same applies to semantics, although the latter is more efficient than phonology in identifying lexical categories. Morphology and syntax are the best determiners of lexical categories: what affixes a word bears (i.e. its morphology) and what word precedes and follows it (i.e. its syntax) reveal a great deal about a word's lexical category.

UNIT 9

Categorization II

Semantics

Semantics is the first criterion in categorization. Every lexical category (N, V, A or Adv) may have a special and common denotation. For example, most nouns may refer to persons (individuals), things (objects) and places (locations) as in (1) below. Thus, one could be led to conclude that any words that pertain to individuals, objects, and locations are predictably nouns. However, this test is not foolproof because abstract nouns such as *love* and *idea* are not persons, things or places, yet they are still nouns.

1. | **nouns** | examples |
    |---|---|
    | persons (individuals) | *Ahmed, Fatima, Mary, John, etc.* |
    | things (objects) | *table, chair, door, car, etc.* |
    | places (locations) | *school, market, park, hospital, etc.* |

As for verbs, it is well-known that they designate actions, sensations, states and occurrences as in (2) below. Thus, any word that relates to these semantic properties may arguably be a verb. Yet, this test is not infallible either. Actions are not exclusive to verbs; there are nouns denoting actions such as *a push, a hit, a run, a jump*, etc.

2. | **verbs** | examples |
    |---|---|
    | actions | *push, hit, run, jump, etc.* |
    | sensations | *feel, hear, see, smell, etc.* |
    | states | *be, become, remain, etc.* |
    | occurrences | *happen, come, leave, etc.* |

As for adjectives and adverbs, they typically express the attributes of nouns and verbs respectively. Adjectives modify persons, things or places (i.e. nouns) as in (3) below, while adverbs modify actions, sensations, states, and occurrences (i.e. verbs) as in (4).

3. | **adjectives** | examples |
    |---|---|
    | properties of persons (individuals) | *smart, clever, stupid, successful, etc.* |
    | properties of things (objects) | *short, tall, big, small, circular, etc.* |
    | properties of places (locations) | *far, close, away, etc.* |

4. | **adverbs** | examples |
    |---|---|
    | properties of actions | *quickly, slowly, gradually, steadily, etc.* |
    | properties of sensations | *suddenly, abruptly, unexpectedly etc.* |
    | properties of states | *well, badly, truly, nearly, etc.* |
    | properties of occurrences | *always, never, rarely, seldom, etc.* |

Yet, these tests are not wholly reliable either due to the above-mentioned difficulties related to nouns and verbs. In short, semantics alone is not enough for word categorization.

UNIT 10

Categorization III

Morphology

Although semantics is a problematic criterion, morphology is less problematic and more efficient in determining the lexical category of a word. With the aid of morphology, we can identify the lexical category of a word based on the word's position in relation to its neighboring morphemes/affixes. Morphemes can be exclusive to certain lexical categories. For instance, *-ment* is a nominal suffix, and most words that bear this suffix are nouns. We will term the word's position with respect to its morphemes its **MORPHOLOGICAL CONTEXT**, i.e. the morphological environment in which a given word occurs.

Derivational vs. Inflectional Morphemes

There are two types of morphemes: (i) **DERIVATIONAL** and (ii) **INFLECTIONAL**. Derivational morphemes are affixes added to words resulting in changing their lexical categories into different ones. The derivational morphemes in **bold** in (1) through (6) reveal what lexical category each word belongs to.

	Lexical category	Rule change	Lexical category
1.	suit (V)	V → A	suit-**able** (A)
2.	act (V)	V → N	act-**ion** (N)
3.	faith (N)	N → A	faith-**ful** (A)
4.	hospital (N)	N → V	hospital-**ize** (V)
5.	black (A)	A → V	black-**en** (V)
6.	quick (A)	A → Adv	quick-**ly** (Adv)

In light of (1) through (6), one may conclude that words that bear *-able* and *-full* are adjectives, words ending in *-ion* are nouns, words carrying *-ize* and *-en* are verbs, and words with *-ly* are adverbs. This is a desirable conclusion. As for inflectional morphemes, i.e. the eight suffixes in (7) through (14), they differ from derivational morphemes in that they do not convert a word from one category into another. However, like derivational morphemes, they are helpful in revealing words' categories. For example, words suffixed with *-s* are nouns, words bearing *-er/-est* are adjectives, and words ending with *-s, -ed, -ing, -en* are verbs.

	Inflectional morpheme	Category	Category (no change)
7.	plural -s	book (N)	book**s** (N)
8.	possessive 's	John (N)	John**'s** (N)
9.	comparative -er	smart (A)	smart**er** (A)
10.	superlative -est	smart (A)	smart**est** (A)
11.	3rd sg present tense -s	they sleep (V)	he sleep**s** (V)
12.	past tense -ed	happen (V)	happen**ed** (V)
13.	progressive tense -ing	happen (V)	happen**ing** (V)
14.	past participle -en	take (V)	tak**en** (V)

UNIT 11

Categorization IV

Nouns

Let us investigate more morphemes that are specific to certain categories. For example, one can conclude that a word is a noun if it takes one of the following derivational morphemes in blue. These morphemes are exclusively added to nouns:

realiz**ation**, protec**tion**, happ**iness**, stupid**ity**, govern**ment**, friend**ship**, typ**ist**, defend**ant**, employ**ee**, brother**hood**, terror**ism** etc.

However, some derivational/inflectional morphemes are not exclusive to nouns as in (1) below. These morphemes need to be carefully interpreted because they look similar to other morphemes related to other categories. The section 'Be careful!' in (1) illustrates these difficulties, although it can be ignored for the sake of simplicity and for teaching purposes.

1. **N- morphemes**   **Examples:**   **Be careful!**
   plural -s   books/bags   present tense -s (e.g. *hits*)
   nominal -er   teacher/helper   comparative -er (e.g. *bigger*)
   nominal -ing   the swimm**ing**   adjectives (e.g. *an interesting question*)
   nominal -al   refus**al**/deni**al**   adjectives (e.g. *normal, vocal, neutral*)

Verbs

As for verbs, one can conclude that a word is a verb if and only if (henceforth iff) it bears one of the following derivational morphemes in blue:

modern**ize**, dead**en**, activ**ate**, **re**think, etc.

Although inflectional morphemes are mostly linked to verbs, similar-looking morphemes can be attached to other categories. Thus, careful interpretation is needed for the verbal morphemes in (2).

2. **V- morphemes**   **Examples:**   **Be careful!**
   3rd sg present -s   he sleep**s**   plural -s (e.g. *balls*)
   past -ed   he wait**ed**   Adjectival -ed (e.g. *a confused student*)
   progressive -ing   he's sleep**ing**   A/N -ing (e.g. *confusing, the swimming*)
   past participle -en   he has tak**en** ...   adjectival -en (e.g. *a stolen car*)
   the negator un-   **un**lock, **un**tie   adjectival un- (e.g. *unhappy*)

It is also noteworthy that verbs do not necessarily bear a morpheme. For examples, irregular verbs are still verbs even though they carry no morphemes, e.g. *ran, came, went, began* etc. This morpheme-less phenomenon is known as **SUPPLETION,** where verbal roots inflect for tense (present/past) by only changing their internal vowels, such as *come-came, run-ran* etc.

UNIT 12

Categorization V

Adjectives

One may conclude that a word is an adjective iff it bears one of the blue morphemes below:

bigg**est** (the superlative), fix**able**, act**ive**, redd**ish**, reck**less**, etc.

Yet, a few morphemes need careful attention as in (1). These morphemes can be added to adjectives, but they can also be attached to other categories.

1. | A- morphemes | Examples: | Be careful! |
    |---|---|---|
    | comparative -er | big**ger**/smart**er** | nominal -er (e.g. *teacher*) |
    | prefix un- | **un**happy/**un**fit | verbal un- (e.g. *unlock*) |
    | -full | faith**ful** | nominal -full (e.g. *a spoonful*) |
    | -ly | friend**ly**/live**ly** | adverbial -ly (e.g. *quickly*) |

Adverbs

One can conclude that a word is an adverb iff it takes the most common adverbial morpheme -ly. Although -ly mostly features in adverbs, it is also attached to adjectives as shown in (2).

2. | Adv- morphemes | Examples: | Be careful! |
    |---|---|---|
    | adverbial -ly | quick**ly**, slow**ly** | adjectival -ly (e.g. *lovely, elderly*) |

The suffix -ly is not essential to mark adverbs either. A few adverbs, such as *work hard, drive slow/fast, stay close* etc., are morpheme-less and known as **FLAT ADVERBS**.

Morphological Contexts

In conclusion, the morphological context of a word (i.e. the morpheme a word bears) can reveal a word's lexical category. We can represent the morphological context in the format set out in (3). The "___" indicates the position where a word occurs.

3. *word*, Lexical Category, [___ + morpheme]

A list of morphological contexts for the lexical categories (N, V, A, Adv) is given below.

4. *word*, N [___ + ation, ness, ity, ment, ship, ant, al, ism, hood, plural -s, er, ing, al]
5. *word*, V [re/un + ___ + ize, en, ate, present -s, past -ed, progressive -ing, participle -en]
6. *word*, A [un+ ___ + comparative -er, superlative -est, able, ive, ish, less, un, full, ly]
7. *word*, Adv [___ + ly]

UNIT 13

Categorization VI

Syntax

When discussing the two earlier criteria of word categorization, we noticed that semantics is more problematic than morphology, which does not escape problems either due to similar-looking morphemes. Syntax—the third criterion—is the least problematic and the most reliable criterion in categorization. We determine the category of a word from a syntactic perspective based on the neighboring words that either precede or follow the word in question. Thus, the test is run based on **SYNTACTIC CONTEXT**, which is the environment where a word occurs. The preceding or following words reveal what category the in-between word belongs to.

Syntactic Positions

One may conclude that a word is a noun iff it occurs in the syntactic positions in (1) below. Though this test may cause some problems, they are not as serious as the morphological ones.

1. | Syntactic positions | Examples | Be careful! |
   |---|---|---|
   | after adjectives | the *big* **book** | Adjectives can! (e.g. *a big red car*) |
   | after a determiner | *a/the/my* **book** | Adjectives can! (e.g. *a big book*) |
   | after prepositions | *at* **home/school** | Determiners can! (e.g. *at the meeting*) |
   | sentence-initially | The **book** *arrives*. | Adverbs can! (e.g. *Suddenly, he stops*) |

One may conclude that a word is a verb iff it occurs in the syntactic environments in (2).

2. | Syntactic positions | Examples | Be careful! |
   |---|---|---|
   | after an auxiliary | *am/is/are* **sleeping** | A/N can! (e.g. *He's brave. He's a man*) |
   | after a modal | *can/may* **come** | Nouns can! (e.g. *Can the student leave?*) |
   | after infinitival 'to' | *want to* **read** | Nouns after Prep *to*! (e.g. *to the market*) |

One may conclude that a word is an adjective iff it occurs in the syntactic contexts in (3).

3. | Syntactic positions | Examples | Be careful! |
   |---|---|---|
   | between D & N | *the* **smart** *man* | ___ |
   | before *than* | **bigger** *than* | ___ |
   | after *less/more/most* | *more* **beautiful** | Nouns can! (e.g. *more/less people*) |

One may conclude that a word is an adverb iff it occurs in the syntactic positions in (4).

4. | Syntactic positions | Examples | Be careful! |
   |---|---|---|
   | before a verb | **quickly** *ran* | Auxiliaries/modals can! (e.g. *is sleeping*) |
   | after a verb | *ran* **quickly** | Nouns can! (e.g. *jumped the fence*) |

UNIT 14

Categorization VII

Syntactic Contexts

The syntactic context of a word can reveal the word's lexical category. We can represent the syntactic context in the format given in (1). The "___" indicates the position where a word occurs.

1. *word*, Lexical Category, [word$_{before}$ + ___ + word$_{after}$]

A list of syntactic contexts for the categories (N, V, A, Adv) is given below.

2. *word*, N [{ determiners / adjectives / prepositions } ___]

3. *word*, V [{ auxiliaries / modals / infinitival *to* } ___]

4. *word*, A [{ determiners / less/more/most } ___ { noun / than }]

5. *word*, Adv [verb ___ verb]

The items between the curly brackets (or braces), i.e. { }, indicate that they may not occur all at once. Each of these items should be considered separately.

Practice

Based on the syntactic contexts above, we can identify the lexical categories of the blue words in (6) through (9) below.

Sentences | Syntactic contexts
6. The landlord prepared a new apartment for them. | *new*, A [D ___ N]
7. The hard test led to all the students' failure. | *test*, N [A ___]
8. The manager has quickly made his decision. | *quickly*, Adv [___ V]
9. We have proposed a new analysis. | *proposed*, V [Aux ___]

UNIT 15

Categorization VIII

Categorization

In summary, categorization (i.e. the identification of the lexical categories or parts of speech of words) is accomplished by means of three criteria: (i) semantics, (ii) morphology and (iii) syntax. It has been observed that semantics is more problematic than morphology which, in turn, is more problematic than syntax. Overall, morphological contexts (the affixes/morphemes a word bears) and syntactic contexts (the words occurring before and after a given word) are the most reliable identifiers of words' lexical categories.

Practice

Let us determine the lexical category of the blue word in the following sentences in light of the information we have discussed in the earlier units. For each answer, we need to provide three pieces of evidence, from semantics, morphology and syntax respectively.

1. The librarian put all the books on the shelves.
   Lexical category: Noun
   Semantics: it is a noun because it denotes a thing (an object).
   Morphological Context: *shelves*, N [___ + plural -*s*]
   Syntactic Context: *shelves*, N [Determiner *the* ___]

2. The kids have taken a driving test.
   Lexical category: Verb
   Semantics: it is a verb because it denotes an action.
   Morphological Context: *taken*, V [___ + past perfect -*en*]
   Syntactic Context: *taken*, V [Auxiliary *have* ___]

3. Those tables are bigger than these ones.
   Lexical category: Adjective
   Semantics: it is an adjective because it denotes a property of an object: *table*.
   Morphological Context: *bigger*, A [___ + comparative -*er*]
   Syntactic Context: *bigger*, A [___ *than*]

4. The actors regularly rehearse the play.
   Lexical category: Adverb
   Semantics: it is an adverb because it denotes a property of an action: *rehearse*.
   Morphological Context: *regularly*, Adv [___ + the adverbial -*ly*]
   Syntactic Context: *regularly*, Adv [___ Verb]

SECTION 2

Phrase Structure

∴

UNIT 16

Heads

Heads

Having discussed the first component of language (i.e. the lexicon: properties of words and their categories), let us turn to grammar (i.e. syntax) and differentiate between a word and a phrase. A phrase is a group of words functioning as a unit.

1. Books arrived. (a word: a noun)
2. The red books about linguistics arrived. (a phrase: a noun phrase)

The noun phrase (NP) *the red books about linguistics* in (2) is simply a composition of several words including the noun (N) *books*. In syntactic theory, every X phrase has to have an obligatory X word. In other words, in every noun phrase, there must be a noun; otherwise it is not NP in the first place. Also, in every verb phrase (VP), adjective phrase (AP), adverb phrase (AdvP) and preposition phrase (PP), there must be a verb (V), an adjective (A), an adverb (Adv) and a preposition (P) respectively. Thus, we can propose the following principle as set out in (3).

3. Every XP must contain X   XP = NP, VP, AP, AdvP, PP, etc.
   X = N, V, A, Adv, P, etc.

Consider the examples (4) through (8).

4. The students read the small books. NP
5. The farmer took a nap. VP
6. The Chelsey team is too strong. AP
7. Students must respond very quickly. AdvP
8. He sleeps at the corner. PP

The blue phrases above are different in category. However, each phrase contains an important word of its kind. In (4), the noun *books* is very important in the NP *the small books*. In (5) through (8), *took* (V), *strong* (A), *quickly* (Adv) and *at* (P) are important words in VP, AP, AdvP and PP respectively. If all these important words are completely removed from the phrases, the sentences become ungrammatical. Compare (4) to (8) with (9) to (13).

9. *The students read the small. NP
10. *The farmer a nap. VP
11. *The Chelsey team is too. AP
12. *Students must respond very. AdvP
13. *He sleeps the corner. PP

All the sentences in the last group are ungrammatical because the blue phrases lack important words. In syntactic theory, we call these important words **HEADS**. Heads determine the lexical category of the whole phrase, and every phrase must have a head of its own kind.

UNIT 17

Specifiers

Specifiers

Any phrase can be a composition of an obligatory element (i.e. head) and other optional elements. The head of a phrase is an essential word that determines the category of that phrase. Let us focus on the left-hand elements of the head in each of the following phrases.

1.	The students read **the small** books.	NP
2.	The farmer **almost** took a nap.	VP
3.	The Chelsey team is **too** strong.	AP
4.	Students must respond **very** quickly.	AdvP
5.	We will meet **right** at the corner.	PP

The left-hand elements in **bold** in (1) through (5) express semantic content. In (1), the determiner *the* and the adjective *small* add specific meanings to the head noun *books*; the determiner makes *books* definite and specific, and the adjective *small* specifies its size. In (2), the adverb *almost* adds to the head verb a specific meaning, giving the process of *taking a nap* a connotation of near-completion. In (3) and (4), the degree words *too* and *very* add affirmative meanings to the head adjective *strong* and the head adverb *quickly* respectively. In (5), the degree word *right* determines the location of the preposition *at* with more precision. All these left-hand words add specific meanings to the heads. Thus, we term them **SPECIFIERS** (cf. specify+er). Specifiers are also known as **MODIFIERS** because they modify heads of phrases. Below is a list of possible specifiers/modifiers for N/V/A/Adv/P heads.

XP	Specifier	Head
NP	Determiners/Adjectives, e.g. *the, an, small, big* etc.	Noun
VP	Adverbs, e.g. *often, perhaps, never, almost, often*, etc.	Verb
AP	Degree word, e.g. *so, too, very, more, quite*, etc.	Adjective
Adv	Degree word, e.g. *so, too, very, more, quite*, etc.	Adverb
PP	Degree word, e.g. *right*, etc.	Preposition

Specifiers/modifiers in English have two characteristics: (i) they occur to the left of the heads and (ii) they are optional. Even if all of them were removed from the above sentences, the sentences would remain grammatical as in (6) through (10).

6.	The students read books.	NP	(Compare with example 1)
7.	The farmer took a nap.	VP	(Compare with example 2)
8.	Chelsey team is strong.	AP	(Compare with example 3)
9.	Students must respond quickly.	AdvP	(Compare with example 4)
10.	We will meet at the corner.	PP	(Compare with example 5)

Unlike heads, the optionality of specifiers means that any XP phrase can be formed without them.

UNIT 18

Complements

Complements

We found that every X phrase is composed of an obligatory head X and optional specifiers to the left. Let us now focus on the elements to the right of the head in each phrase.

1. We have witnessed the destruction **of the city**. NP
2. John often collects **rare stamps**. VP
3. The boy is very afraid **of the dog**. AP
4. We will meet right at **the corner**. PP

In (1), the noun head is *destruction* followed by PP, i.e. *of the city*. The PP *of the city* completes the meaning of the sentence and gives the reader an idea about the destructed entity. In (2), the verb head *collects* is followed by NP, i.e. *rare stamps*. The NP *rare stamps* also completes the meaning of *collect* (i.e. What does John collect? Rare stamps.). In (3), the head adjective *afraid* is followed by PP, i.e. *of the dog*. The PP *of the dog* is essential in completing the meaning of *afraid* (i.e What is the boy afraid of? The dog.). In (4), the head preposition *at* is followed by NP *the corner*, which completes the information of the location (i.e. Where will we meet? Right at the corner.). Given that all the right-hand elements complete the meaning of heads, we call them **COMPLEMENTS**. Complements are always phrases: PP (after N or A) as in (1) and (3), or NP (after V and P) as in (2) and (4).

Unlike obligatory heads and optional specifiers, complements can be either optional or obligatory. The optionality of complements is determined by the head. The head determines whether it needs an obligatory complement (to ensure the grammaticality of the sentence) or an optional complement (which is rather important but their removal does not make a difference). Let us remove all the complements in **bold** from the examples above.

5. We have witnessed the destruction. NP
6. *John often collects. VP
7. The boy is very afraid. AP
8. *We will meet right at. PP

Based on these results, we can conclude that the complements in (1) and (3) are optional because their removal in (5) and (7) does not disturb the sentential grammaticality. On the other hand, the complements in (2) and (4) are obligatory since their removal, as in (6) and (8), would render the sentences ungrammatical.

To recap, a head is an obligatory element that occurs between a specifier and a complement. A specifier specifies the meaning of the head; it is an optional word occurring to the left of the head. A complement is a phrase (XP) that completes the meaning of the head; it occurs to the right of the head. The head determines whether a complement is optional or obligatory based on its role in the grammaticality of the whole sentence.

UNIT 19

Complement Selection 1

Complement Selection

We have seen that heads **select complements** and determine whether these complements are optional or obligatory. We term this process **COMPLEMENTATION** (or **COMPLEMENT SELECTION**). Complementation can be formulated in the formalism in (1) known as **SUBCATEGORIZATION FRAMES**.

1.   *word*, lexical category [___ complement/XP/(XP)]

In (1), the lexical category can be N, V, A, P, etc. The "___" indicates the position of this head/word. A head is followed by a complement. If a complement XP is optional, we write it between brackets: (XP); if obligatory, it is written without brackets: XP.

Sentences	Subcategorization frames
2. We have witnessed the *destruction* **(of the city).**	*destruction*, N [___ (PP)]
3. John often *collects* **rare stamps.**	*collects*, V [___ NP]
4. The boy is very *afraid* **(of the dog).**	*afraid*, A [___ (PP)]
5. We will meet right *at* **the corner.**	*at*, P [___ NP]

Depending on the head selection of complements, complements are classified as either optional or obligatory. In (2) and (4), they are optional because their presence or absence makes little difference; they are thus written in parentheses. In (3) and (5), they are obligatory because their removal would cause ungrammaticality. Thus, they are written without brackets.

Complex Complement Selection

The complementation of every head (N, V, A, P, etc.) in English needs to be expressed within the formalism in (1). Since a complement is another phrase XP with a separate head X, the head that selects a complement may also select the head of the complement itself.

Sentences	Subcategorization frames
6. *Mary is fond *with* picnics.	
7. Mary is fond *of* picnics.	*fond*, A [___ PP$_{[of]}$]
8. *The family relied *at* the father.	
9. The family relied *on* the father.	*relied*, V [___ PP$_{[on]}$]

In (6), the head adjective *fond* selects a PP-complement but with the incorrect preposition *with*. Thus, (6) is ungrammatical. The head *fond* needs a PP-complement with a head P *of* as in (7). The same applies to (8) and (9), where the head verb *relied* requires that its PP-complement take the head P *on*, not *at*. These requirements can be represented in the subcategorization frames with subscript information written beside the complement XP, e.g. XP$_{[head]}$ as in (7) and (9).

UNIT 20

Complement Selection 11

Complement Selection

As discussed in the earlier unit, heads **select the XP-complement** and determine whether it is optional or obligatory. In certain cases, a head selects the head of its complements. **Subcategorization frames** can represent these selections as in (1).

1. *word*, lexical category [___ XP/XP$_{[word]}$ or (XP)/(XP$_{[word]}$)]

Heads are not limited to selecting one complement only, but may select two complements as well. Some complements are optional because their removal does not change the grammaticality of the sentences. The notation *(word) in the following examples means that the starred and bracketed words cannot be removed.

Sentences/phrases | Subcategorization frames
2. The teacher *gave* *(a prize) *(to the student). | *give*, V [___ NP PP]
3. The teacher *handed* *(the student) *(a prize). | *handed*, V [___ NP NP]
4. The jury *deemed* *(his story) *(controversial) | *deemed*, V [___ NP AP]
5. The parents *bought* *(a car) (for their son). | *bought*, V [___ NP (PP$_{[for]}$)]
6. I *talked* (to the doctor) (about my case) | *talked*, V [___ (PP$_{[to]}$) (PP$_{[about]}$)]
7. He *put* *(the bandage) *(on his wrist). | *put*, V [___ NP PP$_{[on]}$]
8. The driver *opened* *(the door) (with a key). | *opened*, V [___ NP (PP$_{[with]}$)]
9. The *discussion* (of the topic) (with Ali) | *discussion*, N [___(PP$_{[of]}$) (PP$_{[with]}$)]
10. The *description* (of the event) (to the audience) | *description*, N [___(PP$_{[of]}$) (PP$_{[to]}$)]

It should be noted that heads do not always need complements as the following examples show. Heads can appear without complements and the sentences will still be grammatical.

Sentences | Subcategorization frames
11. The manager *came*. | *came*, V [___]
12. The worker *slept*. | *slept*, V [___]
13. We bought a new *car*. | *car*, N [___]
14. The traffic light is *red*. | *red*, A [___]
15. The car broke *down*. | *down*, P [___]

None of the heads in (11) through (15) require complements in order to be meaningful. However, one might argue that these heads may also take complements as shown below.

16. The manager *came* yesterday.
17. The worker *slept* early.

The blue phrases in (16) and (17) are not called complements but **ADJUNCTS**. Adjuncts can be added to any head, and are not needed to complete the meaning of the heads.

UNIT 21

Adjunct 1

Complements vs. Adjuncts

We have seen that not all the phrases that follow heads are complements. They might merely be adjuncts. An adjunct is an optional modifier that adds nonessential information to the head. Whereas complements can be optional and obligatory, adjuncts are always optional. Consider the following examples where both complements and adjuncts can follow a head.

Sentences		Subcategorization frames	Type
1.	Ali *believes* in Allah.	believe, V [___ PP$_{[in]}$]	**Complement**
2.	Ali *slept* in the room.	sleep, V [___]	**Adjunct**
3.	*Ali *believes*.		
4.	Ali *slept*.		

Although the phrases *in Allah* and *in the room* are both PPs, and both follow a verb head, the PP *in Allah* is a complement whereas the other PP *in the room* is an adjunct. The deletion of the PP *in Allah* would render sentence (1) ungrammatical as in (3). Thus, we argue that the PP *in Allah* is a complement and should be included in the subcategorization frame of the verb *believed* as in (1). In contrast, the deletion of the PP *in the room* does not affect the grammaticality of sentence (2). Sentence (4) is grammatical even without the PP *in the room*. This proves that the PP *in the room* is an adjunct. Adjuncts are optional elements which do not need to be included in subcategorization frames. Thus, the subcategorization frame of *slept* in (2) is empty. In light of these differences, we conclude that *in Allah* is a complement (because it is obligatory) and *in the room* is an adjunct (because it is optional).

Although complements can be obligatory as in (1), be reminded that they can be optional as well, making the judgement as to whether an XP is an adjunct or a complement much harder.

Sentences		Subcategorization frames	Type
5.	He *smiles* at his friend.	smiles, V [___ (PP$_{[at]}$)]	**Complement**
6.	He *sleeps* at home.	sleeps, V [___]	**Adjunct**

The PP *at his friend* in (5) is a complement although it is an optional element like the adjunct *at home* in (6). In syntactic theory, several diagnostic tests can differentiate between adjuncts and optional complements. The main distinction can be **SEMANTICS**-based as shown below.

> *Test 1: XP is an adjunct iff it is a modifier of the head, i.e. changing the time or location of the event if it is a head verb. However, complements do not have this semantic function. XP is a complement iff it completes the meaning of the head.*

In (6), the PP *at home* is an adjunct because it is a modifier that specifies the location of the event *sleeping*. In contrast, the PP *at his friends* in (5) is a complement because it only completes the meaning of the verb *smiles*.

UNIT 22

Adjunct II

Complements vs. Adjuncts

We have seen that the phrase that follows a head X may be an adjunct or a complement. Since complements can be optional, we need tests to distinguish them from optional adjuncts as in (1) and (2). In Unit 21, we discussed a **SEMANTICS**-based test.

Sentences	Subcategorization frames	Type
1. He *smiles* at his friend.	*smiles*, V [__ (PP$_{[at]}$)]	Complement
2. He *sleeps* at home.	*Sleeps*, V [__]	Adjunct

A second test for complement-adjunct distinction follows from **SELECTION**:

Test 2: If XP occurs freely with many heads, it is an adjunct. If XP is more restricted and selected by certain heads, it is a complement.

In (2), the PP *at home* is argued to be an adjunct because it can appear with many other verbs such as *worked, studied, read, fought* (*at home*) etc. Because adjuncts can occur freely with many verbs, they are mostly time-place phrases like *yesterday, early, at home* etc. In contrast, the PP *at his friends* in (1) is a complement because it is restricted to a few verbs such as *stared* and *looked*. The PP *at his friend* cannot be added to verbs such as *sleep* as in **sleep at his friends*. Thus, we conclude that the PP *at his friend* is a complement, not an adjunct.

The third test is based on **ORDERING**:

Test 3: Complements must precede adjuncts. XP is a complement iff it cannot follow an adjunct. XP is an adjunct iff it cannot precede a complement.

In (2), for instance, we cannot put the PP-adjunct *at home* before the PP-complement *at his friends*, because adjuncts may not precede complements. This evidence suggests that the PP *at home* is an adjunct as in (3) whereas the PP *at his friend* is a complement as in (4).

3. *He smiled [$_{adjunct}$ at home] [$_{complement}$ at his friends]. (ungrammatical)
4. He smiled [$_{complement}$ at his friends] [$_{adjunct}$ at home]. (grammatical)

Applying these three tests (semantics, selection and ordering), distinguishing between adjuncts and complements is now possible. One more test that distinguishes complements from adjuncts is **ITERATIVITY**. A head can select a maximum of two complements as in (5). In contrast, adjuncts iterate freely; we can have as many as four adjuncts as in (6).

5. Ali gave [$_{NP}$ Ahmed] [$_{NP}$ a pen] *[$_{NP}$ ~~a book~~]. (only two complements are allowed)
6. He *sleeps* [$_{PP}$ in the bed] [$_{PP}$ at home] [$_{PP}$ at 8:00] [$_{PP}$ in most cases]. (All adjuncts)

UNIT 23

Summary

Complement Selection

To determine what a head **selects as a complement** requires more practice, given that some complements are obligatory and others are optional. If optional, more problems ensue, as adjuncts are also optional elements. However, we learned four tests to distinguish complements from adjuncts. Once you identify what complements are selected by a given head, these complements should be put within **subcategorization frames** such as (1) below.

1. word, lexical category [__ XP/XP$_{[word]}$ or (XP)/(XP$_{[word]}$)]

To be able to write the correct subcategorization frames for a given verb, noun, adjective etc., we need more knowledge of the language we work on. We need to list all possible and impossible sentences, including the verb, noun, adjective etc. in question. However, we should avoid adding time-place adjuncts to our compiled list.

Suppose you want to find the appropriate subcategorization frame for the verb *present*. List all the possible and impossible sentences featuring *present* as a verb, but be careful not to add any time-place adjuncts to them such as *at night, at the corner* etc. The list may include the following sentences.

2. *I presented.   *presented* cannot select nothing.
3. I presented prizes.   *presented* must select NP
4. I presented prizes to the winners   *presented* selects NP and also PP$_{[to]}$
5. They presented me with a watch.   *presented* selects NP and also PP$_{[with]}$
6. *I presented to the winners.   *presented* cannot select PP$_{[to]}$ alone.
7. *I presented with a watch.   *presented* cannot select PP$_{[with]}$ alone.
   No more examples.

Thus far, we are sure that we have included all possible and impossible examples for the verb *present* as shown in (2) through (7). It is clear that the verb *present* must select NP as in (2) and (3). The verb *present* cannot select PP alone as in (6) and (7), but it can select optional PP$_{[to]}$ or PP$_{[with]}$ after it obligatorily selects NPs as in (4) and (5). In light of the facts above, we can conclude that the subcategorization frame of the verb *present* is the one in (8).

8. *present*, V [__ NP (PP$_{[to/with]}$)]

The same steps can be followed for other verbs. For instance, the subcategorization frame of the verb *put* illustrated in (9) is based on the facts in (10) through (12).

9. *place*, V [__ NP PP$_{[on/below/around]}$]

10. *I put.
11. *I put plates.
12. I put plates on/below/around the table.

UNIT 24

Constituency

Constituency

In the previous units, we have seen that phrases are compositions of words. Every XP (i.e. NP, VP, PP etc.) typically consists of (i) an optional specifier, (ii) an obligatory head and (iii) (an) obligatory or optional complement(s)—in the given order. These elements (specifiers, heads and complements) make the whole XP function as a **CONSTITUENT**.

A constituent is a group of words that functions as a unit. Consider the following blue constituents in (1) through (3).

1. [NP The student] wrote [NP a wonderful essay] [PP in the class].   CONSTITUENTS
2. The student [VP wrote a wonderful essay] in [NP the class].   CONSTITUENTS
3. The student [VP wrote a wonderful essay in the class].   CONSTITUENT

Our intuitive knowledge of English makes it easy for us to understand why all the bracketed blue phrases above are constituents. Each one of these constituents forms a single unit. In (1), the phrases *the student* and *a wonderful essay* are clearly NPs while the phrase *in the class* is PP. Such phrases are constituents and categorially defined. In (2) and (3), the phrase *the class* is NP while the phrases *wrote a wonderful essay* and *wrote a wonderful essay in the class* are VPs forming separate constituents as well. Consider the non-constituents in (4).

4. The [?P student wrote] a [?P wonderful essay in] the class.   NON-CONSTITUENTS

In (4), the phrases *student wrote* and *wonderful essay in* are not constituents (i.e. they do not function as single units because their words are not related). These phrases do not represent any lexical category; what would be the lexical category of the phrase *student wrote*? NP or VP? What would be the lexical category of the phrase *wonderful essay in*? NP or PP?

Similar to categorization and subcategorization/complementation, constituency is a central tenet in syntactic theory. Since it is important to identify the lexical category of a word and the subcategorization of a head, it is also important to determine whether or not a group of words functions as a single constituent. In Units 8 through 15, we have learned three criteria for categorizing words, namely semantics, morphology and syntax. In Units 19 through 23, we have learned four diagnostic tests that distinguish complements from adjuncts, namely semantics, selection, ordering and iterativity. For constituency, we also have tests that determine whether a group of words is a constituent or not.

5. a. Stand-Alone Test
   b. Substitution Test
   c. Displacement Test
   d. Coordination Test

The four constituency tests above are not always fool-proof; they may lead to an incorrect conclusion. However, the application of these four diagnostic tests all together to a given phrase confirms its constituenthood in a more accurate manner.

UNIT 25

Stand-Alone Test

Stand-Alone Test

To determine whether a group of words is a constituent or not is an important step prior to syntactic analysis. One piece of evidence that a group of words is a constituent follows from the fact that it can stand alone. If a group of words stands alone without grammaticality problems, it is a constituent; if it cannot, it is not a constituent. The **STAND-ALONE TEST** can draw these results because it examines whether or not a sequence of words stands alone as an answer to a question. This test is also known as **ANSWER ELLIPSIS** or **ANSWER FRAGMENT**.

To apply the stand-alone test, a question should be carefully formed in a way that the group of words under investigation becomes an answer to it. If the phrase stands alone as answer to the formed question, it is a consistent. If it cannot stand alone and becomes ungrammatical or awkward, it is not a constituent. In Unit 24, we concluded that the bracketed blue phrases in (1) through (3) were constituents. Let us verify this conclusion by applying the stand-alone test.

1. [$_{NP}$ The student] wrote [$_{NP}$ a wonderful essay] [$_{PP}$ in the class].   CONSTITUENTS
2. The student [$_{VP}$ wrote a wonderful essay] in [$_{NP}$ the class].   CONSTITUENTS
3. The student [$_{VP}$ wrote a wonderful essay in the class].   CONSTITUENT

For each bracketed phrase in (1) through (3), we should create a question to which the phrase in question becomes a well-formed answer. As shown in (4) through (9), all the blue phrases in (1) through (3) can stand alone as answers to their questions. This is taken as evidence that they are actually constituents.

Question: CONSTITUENTS   **Answer: CONSTITUENTS**
4. Who wrote a wonderful essay in the class?   *the student* (e.g. 1)
5. What did the student write in the class?   *a wonderful essay* (e.g. 1)
6. Where did the student write a wonderful essay?   *in the class* (e.g. 1)
7. What did the student do in the class?   *wrote a wonderful essay* (e.g. 2)
8. Where did the student write an essay?   *the class* (e.g. 2)
9. What did the student do?   *wrote a wonderful essay in the class* (e.g. 3)

Now consider the blue bracketed phrases in (10). In Unit 24, we concluded that they were not constituents, neither were they categorially determined.

10. The [$_{?P}$ student wrote] a [$_{?P}$ wonderful essay in] the class.   NON-CONSTITUENTS

The stand-alone test provides the evidence for this claim. As shown in (11) and (12), the blue phrases in (10) cannot stand alone as answers to their formed questions. Thus, they are, in fact, non-constituents

Question: NON-CONSTITUENTS   **Answer: NON-CONSTITUENTS**
11. What did the student do in the class?   **student wrote* (e.g. 10)
12. What did the student write in the class?   **wonderful essay in* (e.g. 10)

UNIT 26

Substitution Test

Substitution Test

The **SUBSTITUTION TEST** or **REPLACEMENT TEST** is a test that examines whether a sequence of words can be substituted with or replaced by a single word while their relevant sentences remain grammatical. Only constituents can be substituted with pro-forms. A **PRO-FORM** is a function word that replaces a phrase and expresses its whole content. In English, there is a pro-form for each phrase as shown in (1) through (4).

	Phrases	Can be substituted with pro-forms like
1.	Noun Phrases	pronouns like *he, she, it, they, them, him* etc.
2.	Verb Phrases	*do, did, does so*
3.	Adjective Phrases	*so/such*
4.	Preposition Phrases	*here/there* (for places) and *then* (for time)

Let us consider the following sentence.

5. [NP The student] wrote [NP a wonderful essay] [PP in the class] [PP in the morning].

All the blue phrases in (5) are constituents, and the evidence follows from the substitution test. These phrases in (5) can be all replaced by appropriate pro-forms as in (6).

6. [NP *He*] wrote [NP *it*] [PP *here*] [PP *then*].   (Substitution Test)

The NP *the student* and *a wonderful essay* are constituents because they are replaceable by their respective pro-forms/pronouns *he* and *it* whereas the PP *in the class* and *in the morning* are constituents because they can be substituted with their respective pro-forms *here* and *then*. Consider more examples below.

7. The student [VP wrote a wonderful essay in the class].
8. The essay is [AP very wonderful].
9. The student [VP did so].   (Substitution Test)
10. The essay is [AP so].   (Substitution Test)

The blue VP *wrote a wonderful essay in the morning* in (7) is a constituent because it can be wholly replaced by a pro-form such as *did so* in (9). As for the AP *very wonderful* in (8), it is also a constituent because it is substitutable by the pro-form *so* in (10). Consider the following examples, which include non-constituent phrases.

11. The [?P student wrote] a [?P wonderful essay in] the class.
12. *The *he* a *it* the class.   (Substitution Test)

When the blue phrases in (11) are substituted with pro-forms as in (12), the sentence becomes ungrammatical. The ungrammaticality of sentence (12) is taken as proof of the fact that these phrases are non-constituents.

UNIT 27

Displacement Test

Displacement Test

The **DISPLACEMENT TEST** or **MOVEMENT TEST** is a test that examines whether a sequence of words can be displaced or moved to the front of the sentence while the resulting sentence remains grammatical. Only constituents can be moved to a clause-initial position. There are several common means of displacement in English.

1. **TOPICALIZATION** (or **FRONTING**) involves the movement of a sequence of words to the front of the sentence.
    - He will not eat [that pasta]. (Base)
    - [That pasta], he will not eat. (Topicalization)
    - The kids ice-skate [for entertainment]. (Base)
    - [For entertainment], the kids ice-skate. (Topicalization)

2. **CLEFTING** involves the placement of a sequence between (*it is/was ... that*) or (*they are/where ... that*).
    - He bought [a fashionable bag] from the store. (Base)
    - *It is/was* [a fashionable bag] *that* he bought from the store. (Clefting)

3. **PREPOSING** (or **PSEUDOCLEFTING**) involves the placement of a sequence before the predicates (*.... is/was/are/were what/who*).
    - [This student] answered [the tricky questions]. (Base)
    - [This student] *was who* answered the tricky questions. (Preposing)
    - [The questions] *were what* this student answered. (Preposing)

By using these displacement tests, we can determine whether a group of words is a constituent or not. If a phrase can be displaced to the front, it is a constituent.

4. [NP The student] wrote a wonderful essay in the class.
    TEST: *It is the student who* wrote a wonderful essay in the class. (Clefting)

5. The student wrote [NP a wonderful essay] in the class.
    TEST: A wonderful essay *is what* the student wrote in the class. (Preposing)

6. The student wrote a wonderful essay [PP in the class].
    TEST: In the class, the student wrote a wonderful essay. (Topicalization)

The displacement test does not work for VPs as in (7). The failure of the displacement test, however, does not mean that a given VP is not a constituent. Other tests should be consulted.

7. The student [VP wrote a wonderful essay] in the class.
    TEST: **wrote a wonderful essay*, the student in the class. (Topicalization)

PHRASE STRUCTURE

UNIT 28

Coordination Test

Coordination Test

The **COORDINATION TEST** is a test that examines whether a sequence of words can be coordinated with another sequence of the same lexical category. Only constituents of the same lexical category can be coordinated as in (1) through (5). This is known as **COORDINATE CONSTITUENT CONSTRAINT** (Chomsky, 1965; Williams, 1978; Schachter, 1977).

Sentences		Conjoined phrases		
1.	The landlord **and** the tenant met.	NP	and	NP
2.	The doctor did come **but** has left.	VP	but	VP
3.	Is the tycoon very smart **or** very lucky?	AP	or	AP
4.	He visits us in the morning **and** in the evening.	PP	and	PP
5.	We should prepare for the marathon slowly **but** surely.	AdvP	but	AdvP

Thus, we can determine the constituenthood of phrases via their ability to be coordinated. If a phrase can be coordinated with another conjunct of a similar category, it is a constituent.

6. The student wrote a wonderful essay in the class.
   TEST: [$_{NP}$ the student] and [$_{NP}$ the teacher] wrote a wonderful essay in the class.

7. The student wrote a wonderful essay in the class.
   TEST: The student wrote [$_{NP}$ a wonderful essay] and [$_{NP}$ a short story] in the class.

8. The student wrote a wonderful essay in the class.
   TEST: The student wrote a wonderful essay [$_{PP}$ in the class] and [$_{PP}$ at home].

9. The student wrote a wonderful essay in the class.
   TEST: The student [$_{VP}$ wrote a wonderful essay] and [$_{VP}$ presented it] in the class.

10. The student wrote a wonderful essay in the class.
    TEST: *The [$_{?P}$ student wrote] and [$_{?P}$ teacher made] a wonderful essay in the class.

All blue phrases in (6) through (9) are constituents because they can be coordinated with other made-up phrases of the same category. In (10), the categorially undefined phrase *student wrote* cannot be coordinated with another phrase of the same category, therefore it is not a constituent. The coordination above is known as **ORDINARY COORDINATION**.

Another type of coordination is called **SHARED COORDINATION** (or **RIGHT NODE RAISING**). In shared coordination, only constituents can be shared across coordinated sentences. The blue phrases in (11) and (12) are constituents because they are shared by each conjunct.

11. He loves ~~writing essays~~ but she hates [$_{VP}$ writing essays].   CONSTITUENT
12. John denied ~~the crime~~ but Sam admitted [$_{NP}$ the crime].   CONSTITUENT

SECTION 3

Phrase Structure Rules

∴

UNIT 29

Basics 1

Reminder

Thus far, we have learned about words' lexical categories (Is a word N, V, A, Adv etc.?), their complementation or subcategorization frames (What phrases do heads N, V, A etc. select as complements, and how many complements are there, one or two?), and whether these words and phrases (consisting of specifiers, heads and complements) form a constituent or not. This information is very helpful in understanding how sentences are constructed.

Phrase Structure Rules

To recap, there are two basic components in every human language: (i) the lexicon, which comprises morphemes and words and (ii) grammar, which is a rule-based system that builds phrases and sentences. Without the support of grammar, the lexicon does not produce grammatical sentences. In other words, the production of random words does not generate well-formed sentences as shown in (1).

1. *on the answered the all smart test the questions student.
2. The smart student answered all the questions on the test.

Although we have well-formed words in (1), their ordering yields an ungrammatical sentence. For grammaticality, these words must be arranged as in (2). The organization of words into well-formed phrases is accomplished through grammar. Grammar has a finite number of syntactic rules known as **PHRASE STRUCTURE RULES** (PSRs). They are the backbone of the system known as **GENERATIVE SYNTAX**. They must be able to **generate** an infinite number of grammatical phrases/sentences.

Every phrase and sentence is constructed through a PSR. Some PSRs build phrases (such as NP, VP, AP, Adv etc.) and others make up sentences. PSRs take the format in (3).

3. XP → W X YP

PSR (3) is read as follows: the X phrase consists of the specifier (W), the head (X) and the complement (YP). The arrow in (3) means 'consists of'. Because we know that a noun phrase (NP) such as *the table of contents* consists of an optional determiner (D) as a specifier, an obligatory noun (N) as a head, and an optional preposition phrase (PP) as a complement, we can easily formulate a PSR that generates English noun phrases similar in construction to *the table of contents*. Such a PSR is represented in (4).

4. NP → (D) N (PP)

As shown in (4), optional elements are written between brackets ( ). PSR (4) can generate many other NPs such as *an apple, Game of Thrones, the destruction of the city* etc.

UNIT 30

Basics 11

Construction of PSRs

To develop a syntax (i.e. a rule-based system) that generates an infinite number of phrases and sentences, we need to construct the rules of this syntax, i.e. the Phrase Structure Rules (PSRs). PSRs can be built through observation. That is, we can formulate rules based on the actual phrases and sentences that we encounter in a given language. To write a PSR for an X phrase, for example, we need to list all possible grammatical and ungrammatical X phrases in that language. Putting the PSR to the test, we should ensure that it generates only grammatical X phrases, and at the same time does not generate ungrammatical ones. Suppose we have the following phrases (XPs) in language L, where X, Y, Z are words.

1. X Y Z (grammatical XP)
2. X Z   (grammatical XP)
3. *Y Z   (ungrammatical XP)
4. *Y X Z (ungrammatical XP)

In light of the grammatical and ungrammatical XP above, we can construct a generative PSR. Comparing (1) and (2), it is clear that the element Y is optional. XP is always grammatical in (1) and (2) irrespective of the presence of Y. Whether Y is present as in (1) or absent as in (2), is not important for the grammaticality of XP. However, if we remove X as in (3), XP becomes ungrammatical. Thus, we can conclude that X is an obligatory element for the grammaticality of XP. In (4), if we put Y before X, XP becomes ungrammatical as well. That is, there is a strict ordering where X must precede Y as in (1). Under these assumptions, we can formulate PSR (5). In PSR (5), Y is put between brackets because it is an optional element. Also, X precedes Y and Z as dictated by (1) and (4). Thus, we are now sure that we have a PSR that generates grammatical XPs and excludes ungrammatical XPs in language L.

5. XP → X (Y) Z

Now consider the following grammatical and ungrammatical XPs in Language W.

6. Y X (grammatical XP)
7. Z X (grammatical XP)
8. *Y Z X (ungrammatical XP)
9. *Z Y X (ungrammatical XP)

To formulate a PSR in light of the examples in (6) through (9), we should first observe that grammatical XPs must not consist of Y and Z together as in (8) and (9). Whatever the order of Y and Z in (8) and (9), the presence of both Y and Z yields ungrammatical XPs. However, if only one, either Y or Z, is present, XP becomes grammatical as in (6) and (7). Thus, to formulate a PSR that generates (6) and (7) and does not generate (8) and (9), we can use the braces { } as in PSR (10). Braces dictate that either Y or Z should be present, but not both.

10. $XP \rightarrow \begin{Bmatrix} Y \\ Z \end{Bmatrix} X$

UNIT 31

Noun Phrase 1

PSRs for Noun Phrases

In English, a noun phrase (NP) must contain at least a head noun (N). It may as well contain elements such as specifiers or complements. To formulate PSRs for English NPs, we need to list all possible grammatical NPs in English. Consider the following noun phrases in (1) through (7).

1. Ahmed arrived.
2. He/they/it arrived.
3. Books arrived.
4. *The/my/these* books arrived.
5. The/my/these *big/red* books arrived.
6. The/my/these *very* big/red books arrived.
7. The/my/these very big/red books *on linguistics* arrived.

In (1) through (3), NP consists of only one element: either (i) a **PROPER NOUN** as in (1), (ii) a **PRONOUN** as in (2) or a **COMMON NOUN** as in (3). To generate other NPs similar to those in (1) through (3), we should propose the two PSRs in (8) and (9). PSR (8) states that 'a noun phrase (NP) consists of a proper/common noun (N)' whereas PSR (9) states that 'a noun phrase (NP) consists of a pronoun (Pron)'.

8. NP → N
9. NP → Pron

PSR (8) is responsible for generating many other NP (proper or common nouns) such as *Mary, John, ideas, love, truth*, etc. PSR (9) generates all English pronouns such as *she, you, we, her*, etc. It is worth noting that a (proper/common) noun and a pronoun do not co-occur in English. English noun phrases should include either a pronoun or a proper/common noun as in (1) or (2), but not both as in (10).

10. a. *Ahmed he arrived.   (proper name + pronoun)
    b. *Books they arrived.   (common noun + pronoun)

In light of these facts, we can collapse PSR (8) and (9) into PSR (11) by using braces.

11. NP → $\left\{ \begin{array}{c} N \\ Pron \end{array} \right\}$

PSR (11) reads as follows: any English noun phrase (NP) consists of either a proper/common noun (N) or a pronoun (Pron), but not both. This rule ensures that ungrammatical sentences like (10) are not generated by our syntax.

UNIT 32

Noun Phrase II

PSRs for Noun Phrases

To formulate more PSRs for NP, we need to consider the remaining possible NPs below.

1. **Books** arrived.
2. The/my/these **books** arrived.
3. The/my/these big/red **books** arrived.
4. The/my/these very big/red **books** arrived.
5. The/my/these very big/red **books** on linguistics arrived.

All noun phrases in (1) through (5) consist of *books* as a head noun. Comparing (1) and (2), a determiner such as *the/my/these* can optionally precede *books*. The presence or absence of these determiners does not affect the grammaticality of the sentence. Both (1) and (2) are grammatical. Thus, we can formulate a PSR that puts an optional determiner before N as in (6).

6. NP → **(D)** N

PSR (6) states that 'a noun phrase may consist of an optional determiner (D) followed by a noun (N)'. This rule can generate other English NPs such as *an apple, your hat, this pen*, etc.

Now consider (3) and (4). It is obvious that an adjective phrase (AP) can be inserted between the optional determiner (D) and the head noun (N). It is optional because its absence from (2) does not disturb the grammaticality of the sentence. It is an adjective phrase (AP) because it can consist of a degree word (Deg) such as *very* and a head adjective (A) such as *big/red*. Thus, PSR (6) can be expanded to include this optional AP as shown in (7).

7. NP → (D) **(AP)** N

In (5), the head noun *books* can be followed by a preposition phrase (PP), namely *on linguistics*. It is an optional PP-complement because its absence from sentences (1) through (4) does not render these sentences ungrammatical. Thus, PSR (7) can be expanded to include this optional PP as shown in (8).

8. NP → (D) (AP) N **(PP)**

PSR (8) can now generate all possible NPs in English. Taking into account rule (11) which presented in Unit 31, the final generative PSR of English NPs is given in (9).

9. NP → $\left\{ \begin{array}{c} \text{(D) (AP) N (PP)} \\ \text{Pron} \end{array} \right\}$

Random Phrases

UNIT 33

PSRs for Preposition Phrases

To formulate PSRs for Preposition Phrase (PP), we need to list all possible PPs in English.

1. *He is* in.
2. *He is* in the boot.
3. *He is* right in the boot.

All preposition phrases in (1) through (3) consist of the P *in* as the head preposition. A preposition can stand alone constituting the whole PP as in (1). In (2), the head preposition is followed by an optional NP, namely *the boot*. This NP has its own PSR as discussed in Unit 32; that is, NP can be *the big boot, the very big boot of the car, it,* etc. What concerns us is that the head preposition can be followed by an optional NP, whatever it is, because its absence from (1) does not render the sentence ungrammatical. In (3), a degree word (Deg) such as *right* precedes the preposition *in*. It is an optional element because its absence does not render the sentences (1) and (2) ungrammatical. In light of these facts, we can formulate PSR (4). PSR (4) states that 'a preposition phrase (PP) consists of an optional degree word (Deg), followed by an obligatory preposition (P), followed by an optional noun phrase (NP)'.

4. PP → (Deg) P (NP)

PSRs for Adjective and Adverb Phrases

To formulate PSRs for Adjective Phrase (AP) and Adverb Phrase (AdvP), we need to consider all possible APs and AdvPs in English.

5. *He is* afraid.   (AP)
6. *He is* so afraid.   (AP)
7. *He is* so afraid of the dog. (AP)
8. *He came* quickly.   (AdvP)
9. *He came* very quickly.   (AdvP)

All the adjective phrases in (5) through (7) consist of *afraid* as the head adjective. An adjective can stand alone making up the whole AP as in (5). In (6), the head adjective is preceded by an optional degree word *so*. In (7), the head adjective is also followed by an optional PP, namely *of the dog*. Based on these facts, we can formulate PSR (10) for English APs. PSR (10) can generate many other APs such as *very curious about the issue, so angry at him* etc. As for adverb phrases (AdvP), they consist of either the adverb head alone as in (8) or the adverb head preceded by an optional degree word *very* as in (9). Thus, English AdvPs can be generated through PSR (11) which yields many other AdvPs such as *so rapidly, quite clearly* etc.

10. AP → (Deg) A (PP)
11. AdvP → (Deg) Adv

UNIT 34

Verb Phrase 1

PSRs for Verb Phrases

Let us now formulate PSRs for Verb Phrase (VP). Consider all possible VPs in English.

1. He ate.
2. He ate a hamburger.
3. *He devoured.
4. He devoured a hamburger.
5. He talked to the man.
6. He talked.
7. He dashed to the room.
8. *He dashed.

All the verb phrases (VPs) in (1) through (6) differ in respect of their complement selection. In (1), the verb *ate* can stand alone making up the whole VP, but it can be followed by one optional NP such as *a hamburger* in (2). The absence of this NP does not render (1) ungrammatical. In (3), the head verb *devoured* cannot stand alone; rather, it needs an obligatory NP as in (4). In (5), the head verb *talked* takes an optional PP *to the man* which can be absent from the sentence without affecting the grammaticality thereof, e.g. (6). As for the head verb *dashed* in (7), it takes an obligatory PP *to the room*. If this PP is removed, the sentence becomes ungrammatical as in (8).

Thus, to generate all the VPs above, we only need the two PSRs in (9) and (10).

9. VP → V (NP) for examples (1), (2) & (4)
10. VP → V (PP) for examples (5), (6) & (8)

PSR (9) states that 'a verb phrase (VP) consists of a verb and an optional noun phrase (NP)'. This NP is optional for (2) but obligatory in (4). As for PSR (10), it states that 'a verb phrase (VP) consists of a verb (V) followed by an optional preposition phrase (PP)'. Similarly, this PP is optional for (5) but obligatory in (7). The presence of NP or PP in the above PSRs heavily relies on the head's complement selections or subcategorization frames (See Unit 19 and 20). Given that PSR (9) and (10) are similar but different in respect of the second element, they can be reduced to one PSR using braces as in (11).

11. $\text{VP} \rightarrow \text{V} \begin{Bmatrix} \text{(NP)} \\ \text{(PP)} \end{Bmatrix}$

PSR (11) states that 'every verb phrase (VP) consists of a verb (V) followed by either a noun phrase (NP) or a preposition phrase (PP)'. This PSR can generate all the VPs in (1) through (8) and many others.

PHRASE STRUCTURE RULES

UNIT 35

Verb Phrase II

PSRs for Verb Phrases

In addition to the earlier VPs, consider more possible VPs in English.

1. He gave Ahmed a letter.
2. *He gave Ahmed.
3. *He gave a letter
4. He gave a letter to Ahmed.
5. *He gave to Ahmed.
6. He deemed these steps very necessary.
7. *He deemed these steps.
8. *He deemed very necessary.
9. He talked to the man about the issue.
10. He talked.
11. He talked to the man.
12. He talked about the issue.

In (1), the head verb *gave* selects two obligatory NPs (NP+NP): *Ahmed* and *a letter* respectively. If we remove one of these two NPs, the sentence becomes ungrammatical as in (2) and (3). In (4), the same verb takes different obligatory complements, namely NP and PP: *a letter* and *to Ahmed* respectively. The removal of one of these complements would also make the sentence ungrammatical as in (3) and (5). In (6), the verb *deemed* selects two obligatory complements: the NP *these steps* and the AP *very necessary*. These complements are obligatory because the removal of either one would lead to ungrammatical sentences as in (7) and (8). In (9), the head verb *talked* takes two optional complements: the PP *to the man* and the PP *about the issue*. These complements are optional because the removal of all, or only one, of them does not yield ungrammaticality as in (10) through (12). In light of these facts, we can formulate the following VP rules:

13. VP → V NP NP   example (1)
14. VP → V NP PP   example (4)
15. VP → V NP AP   example (6)
16. VP → V (NP) (PP) examples (9), (10), (11) & (12).
17. VP → V (NP)   old rule from Unit 34
18. VP → V (PP)   old rule form Unit 34

Considering these new PSRs along with the old rules we formulated in Unit 34, we can reduce all of them to PSR (19) that covers all possible verb phrases in English.

19. $\text{VP} \rightarrow \text{V} \left(\begin{Bmatrix} \text{(NP)} \\ \text{(PP)} \end{Bmatrix} \right) \left(\begin{Bmatrix} \text{NP} \\ \text{AP} \\ \text{(PP)} \end{Bmatrix} \right)$

UNIT 36

Sentence I

PSRs for Sentences

To formulate PSRs for sentences, let us consider all possible sentences in English.

1. *The girl* devours a sandwich.
2. *The girl* devoured a sandwich.
3. **The girl* (as a sentence).
4. *devoured a sandwich (as a sentence).
5. *The girl* **does** devour a sandwich.
6. *The girl* **did** devour a sandwich.
7. *The girl* **is** devouring a sandwich.
8. *The girl* **had** devoured a sandwich.
9. *The girl* **will** devour a sandwich.
10. *The girl* **can** devour a sandwich.
11. *The girl* **may** devour a sandwich.
12. *The girl* **should** devour a sandwich.

All the sentences in (1) through (12) are grammatical except (3) and (4). Sentences (1) and (2) consist of only two phrases: an obligatory NP *the girl* and an obligatory VP *devours/devoured a sandwich*. The removal of either one of these obligatory elements in (1) and (2) would render the whole construction ungrammatical as illustrated in (3) and (4).

In (5) and (6), the words *does* and *did* appear between the obligatory NP and VP. These words mark the tense of the sentence: **PRESENT** (if *does*) or **PAST** (if *did*). Although sentences (1) and (2) do not contain these words, they are still tensed as manifested in the morphemes attached to the verb *devour*: **PRESENT** (if *devours*) or **PAST** (if *devoured*). In fact, (1) and (2) are similar in meaning to (5) and (6), but their tense representations differ: either morphologically (verb + -*s* or -*ed*) or syntactically (*does* or *did* + verb in bare form).

AUXILIARIES such as *is* and *had* can also appear between NP and VP as shown in (7) and (8). Additionally, **MODALS** such as *will, can, may* and *should* may appear in the exact same position as shown in (9) through (12). Thus, we can call these words (*Do/Does/Auxiliaries/Modals*) **TENSE WORDS** because they express the tense of the whole sentence and they all appear in the same position, i.e. between NP and VP.

In light of the above facts, we can state that an English (S)entence consists of three elements: an obligatory NP (e.g. *the girl*); an optional Tense word (e.g. *does/did/is/has/will/can/may/should*) (they are optional because they can be absent as in (1) and (2)); and finally an obligatory VP (i.e. *devour/devours/devoured/devouring*). We assume that the formulated PSR in (13) can generate all the sentences above and many others.

13. S → NP (Tense word) VP   examples (1) through (12)

UNIT 37

Sentence II

PSRs for Sentences

Recall that PSR (11) is proposed to account for the sentences below.

1. *The girl* devours a sandwich.
2. *The girl* devoured a sandwich.
3. *The girl* does devour a sandwich.
4. *The girl* did devour a sandwich.
5. *The girl* is devouring a sandwich.
6. *The girl* had devoured a sandwich.
7. *The girl* will devour a sandwich.
8. *The girl* can devour a sandwich.
9. *The girl* may devour a sandwich.
10. *The girl* should devour a sandwich.

11. S → NP (Tense word) VP   examples (1) through (10)

Although PSR (11) generates the above examples, it is problematic in two respects. First, the element S that refers to 'sentence' is not a phrase. Put differently, S is not an XP like other phrases: NP, VP, PP, AP, etc. All the PSRs proposed earlier are XPs except PSR (11). Another disadvantage follows from the fact that S does not have a head of its kind. In all the earlier PSRs, XP consisted of X: NP consisted of N, VP consisted of V, AP consisted of A etc. However, S did not consist of a head S on the right side. To resolve these problems, syntacticians propose that all sentences in English be considered **TENSE PHRASES** (TP). Tense is the main element in sentences that sets it apart from other XPs such as NP, AP, AdvP, VP etc. Without tense, a sentence cannot stand. Thus, Tense Phrase (TP) can now consist of a head of its kind, namely T; PSR (11) is revised as follows.

12. TP → NP (T) VP

PSR (12) is better than PSR (11) in that TP is a phrase like other phrases, and it has a head of its kind, i.e. T (for Tense Word). However, there is yet another problem with PSR (12). The head T is optional, which is not common in other PSRs. Heads are obligatory elements and their removal leads to ungrammaticality. This optionality of the head T in (12) is suggested as a result of comparing sentences (1) and (2) with other examples that have tense words. For consistency purposes and to enforce the obligatoriness of the head T, syntacticians propose that the morphological *-s* and *-ed* in (1) and (2) appear in the head T as well, but they are attached to the end of verbs at a later stage (see this analysis in Unit 104). Under this view, the head T, like other heads, is obligatory in all sentences. PSR (12) will thus be revised accordingly as in (13).

13. TP → NP T VP

UNIT 38

Complementizer

PSRs for Complementizer Phrase (CP)

Sentences or Tense Phrases (TPs) can be more complex. Consider the following examples.

1. The man will believe **that** *the girl has devoured a sandwich.*
2. The man may wonder **whether** *the girl has devoured a sandwich.*
3. The man has asked **if** *the girl has devoured a sandwich.*

In (1) through (3), we have two sentences (or two TPs) in each example. The blue words are sentences because they are made up of NP *the man*, a tense word *will/may/has* and a verb phrase *believe/wonder/asked*. These sentences are called **MATRIX** (or **MAIN**) **CLAUSES**. The words in italics also form sentences: NP *the girl*, a Tense word *has* plus a verb phrase *devoured a sandwich*; and they are known as **EMBEDDED** (or **SUBORDINATE**) **CLAUSES**. The two clauses in each example above are separated by words called **COMPLEMENTIZERS**: *that/whether/if*. Complementizers (C) behave like linking words between clauses, and they may introduce an infinite number of clauses as in (4) below.

4. He believes **that** Ali knows **that** Fahd suggested **that** Nada should announce **that** …

To generate sentences (1) through (4), we need the two PSRs in (5) and (6).

5. CP → C TP
6. VP → V CP

PSR (5) states that 'a complementizer phrase (CP) consists of an obligatory complementizer (C) such as *that/whether/if*, followed by a TP (whose PSR is: TP → NP T VP)' whereas PSR (6) states that 'a verb phrase (VP) consists of a verb (such as *believe, wonder, ask, know, suggest* etc.) followed by a complementizer phrase (CP) (whose PSR is CP → C TP)'. Verbs such as *believe, wonder* and *asked* in (1) through (3) must be followed by CPs. Otherwise, the sentences would become ungrammatical or less meaningful as in (7) through (9).

7. *The man will believe.
8. *The man may wonder.
9. *The man has asked.

The awkwardness of (7), (8) and (9) suggests that CPs are obligatory complements for the verbs *believe, wonder* and *asked*. This information should be listed in the subcategorization frames of such verbs as shown in (10) through (12).

10. The man will believe *that the girl has devoured a sandwich.*   believe, V [___CP]
11. The man may wonder *whether the girl has devoured a sandwich.*   wonder, V [___CP]
12. The man has asked *if the girl has devoured a sandwich.*   asked, V [___ CP]

UNIT 39

Conjunction

PSRs for Conjunction Phrase (ConjP)

The following examples consist of Conjunction Phrases (ConjP).

Sentences		**Conjoined phrases**		
1.	The man **and** the woman came.	NP	and	NP
2.	The man did come **but** has left.	VP	but	VP
3.	Is the man very strong **or** very weak?	AP	or	AP
4.	He visits us in the morning **and** in the evening.	PP	and	PP
5.	We should cram for the exam slowly **but** surely.	AdvP	but	AdvP
6.	The man came **but** the women left.	TP	but	TP
7.	I believe that he can come **and** that she can leave.	CP	and	CP
8.	*The man **and** so strong came.	*NP	and	AP
9.	*He came **or** quickly.	*VP	and	AdvP
10.	*The man came **but** that he can.	*TP	but	CP

Each sentence in (1) through (7) contains a conjunct phrase. Conjunctions are written in bold: **and**, **but** and **or**. In (1), two NPs are conjoined with *and* whereas two VPs are conjoined with *but* in (2). In (3) and (4), two APs and two PPs are conjoined with *or* and *and* respectively. In (5), two AdvPs are conjoined with *but*. Not only small phrases can be conjoined, but entire sentences (TPs) as well, e.g. (6). Complementizer phrases (CPs) are also conjoined with *and* as in (7). In (1) through (7), the two conjoined phrases are of the same category. This is according to **COORDINATE CONSTITUENT CONSTRAINT** (Chomsky, 1965; Williams, 1978; Schachter, 1977). As put by Gazdar (1981:172), 'only items of the same syntactic category can be conjoined'. If these conjuncts are of different categories, the resulting sentences become ungrammatical as in (8) through (10). Consider the PSRs below, and also consider the generalized PSR (18) which can compensate for all the PSRs in (11) through (17).

11. ConjP → NP Conj NP   for example (1)
12. ConjP → VP Conj VP   for example (2)
13. ConjP → AP Conj AP   for example (3)
14. ConjP → PP Conj PP   for example (4)
15. ConjP → AdvP Conj AdvP   for example (5)
16. ConjP → TP Conj TP   for example (6)
17. ConjP → CP Conj CP   for example (7)
18. **ConjP → XP Conj XP**   where XP = XP

Note that both conjoined phrases are obligatory. They cannot be optional; if they were, the sentences would become ungrammatical as in (19) and (20) in contrast to (1).

19. *The man **and** ___ came.   NP and ~~NP~~
20. *___ **and** the women came.   ~~NP~~ and NP

UNIT 40

Adjunction

PSRs for Adjuncts

In the earlier units, PSRs were devised to arrange the heads along with their specifiers and complements, either obligatory or optional. Let us consider adjuncts that are always optional.

1. The girl has recently devoured a sandwich.
2. The girl has *devoured a sandwich* recently.
3. The girl *read the books* in the room.
4. The girl, in the room, *read the books*.

All the sentences in (1) through (4) are grammatical in English. In (1), the AdvP *recently* is an optional adjunct preceding not only a verb, but a verb phrase (VP) *devoured a sandwich*. In (2), the same AdvP *recently* follows the VP *devoured a sandwich*. The same applies to (3) and (4), where the adjunct PP *in the room* is optional and either follows or precedes the VP *read the books*. These adjuncts can take the PSRs below.

5. VP → AdvP VP   for example (1)
6. VP → VP AdvP   for example (2)
7. VP → VP PP   for example (3)
8. VP → PP VP   for example (4)

It is important to note that these PSRs do not have a head. This is because adjuncts modify the whole phrase (head plus complements), not only the head. Adjuncts can modify bigger phrases such as TPs as in the following examples.

9. Recently, *the girl has devoured a sandwich*.
10. *The girl has devoured a sandwich*, recently.
11. In the room, *the girl read the books*.
12. *The girl read the books* in the room.

The adjunct AdvP *recently* can modify the whole sentence, preceding or following it as in (9) and (10). Similarly, the adjunct PP *in the room* can precede or follow a TP, e.g. (11) and (12). The appropriate PSRs for examples (9) through (12) are given below.

13. TP → AdvP TP   for example (9)
14. TP → TP AdvP   for example (10)
15. TP → PP TP   for example (11)
16. TP → TP PP   for example (12)

The distinction between examples (1) and (2), on the one hand, and (9) and (10), on the other, follows from the scope of modification: the adjunct AdvP *recently* only modifies VP in (1) and (2), but it covers TP in (9) and (10). The same applies to the adjunct PP *in the room*.

Summary 1

Summary of PSRs

In light of the previous discussions, all the PSRs follow the formats in (1), (2) and (3) below.

Generalized Complementation Rule
1. XP → Specifier X Complements

   Where
   XP = NP, VP, AP, AdvP, PP, TP, CP or ConjP
   Specifier = (D) for NP, (Deg) for AP/AdvP/PP, (NP) for TP, (XP) for ConjP
   X = N, V, A, Adv, P, T, C, or Conj
   Complements: XP such as NP, PP, VP, CP, etc.

   Generalized Adjunction Rule:
2. XP → XP YP
3. XP → YP XP

   Where
   XP = TP or VP
   YP = PP or AdvP

A summary of the formulated PSRs is given below with examples.

PSRs

Noun Phrases (NP):

4. NP → { (D) (AP) N (PP) / Pron }

   1. $_N$ John (proper noun)
   2. $_N$ cars (common noun)
   3. ($_D$ the) $_N$ cars
   4. ($_D$ the) ($_{AP}$ very black) $_N$ car
   5. ($_D$ the) ($_{AP}$ very black) $_N$ car ($_{PP}$ of the police)
   6. $_{Pron}$ he

Preposition Phrases (PP):

5. PP → (Deg) P (NP)

   1. $_P$ in
   2. $_P$ in ($_{NP}$ the boot)
   3. ($_{Deg}$ right) $_P$ in ($_{NP}$ the boot)

Adjective Phrase (AP):

6. AP → (Deg) A (PP)

   1. $_A$ curious
   2. $_A$ curious ($_{PP}$ about the event)
   3. ($_{Deg}$ so) $_A$ curious ($_{PP}$ about the event)

Adverb Phrase (AdvP):

7. AdvP → (Deg) Adv

   1. $_{Adv}$ rapidly
   2. ($_{Deg}$ so) $_{Adv}$ rapidly.

UNIT 42

Summary II

Summary of PSRs

Tense Phrase (TP):

1. TP → NP T VP

1. $_{NP}$ Ahmed $_T$ can $_{VP}$ read a book.
2. $_{NP}$ The student $_T$ will $_{VP}$ develop an idea.

Verb Phrases (VP):

2. VP → V ({ (NP) / (PP) }) ({ NP / (AP) / (PP) })

1. He $_V$ reads.
2. He $_V$ reads ($_{NP}$ a book).
3. He $_V$ cuts $_{NP}$ the meat.
4. He $_V$ gestured ($_{PP}$ to him)
5. He $_V$ looked $_{PP}$ at him
6. He $_V$ sent $_{NP}$ Ali $_{NP}$ a letter.
7. He $_V$ sent $_{NP}$ a letter $_{PP}$ to Ali.
8. He $_V$ talked ($_{PP}$ to Ahmed) ($_{PP}$ about it).
9. He $_V$ deemed $_{NP}$ this step $_{AP}$ very necessary.

Complementizer Phrase (CP)

3. CP → C TP

1. He believed $_C$ that $_{TP}$ the man may come.
2. He asked $_C$ if $_{TP}$ the man will come.
3. He wondered $_C$ whether $_{TP}$ the man came.

Verb Phrase (VP)

4. VP → V CP

1. He $_V$ believed $_{CP}$ that the man may come.
2. He $_V$ asked $_{CP}$ if the man will come.
3. He $_V$ wondered $_{CP}$ whether the man came.

Conjunction Phrase (ConjP)

5. ConjP → XP Conj XP
XP = NP, VP, AP, AdvP
PP, TP, CP

1. $_{NP}$ The students $_{Conj}$ and $_{NP}$ the teachers came.
2. He $_{VP}$ came $_{Conj}$ but $_{VP}$ left.
3. He is $_{AP}$ so strong $_{Conj}$ or $_{AP}$ so patient.
4. He is studying $_{AdvP}$ slowly $_{Conj}$ but $_{AdvP}$ surely.
5. He stays $_{PP}$ at home $_{Conj}$ but $_{PP}$ at night.
6. $_{TP}$ He came $_{Conj}$ and $_{TP}$ she left.
7. I ask $_{CP}$ if he came $_{Conj}$ and $_{CP}$ if she left.

Adjunction Rules

6. VP → AdvP VP
7. VP → VP AdvP
8. VP → VP PP
9. VP → PP VP
10. TP → AdvP TP
11. TP → TP AdvP
12. TP → PP TP
13. TP → TP PP

1. He $_{AdvP}$ quickly $_{VP}$ visited his relatives.
2. He $_{VP}$ visited his relatives $_{AdvP}$ quickly.
3. He $_{VP}$ visited his relatives $_{PP}$ in the morning.
4. He, $_{PP}$ in the morning, $_{VP}$ visited his relatives.
5. $_{AdvP}$ Recently, $_{TP}$ he visited his relatives.
6. $_{TP}$ He visited his relatives, $_{Adv}$ recently.
7. $_{PP}$ In the past, $_{TP}$ he visited his relatives.
8. $_{TP}$ He visited his relatives, $_{PP}$ in the past.

SECTION 4

Tree Structure

∴

UNIT 43

Representation

Representations of PSRs

Having discussed the Phrase Structure Rules (PSRs), it is now time to see how they are structurally represented. There are two ways to represent PSRs: via (i) tree structures or (ii) bracketing. Consider (1) and (2).

1. PSR (i) Tree Structure (ii) Bracketing

    NP → (D) (AP) N (PP)

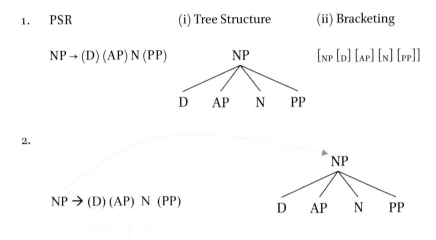

2. NP → (D) (AP) N (PP)

A PSR can be correctly diagrammed in a tree format based on the position of the arrow (→). As illustrated in (2), the left-hand element of the arrow, NP, is put at the top of tree, and the right-hand elements of the arrow are spread in the same order as dangling branches. As for bracketing in (1ii) above, it is not that different from the PSR format; after removing the arrow, each right-hand element is bracketed inside the main brackets of the left-hand element.

Kinship terminology is used for PSRs and tree structures as shown below.

3. PSR Tree Structure Bracketing

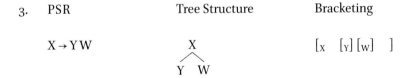

i. X is the **mother** of Y and W iff X appears on the left side of a PSR and Y and W appear on the right side. In a tree structure, X is the **mother** of Y and W iff X appears above Y and W.

ii. Y and W are the **daughters** of the mother X iff Y and W appear on the right side of a PSR and X appears on the left side. In a tree structure, Y and W are the daughters of X iff both Y and W appear side by side under X.

iii. Y is a **sister** of W iff both Y and W appear on the right side of a PSR. In a tree structure, Y is a **sister** of W iff both Y and W appear side by side under X.

UNIT 44

Nodes and Branches

Tree Structure Terminology

Tree structures are syntactic representations of PSRs. Note that PSRs in (1) are represented in the tree in (2) preserving the same ordering of the elements. The optional elements in (1), such as (D), (AP), (Deg) and (NP), are represented in (2) without brackets. Brackets should not be added to the optional elements in tree diagrams. If these optional elements appear in a given phrase, they should be represented in bare form like obligatory ones.

1. PSRs 2. Tree Structure

NP → (D) (AP) N (PP)
AP → (Deg) A
PP → P (NP)

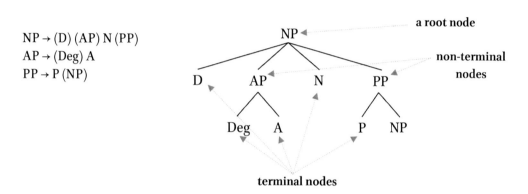

As shown above, syntactic tree (2) consists of **nodes** and **branches**. A **node** is the base or end of a branch. **Branches** are the lines that meet at the node. Each node in (2) has a **label** (an identifying name) such as NP, D, AP, Deg, A, N, PP, P and NP.

i. A **root node** is the node with no branches above. It is the base of the whole tree and the highest node in it. The highest NP in tree (2) is a root node because there are no branches above NP.
   – *If we inverted the tree, NP would be like the base or the root of a tree with many branches.*

ii. A **terminal node** is the node with no branches below it. In tree (2), D, Deg, A, N and P have no branches below them. They are thus terminal nodes.
   – *Terminal nodes are like the leaves on the branches.*

iii. A **non-terminal node** is neither a root node nor a terminal node. It is the node that has branches both below and above it. In tree (2), only AP and PP have branches both below and above them. Thus, they are non-terminal nodes.
   – *Non-terminal nodes are like the joints of nodes in a tree.*

UNIT 45

Dominance

Dominance

Let us now consider a few syntactic relations in tree structures. **DOMINANCE** is a structural relation between tree nodes, and it is represented in terms of top-down order.

1. Dominance Relations:

    i. A dominates B iff A appears above B in the tree.
    ii. If A dominates B, and B dominates C, then A **automatically dominates** C. (*Transitive-Relation Dominance*).
    iii. If A **immediately dominates** B, then A is right above B in the tree, and there is no intervening node C between A and B. That is, A must be the closest dominant node of B. (*Immediate Dominance*)

2. PSRs   3. Tree Structure

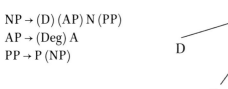
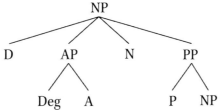

In light of the relations in tree (3) above, we can make the following statements:
– The highest NP dominates all of the following elements: D, AP, Deg, A, N, PP, P, NP.
– The highest NP immediately dominates D, AP, N and PP.
– AP immediately dominates Deg and A.
– PP immediately dominates P and the lowest NP.
– D does not dominate AP, AP does not dominate D, N does not dominate PP, and PP does not dominate N.
– P does not dominate PP, and A does not dominate AP.

In short, and using kinship terminology, all mothers in trees must dominate their daughters. Daughters do not dominate their mothers, and sisters do not dominate each other.

UNIT 46

Precedence

Precedence

PRECEDENCE (i.e. what precedes which?) is another structural relation between tree nodes, and it is represented in terms of left-to-right order.

1. Precedence Relations:

    i. A precedes B iff A appears on the left of B.
    ii. If A precedes B, and B precedes C, then A **automatically precedes** C as well. (*Transitive-Relation Precedence*).
    iii. If A **immediately precedes** B, then A is immediately to the left of B, and there is no intervening node C between A and B. That is, A is the closest branch of B to the left. (*Immediate Precedence*)

2. PSRs

    NP → (D) (AP) N (PP)
    AP → (Deg) A
    PP → P (NP)

3. Tree Diagram

    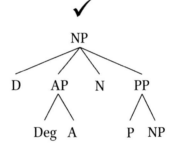

4. No crossing branches

    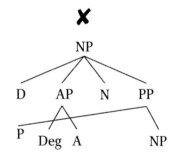

In light of the relations in tree (3) above, we can formulate the following statements:
- D precedes all of the following elements: AP (Deg, A) N and PP (P, NP).
- D immediately precedes AP.
- AP precedes N and PP (P, NP).
- AP immediately precedes N.
- N immediately precedes PP.
- AP does not precede D, and PP does not precede N.

In tree (4), P is not allowed to cross or precede Deg. Branches in syntactic representations should respect precedence and represent the linear order of the elements as formulated in the PSRs. To capture the constituenthood of phrases, branches should not cross each other; this is known as **NO CROSSING CONSTRAINT**.

UNIT 47

Noun Phrases

Tree Structures for Noun Phrases

Let us now convert all the PSRs discussed earlier into tree diagrams. In English, a noun phrase (NP) has the following PSRs, which can be diagrammed in tree structures as follows.

1. NP → N
   e.g. *John*

   NP
   |
   N
   John

2. NP → N
   e.g. *cars*

   NP
   |
   N
   cars

3. NP → pron
   e.g. *they*

   NP
   |
   Pron
   they

4. NP → (D) N
   e.g. *the cars*

   NP
   / \
   D   N
   the cars

5. NP → D (AP) N
   e.g. *the very good cars*

   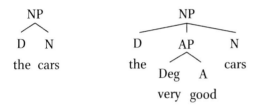

6. NP → (D) (AP) N (PP)
   e.g. *the very big books of linguistics*   e.g. *the very black cars of the police*

   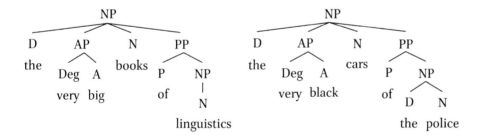

It is important to note that the structural representations above preserve the linear ordering of the words in their relevant NPs (i.e. precedence). That is, the words in each tree diagram above are read from left to right as a grammatical NP. The incorrect ordering of the words in a syntactic tree indicates that there is a violation of precedence, and that the tree is incorrectly drawn.

UNIT 48

Random Phrases

Prepositional Phrase

In English, a preposition phrase (PP) has the following PSRs, which can be diagrammed as follows.

1. PP → P
    e.g. *at*

2. PP → (Deg) P
    e.g. *right at*

3. PP → (Deg) P (NP)
    e.g. *right at the corner*

```
     PP              PP                    PP
     |              /  \                 / | \
     P            Deg   P              Deg P  NP
     at          right at             right at / \
                                              D   N
                                              the corner
```

Adjective Phrase

Adjective Phrase (AP) also has PSRs, which can be graphically represented as follows.

4. AP → A
    e.g. *afraid*

5. AP → (Deg) A
    e.g. *so afraid*

6. AP → (Deg) A (PP)
    e.g. *so afraid of the dog*

```
     AP              AP                    AP
     |              /  \                 / | \
     A            Deg   A              Deg A   PP
     afraid       so   afraid          so afraid / \
                                                P   NP
                                                of  / \
                                                   D   N
                                                   the dog
```

Adverb Phrase

PSRs of Adverb Phrase (AdvP) can be structured as follows.

7. AdvP → Adv
    e.g. *quickly*

8. AdvP → (Deg) Adv
    e.g. *very quickly*

```
     AdvP            AdvP
     |              /    \
     Adv           Deg   Adv
     quickly       very  quickly
```

UNIT 49

Verb Phrases

Verb Phrase

The PSRs of Verb Phrase (VP) can also be diagrammed in tree formats as follows.

1. VP → V
    e.g. *ate*

    ```
    VP
    |
    V
    ate
    ```

2. VP → V (NP)
    e.g. *ate a sandwich*

    ```
         VP
        /  \
       V    NP
      ate  /  \
          D    N
          a  sandwich
    ```

3. VP → V PP
    e.g. *dashed to the room*

    ```
          VP
         /  \
        V    PP
    dashed  /  \
           P    NP
           to  /  \
              D    N
             the  room
    ```

4. VP → NP PP
    e.g. *gave a present to the student*

    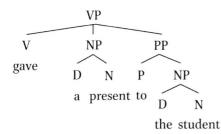

5. VP → NP NP
    e.g. *gave the student a present*

    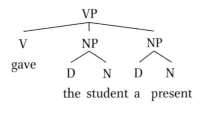

6. VP → (NP) (PP)
    e.g. *talked to the boss about my issue*

    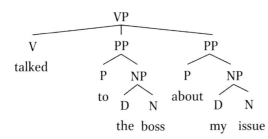

7. VP → NP AP
    e.g. *deemed these steps very necessary*

    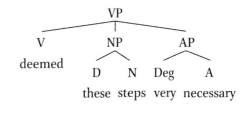

UNIT 50

Sentences

Verb Phrase

PSR (1) below is the only syntactic rule for sentences.

1. TP → NP T VP

In our preliminary analysis, we will assume that the head T is filled with {present} if the verb is in the present tense (e.g. *makes*) as in (2), or with {past} if the verb is in the past tense (e.g. *dashed*) as in (3). If sentences consist of auxiliaries such as *is, am, are, etc.* or modals such as *can, could, may, might, will, would*, T will be filled with these tense words as illustrated in (4) and (6).

2. TP → NP T VP
    e.g. *The chef makes a sandwich*

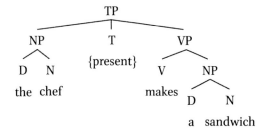

3. TP → NP T VP
    e.g. *He dashed to the room*

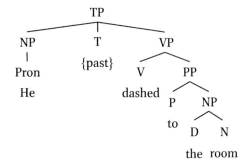

4. TP → NP T VP
    e.g. *The student is doing his homework*

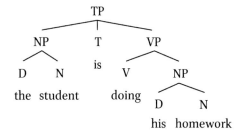

5. TP → NP T VP
    e.g. *Ali may give them an award*

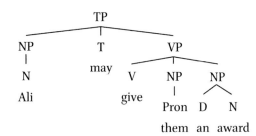

TREE STRUCTURE

UNIT 51

Complementizer Phrases

Verb Phrase

In addition to PSR (1) formulated for sentences, PSRs (2) and (3) are the only syntactic rules that generate clauses with the complementizers *that, if,* and *whether*.

1. TP → NP T VP   (for sentences)
2. VP → V CP   (for verbs followed by CP like *believe, think*)
3. CP → C TP   (for *that/if/whether*-clauses)

These PSRs can be demonstrated in tree structures as follows.

4. TP → NP T VP ||| CP → C TP
   e.g. ... *that the father opened the door*

5. TP → NP T VP ||| CP → C TP
   e.g. ... *if the train has stopped*

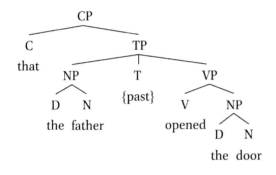 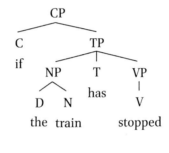

6. VP → V CP ||| CP → C TP ||| TP → NP T VP
   e.g. *Ali may ask whether Fatima visited her relatives.*

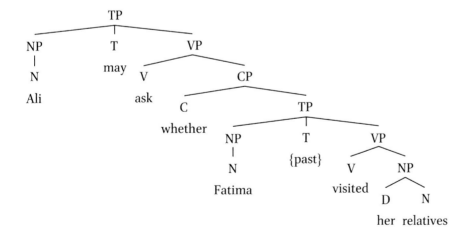

UNIT 52

Conjunction Phrases

Conjunction Phrase

Conjunction Phrases can be structurally drawn according to their PSRs as follows.

1. ConjP → NP Conj NP
   e.g. *the father and the mother*

2. ConjP → AP Conj AP
   e.g. *so afraid but very smart*

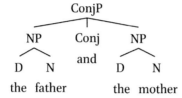
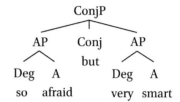

3. ConjP → VP Conj VP
   e.g. *take the biscuit or leave it*

4. ConjP → AdvP Conj AdvP
   e.g. *slowly but surely*

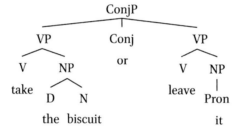
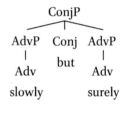

5. ConjP → TP Conj TP
   e.g. *The manager has left but his secretary will come.*

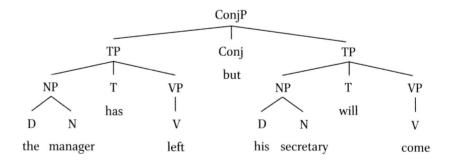

UNIT 53

Adjoined Phrases

Adjoined Phrases

Adjoined phrases or adjuncts are either AdvP or PP, and they can be represented according to their PSRs as follows.

1. VP → VP AdvP
   e.g. *He left the room suddenly.*

   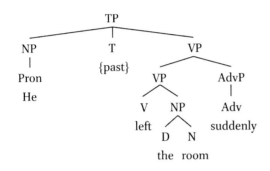

2. VP → AdvP VP
   e.g. *He suddenly left the room.*

   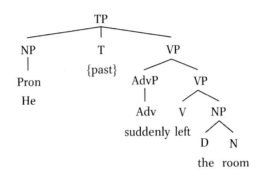

3. VP → VP PP
   e.g. *He paid the rent in the morning*

   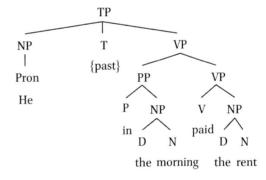

4. VP → AdvP VP
   e.g. *He, in the morning, paid the rent*

   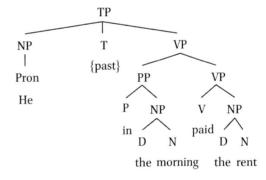

5. TP → PP TP
   e.g. *At night, he attends classes*

   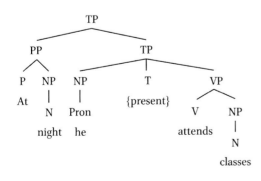

6. TP → AdvP TP
   e.g. *Recently, he has attended classes*

   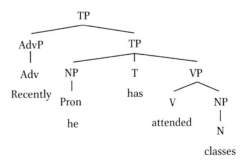

UNIT 54

Tree Drawing 1

Tree Drawing

To draw a syntactic tree, you should always take into consideration the fact that every sentence is created from two sources of information: (i) the lexicon (that includes words) and (ii) grammar (that includes PSRs). Thus, tree drawing requires knowledge about the words in the lexicon (i.e. what is a word's lexical category? What—and how many—complements does a head select? What is a word's subcategorization frame?) and the PSRs. Consider (1) below.

1. The professor delivered a lecture about this issue.

To generate (1), we need to list all the subcategorization frames of the heads (N, V, P): *professor, delivered, lecture, about, issue*.

2. The heads in sentence (1)   Subcategorization frames
   a. *professor*   *professor*, N [__]
   b. *delivered*   *delivered*, V [__ NP]
   c. *lecture*   *lecture*, [__ (PP$_{[about]}$)]
   d. *about*   *about*, P [__ NP]
   e. *issue*   *issue*, N [__]

The subcategorization frames in (2) are based on our knowledge of English in general, and sentence (1) in particular. For instance, we know that the verb *delivered* selects an obligatory NP because we routinely come across phrases such as [*delivered a speech, a sermon*, etc.]; thus its subcategorization frame includes NP in (2b). As for the noun *lecture*, we are familiar with phrases such as [*lecture about this topic/subject* etc.]; we therefore allow this noun to take an optional PP in (2c). We also know that the preposition *about* selects NP as in [*about the issue/topic* etc.]; thus we propose (2d). Regarding the nouns *professor* and *issue*, we rarely encounter complements after them, especially in (1); they are therefore represented without complements in (2a) and (2e).

Another important source of information is the PSRs. In the previous units, we devised a set of PSRs whereby we could construct similar phrases to the ones in sentence (1).

3. Phrases in sentence (1)   PSRs
   the professor   NP → D N
   delivered a lecture about this issue   VP → V NP
   a lecture about this issue   NP → D N PP
   about this issue   PP → P NP
   this issue   NP → D N

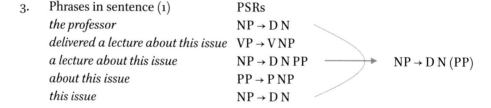

Although some PSRs are repeated in (3), they can be reduced to one rule as shown in the right-hand PSR of NP, referring to the three similar PSRs on the left side.

UNIT 55

Tree Drawing 11

Tree Drawing

In sum, sentence (1) can be generated if we know (i) the subcategorization frames of its heads and (ii) the appropriate PSRs that generate its phrases. This information is laid out in (2).

1. The professor delivered a lecture about this issue.

2. Subcategorization frames PSRS frames
   a. *professor*, N [___]   a. NP → D N
   b. *delivered*, V [___ NP]   b. PP → P NP
   c. *lecture*, [___ (PP$_{[about]}$)] c. NP → D N PP
   d. *about*, P [___ NP]   d. VP → V NP
   e. *issue*, N [___]   e. TP → NP T VP
                                      f. NP → D N

3. Tree for (1)

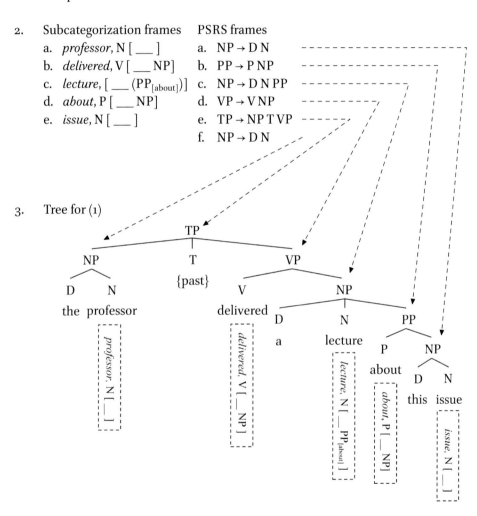

Using the information in (2), sentence (1) can be drawn as shown in (3). It is important to note that every head in (3) respects its subcategorization frames in (2), and represents it accordingly. For instance, the verb *delivered* in (3) is structurally positioned before NP as formulated in its subcategorization frame [___ NP]. Likewise, the noun *professor* appears in a separate node in accordance with its subcategorization frame [___] in (2). Concerning the PSRs, they are accurately mapped onto structure (3) without any violation.

UNIT 56

Tree Drawing III

Tree Drawing

In Unit 55, we represented sentence (1) as shown in (2).

1. The professor delivered a lecture about this issue.

2. Tree for (1)

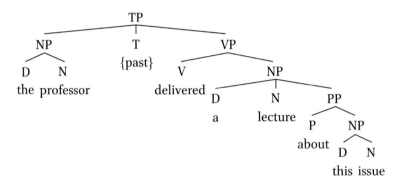

In the coming units, we will draw more trees. It is therefore important to learn a new approach to reduce complex structures. Syntacticians use triangles △ in trees when the internal branches of a given node are irrelevant. Thus, tree (2) can be reduced in several ways as illustrated in (3) through (5). Notice that only XPs are triangled.

3. A reduced tree for (1)

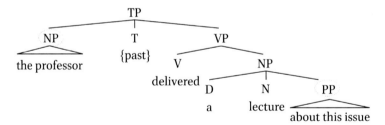

4. A more reduced tree for (1)

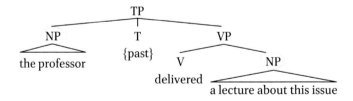

5. The most reduced tree for (1)

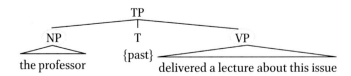

UNIT 57

Ambiguity

Ambiguity

Our knowledge of dominance (i.e. the hierarchical structure of words), precedence (i.e. the linear order of words) and constituency (i.e. the union of words) can now explain ambiguous sentences. In certain cases, one sentence may have multiple meanings as in (1).

1. The child does not run like his father.

Sentence (1) has three meanings:

2. The child does not run like his father **who does not run**. (= neither runs)
3. The child does not run like his father **who runs**. (= the father runs)
4. The child does not run **in the same speed** his father runs. (= both run).

Constituency and dominance account for the interpretation of any ambiguous sentence from a structural perspective. Consider the following ambiguous example.

5. Fatima saw the man with the binoculars.

Sentence (5) has two meanings. Through the rearrangement of the PP *with the binoculars*, we can illustrate the two meanings as in (6) and (7).

6. Fatima [saw with the binoculars] the man.
7. Fatima saw [the man with the binoculars].

In (6), Fatima used the binoculars and saw the man. In (7), Fatima saw the man who was carrying the binoculars with him. The ambiguity follows from the function of the PP *with the binoculars* in the structure. If it functions as an adjunct as in (6)–(8), it modifies the verb phrase *saw the man*. If it serves as a complement as in (7)–(9), it completes the meaning of the head noun *man*.

8. Meaning (6)   9. Meaning (7)

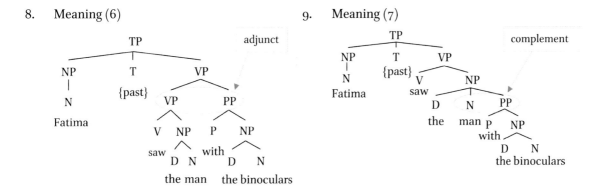

SECTION 5

X-Bar Theory

∴

X-BAR THEORY

UNIT 58

Motivation I

X-Bar Theory

X-BAR THEORY is a theory developed by Noam Chomsky (1970) to account for all the syntactic structures in the world languages. All the PSRs in the previous units are English-specific, and therefore cannot be applied to other languages like Arabic, French, Sanskrit etc. Moreover, for each English syntactic category (NP, VP, AP, AdvP etc.), a different set of PSRs is developed; these PSRs have nothing in common, neither are they uniform. X-bar theory aims to propose a **GENERAL SCHEME** that can be carried over to all categories in English as well as other languages. In doing so, it aims to develop a grammar for English and, through generalizations and principles, to construct a **UNIVERSAL GRAMMAR** (UG) that is applicable to all languages. This is the ultimate goal of all syntacticians.

Constituency

We can only realize the importance of X-bar theory if we consider the problems arising from old grammar discussed earlier. In the previous units, it was argued that every phrase in a sentence must be a constituent as shown in (1) and (2).

1. [NP The student] wrote [NP a wonderful essay] [PP in the class]
2. [*He*] wrote [*it*] [*there*].   (Substitution Test)

The blue phrases in (1) are constituents because they can be replaced with their respective proforms in (2). The pronouns *he* and *it* replace the NPs while *there* replaces the PP. If these phrases are really constituents, we predict that every constituent will be structurally captured in the tree. Each constituent must be under a separate node as in (3).

3. Tree for (1)

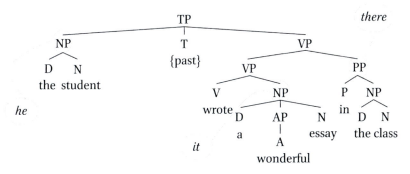

In (3) each constituent is structurally singled out under a separate node. The whole node of a constituent can be replaced by one proform. The NPs *the students* and *a wonderful essay* can be replaced by *he* or *it* respectively; and the PP *in the class* can be replaced by *there*. Although this is a desirable finding, our old grammar cannot always yield similar results.

UNIT 59

Motivation II

X-Bar Theory

Consider the NP *that book of Linguistics*, which presents a challenge to constituency tests.

1. That *book of Linguistics* arrived.

This NP consists of phrases functioning as separate constituents.

2. That *one of Linguistics* arrived.   = *one* replaces *book* only.
3. That *one* arrived.   = *one* replaces *book of Linguistics*

As shown in (2) and (3), the noun phrase *that book of Linguistics* involve two constituents: (i) *book* and (ii) *book of Linguistics*. The evidence that they are constituents comes from the **ONE-REPLACEMENT TEST**, which is a test that determines whether a group of words is a constituent by substituting the whole phrase with the proform *one*. The phrase *book* is a constituent because it can be replaced by *one* in (2). The phrase *book of Linguistics* is also a constituent because it can be fully substituted with *one* in (3). If these phrases (*book*, and *book of Linguistics*) are really two constituents as they are according to the one-replacement test, we predict that they will be structurally singled out in separate nodes. However, this prediction is not borne out as shown in our old structure (4).

4. Tree for (1)   5. Tree for (1)

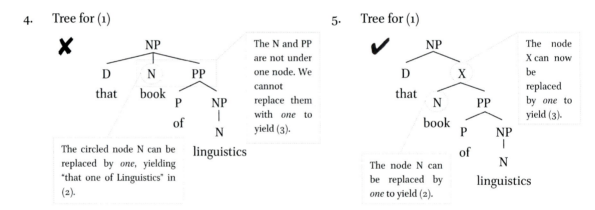

In (4), the circled N *book* is a constituent because it is singled out under a separate node (N), and thus can be substituted with *one*. Although the phrase *book of Linguistics* is also a constituent, based on the one-replacement test in (3), this phrase cannot be a constituent from a structural perspective because N *book* is in a separate node from the node where PP *of Linguistics* occurs; the two phrases *book* + *of Linguistics* cannot be grouped together or alone under one single node. In light of this constituency problem, X-bar theory argues that our old structure (4) is insufficient because it cannot capture all constituents structurally. Alternatively, it proposes a new structure roughly like the one in (5) that can at least separate each constituent in (2) and (3) under separate nodes. But what is X in (5)?

UNIT 60

Motivation III

X-Bar Theory

To capture the constituents in (2) and (3) below, X-bar theory proposes structure (4).

1. That *book of Linguistics* arrived.
2. That one *of Linguistics* arrived.   = *one* replaces *book* only.
3. That one arrived.   = *one* replaces *book of Linguistics*

4. Tree for (1)   5. Tree for (1)

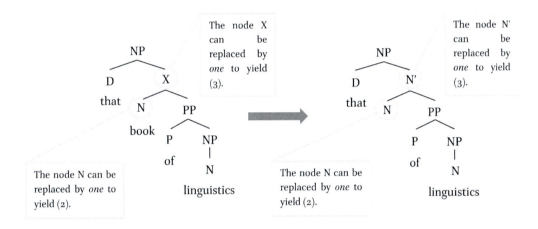

The X in (4) is proposed only to capture the constituent *book of linguistics* in (3), which needs to be under a separate node. In X-bar theory, this new level X is called X' (pronounced as "X-bar"). Although X' is formally written as $\overline{X}$ (with a bar over X), this notation is not easy to type in software tree-drawing programs. Thus, only a prime (') is used after X (i.e. X') in most syntactic works. This X' can be N', V', P', Adv', T', C', Conj' based on the category of the phrase within which it appears. Thus, X' is revised as N' in (5) because it appears within a noun phrase. The X-bar level effectively captures many other constituents as in (6) below, where every square can be substituted with *one*.

6. Every 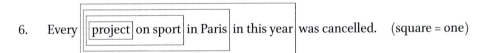 was cancelled.   (square = *one*)

7. Old tree for (5)   8. X'-theory tree for (5)

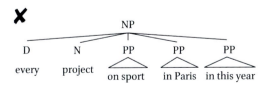
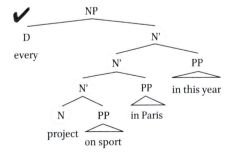

Structure (7) is old and insufficient because it does not capture the constituents squared in (6). The X'-theory structure in (8), where N' iterates to capture every constituent in a single node, is much better.

UNIT 61

Motivation IV

X-Bar Theory

Recall that all the earlier PSRs were written in the following format:

1. **XP → Specifier   X   Complement**
    NP → (D) (AP)   N   (PP)
    PP → (Deg)   P   (NP)
    TP → NP   T   VP
    AP → (Deg)   A   (PP)
    Etc.

The XP in (1) can be NP, VP, PP, AP, AdvP, CP etc. We have shown that the left-hand specifiers are words that precede, and add specific meanings to, the most important word, i.e. the head X. Specifiers include determiners, degree words, etc. Complements, on the other hand, complete the meaning of the head X and include different XPs such as NP, VP, PP, etc. Complements can be optional or obligatory.

X-bar theory proposes that all the PSRs above be reduced to a single scheme as in (2).

2. **X′-Theory Scheme**
    XP → Specifier, X′
    X′ → X, complement

The new level X′ can be N′, V′, V′, P′, A′, Adv′, T′, C′. Consider the old structural representation of rule (1) in (3) and that of the new X′-theory scheme (2) in (4).

3. Rule (1): **OLD STRUCTURE**   4.   Scheme (2): **X′-THEORY**

Given that the presence of X′ level in (4) is proven to be important to capture constituency facts, as discussed in Unit 60, structure (3) should now be abandoned. It is important to know that the X′ level in structure (4) can take different notations as shown in (5) through (7). Nonetheless, we will adhere to the notations in (5) throughout the book.

5.   6.   7.

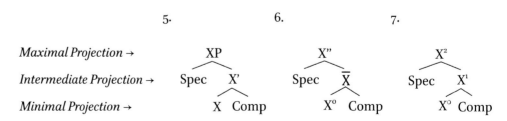

UNIT 62

Motivation V

X-Bar Theory

The difference between the old grammar in (1) and (2), on the one hand, and the X-bar theory grammar in (3) and (4), on the other, lies in the rules and their representative structures.

1. **Old Grammar Rule**

    XP → Specifier X Complement

2. **Flat Tree Structure**

3. **X-bar Theory Scheme**

    XP → Specifier, X'
    X' → X, complement

4. **Hierarchical Tree Structure**

The old structure in (2) is a **FLAT TREE STRUCTURE** with **TERNARY** branching (at most, three branches can be found at any one level). The X'-Theory structure in (4) is a **HIERARCHICAL TREE STRUCTURE** with **BINARY** branching (with two branches at each level). In addition to constituency problems, X'-theory seeks to solve problems related to word orders in the world languages. The old rule (1) is specific only to English or similar languages that require that specifiers precede the head, and that the head is followed by a complement. PSR (1) can generate the English word order (Subject + Verb + Object) in (5).

5. SUBJECT   VERB   OBJECT
    The jaguar   ate   the man

However, other languages do not have the same word order as English. Hixkaryana, a Caribbean language, has the reverse word order (Object + Verb + Subject) as shown in (6).

6. OBJECT   VERB   SUBJECT
    toto   *yononye*   *kamara*
    the-man   ate   the-jaguar
    'The jaguar ate the man'

In (6), the object precedes the verb, which in turn precedes the subject. Sentence (6) has the reverse order of English sentences. Thus, PSR (1) cannot generate sentences in Hixkaryana, not to mention numerous other word orders cross-linguistically. X'-theory aims to develop a universal scheme that generates all possible word orders in all languages.

UNIT 63

Motivation VI

X-Bar Theory

Consider the differing word orders in English and Hixkaryana again in (1) and (2).

1. SUBJECT VERB OBJECT
   The jaguar ate the man

2. OBJECT VERB SUBJECT
   toto yononye kamara
   the-man ate the-jaguar
   'The jaguar ate the man'

The old PSRs needed to generate the above sentences, given in (3), are represented in (4).

3. a. TP → NP T VP
   b. VP → V NP

4.

The rules above can generate English sentence (1) as in (5), but they fail to generate Hixkaryana sentence (2) as in (6).

5. Tree for (1)   6. Tree for (2)

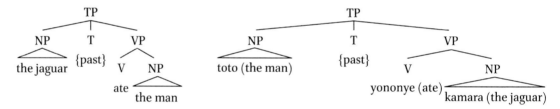

As shown in (6), the PSRs in (3) cannot be applied to Hixkaryana. In (6), the subject *kamara* 'the jaguar' is now in the object position, whereas the object *toto* 'the man' is in the subject position. The tree in (6) means 'the man ate the jaguar', while the intended meaning is 'the jaguar ate the man' as in (2). The problem is exacerbated by the many word orders in different languages shown in the table below (cf. Tomlin, 1986:22). How can we generate all these word orders through the old rules in (3)?

Word order	English equivalent	% of languages	Examples
SOV	She him loves	45%	Hindi, Greek, Latin, Japanese, Korean
SVO	She loves him	24%	English, French, Italian, Mandarin, Russian
VSO	Loves she him	9%	Arabic, Hebrew, Irish, Filipino, Welsh
VOS	Loves him she	3%	Baure, Proto-Austronesian, Malagasy
OVS	Him loves she	1%	Apalaí, Hixkaryana,
OSV	Him she loves	0%	Warao

X-BAR THEORY

UNIT 64

Motivation VII

X-Bar Theory

The ultimate goal of X'-theory is to provide rules that can generate all the possible phrase and sentence structures in the world's languages. The X'-theory scheme in (1) can achieve that.

1. **X-bar Theory Scheme**   2.   **Hierarchical Tree Structure**

   XP → Specifier, X'
   X' → X, complement

   ```
           XP
          /  \
        Spec  X'
              / \
             X  Comp
   ```

Unlike the old rules, the sister elements in scheme (1) are separated by a comma. This comma indicates that there is a free ordering that suits all the possible word orders in all languages. Thus, the X-bar theory scheme can generate all possible structures as shown below.

		English		Hixkaryana
3.	Possible specifier ordering	XP / \\ Spec X'	OR	XP / \\ X' Spec
4.	Possible complement ordering	X' / \\ X Comp	OR	X' / \\ Comp X

The two structures in (3) show all possible specifier ordering: the specifier can precede X' as in English, or follow it as in Hixkaryana. The two structures in (4) show all possible complement ordering: the complement follows the head as in English, or precedes it as in Hixkaryana. Thus, both sentences, in both English and Hixkaryana, can follow the X'-theory scheme in (1). However, their structure will differ in respect of ordering as shown below.

5. English sentence (TP)   6.   Hixkaryana sentence (TP)

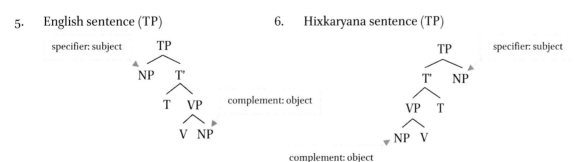

UNIT 65

Motivation VIII

X-Bar Theory

Based on the free ordering between (specifier, X') and (complement, head X) in the X'-theory scheme in (1), the tree for sentence (2) from Hixkaryana will be represented as in (3).

1. **X-bar Theory Scheme**
   XP → Specifier, X'
   X' → X, complement

2. OBJECT   VERB   SUBJECT
   toto   *yononye* *kamara*
   the-man   ate   the-jaguar
   'The jaguar ate the man'

3. Tree for (2)

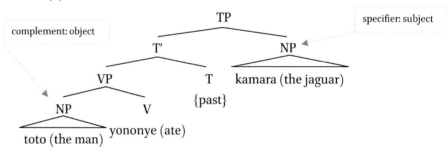

In (3), the subject *kamara* 'the jaguar' now fills the specifier position, i.e. the position of subjects in all languages. As for the object *toto* 'the man', it occupies the complement position of the verb as in other languages. Now, consider the word order in Turkish (Subject + Object + Verb). The structure for this order will be as in (5), where the order of (specifier, X') remains as in English, but the order of (complement, head X) is switched as in Hixkaryana.

4. SUBJECT OBJECT   VERB
   Yousef *elmayi*   *yedi*
   Yousef   the apple ate
   'Yousef ate the apple'

5. Tree for (4)

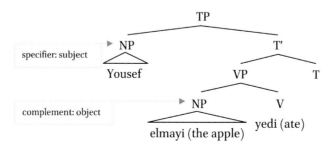

UNIT 66

Motivation IX

X-Bar Theory

To sum up, in X'-theory, we have one general scheme in (1). This scheme applies to all the languages in the world.

1. **X-bar Theory Scheme**
   XP → Specifier, X'
   X' → X, complement

However, the ordering between (specifier, X') or between (X, complement) is not entirely fixed. In many languages, specifiers might precede X' while in other languages X' might precede specifiers. The head X may also precede complements in some languages, but the reverse is attested in other languages. In brief, every language exhibits the appropriate ordering for its structure.

The framework we work within for these variations is known as the **PRINCIPLE-AND-PARAMETER** Framework (Lasnik, 1994; Chomsky & Lasnik, 1995). Principle and Parameters (P&P) is a framework formulated within generative syntax, where all languages are claimed to follow general principles (i.e. abstract rules) and specific parameters (i.e. switches) that are turned on or off for particular languages. For simplification, the general scheme in (1) can be considered as a general principle/rule that occurs in all languages, but the ordering of (specifier, X') or (X, complement) is a parameter. The parameter can be turned on or off to indicate whether a language is head-initial (i.e. X precedes complements) such as English or head-final (i.e. complements precede X) such as Turkish.

The parameters in X'-theory can be demonstrated as on or off switches. Whether a specifier precedes X' or not is dependent on whether the switch is turned on or off for that specific order as demonstrated below.

English		Turkish	
Principles		**Principles**	
Order:	Order:	Order:	Order:
Specifier, X'	X, Complement	Specifier, X'	X, Complement
Parameters		**Parameters**	
Specifier, X'	X, complement	Specifier, X'	X, complement
ON	ON	ON	OFF
X', specifier	Complement, X	X', specifier	Complement, X
OFF	OFF	OFF	ON

UNIT 67

Representation 1

X-Bar Theory

In the previous units, we have demonstrated a few advantages of X-bar theory, some of which are as follows. It can capture constituency, and generate all the possible word orders (sometimes with transformational rules; see Unit 86). It reduces the rules to a minimum through general scheme (1), represented in (2). From now on, we will use the representation in (2) for English data. This representation will not dramatically affect our earlier results nor will it change the whole syntactic scenario.

1. X-bar Theory Scheme   2. X'-Theory Structure

   XP → Specifier, X'
   X' → X, complement

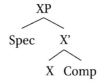

From Old to New Tree Structures

In the coming units, we will draw trees using the X'-theory scheme above. As for subcategorization frames (what does a head select as a complement?), they will remain intact. Let us demonstrate how the trees will be redrawn in accordance with X'-theory.

OLD REPRESENTATION → **X-BAR THEORY REPRESENTATION**

3. General Representation

4. Noun Phrase

5. Preposition Phrase

UNIT 68

Representation II

From Old to New Tree Structures

All our old structures need to be adapted to the new X-bar theory structures as follows.

OLD REPRESENTATION → **X-BAR THEORY REPRESENTATION**

1. Adjective Phrase

```
      AP              →            AP
     /|\                          /  \
   Deg A  PP                    Deg   A'
                                     / \
                                    A   PP
```

2. Adverb Phrase

```
      AdvP            →           AdvP
     /   \                       /    \
   Deg   Adv                   Deg    Adv'
                                       |
                                      Adv
```

3. Verb Phrase 1

```
    VP               →             VP
    |                               |
    V                               V'
                                    |
                                    V
```

4. Verb Phrase 2

```
    VP               →             VP
   / \                              |
  V   NP                            V'
                                   / \
                                  V   NP
```

5. Verb Phrase 3

```
    VP               →             VP
   / \                              |
  V   PP                            V'
                                   / \
                                  V   PP
```

6. Verb Phrase 4

```
     VP              →             VP
    /|\                             |
   V NP PP                          V'
                                   /|\
                                  V NP PP
```

UNIT 69

Representation III

From Old to New Tree Structures

All our old structures need to migrate to the new X-bar theory structures as follows.

OLD REPRESENTATION → **X-BAR THEORY REPRESENTATION**

1. Verb Phrase 5

2. Verb Phrase 6

3. Verb Phrase 7

4. Tense Phrase

5. Complementizer Phrase

```
      CP              →         CP
     /  \                       |
    C   TP                      C'
                               / \
                              C   TP
```

6. Conjunction Phrase

UNIT 70

NP, AP, PP, AdvP, VP

Random Phrases

Let us represent random phrases according to the X'-theory scheme.

1. NP: *the destruction of the city*   2. AP: *so afraid of the project*

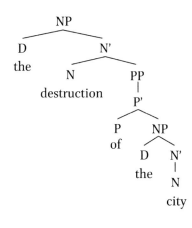 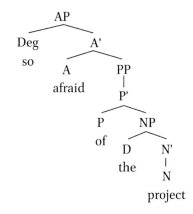

3. PP: *right at the corner*   4. AdvP: *so quickly*

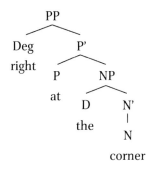 

5. VP: *gave Ali a present*   6. ConjP: *the student and the teacher*

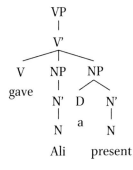 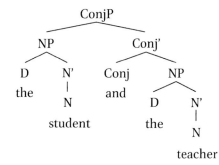

UNIT 71

TP and CP

Random Phrases

Below are TP (a sentence) and CP represented according to X′-theory principles.

1. TP: *The police has arrested the thief.*

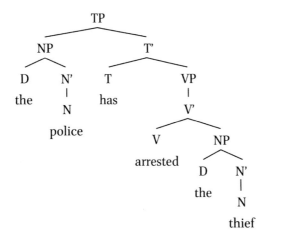

2. TP: *The fans have left the stadium.*

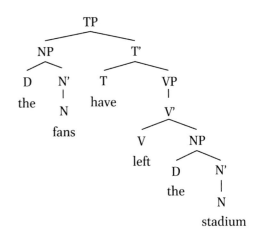

3. CP: *They have inquired whether the match ended.*

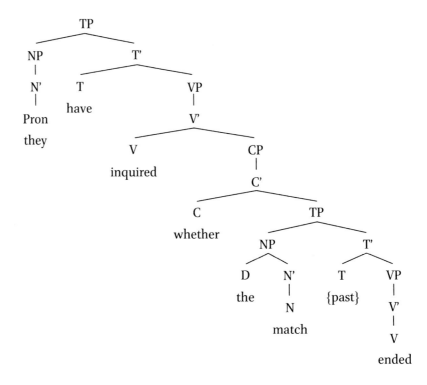

UNIT 72

Adjunction Rules 1

Adjoined Phrases

In the old grammar, adjuncts were PP/AdvP added to phrases such as VP and TP as shown in the following structures. Triangles are used for irrelevant information.

1. VP → AdvP VP   2. VP → VP PP

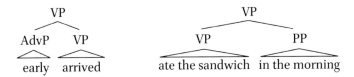

3. TP → AdvP TP   4. TP → PP TP

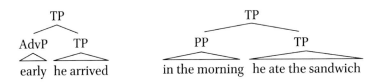

Note that X'-Theory does not propose branches for adjuncts because our old adjunction rules do not require any modification. Syntacticians, however, propose that adjuncts be iteratively attached to the X' level, either to its left as in (6), or to its right as in (7).

5.   6.   7.

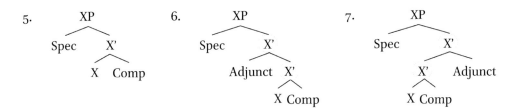

The most important observation about the above structures is that adjuncts are not positioned in a Spec or a Comp position. If an XP is attached to an intermediate X'-level, it is an adjunct. To sum up, adjuncts can be represented in two ways: either (i) through the old PSRs as in (8) and (9), or (ii) using the proposal of X'-Theory as in (10) and (11).

8.   9.   10.   11.

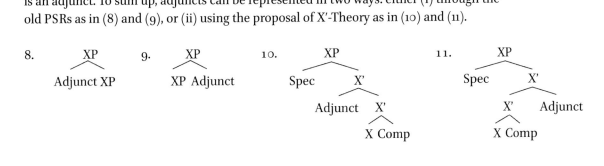

UNIT 73

Adjunction Rules II

Adjoined Phrases

One property of adjuncts is that they can iterate (Bresnan, 1982; Svenonius, 1994; Stroik and Putnam, 2013). Iterativity can be captured in both structures.

1. Old Structure
   (*they*) *read in the bed at night*

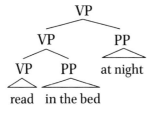

2. X'-Theory Structure
   (*they*) *read in the bed at night*

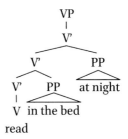

The difference between the old structure and X'-theory follows from the fact that adjuncts are added to an iterative VP in (1), but adjoined to an iterative V' in (2). Yet, we have preliminary evidence that the attachment of adjuncts to the X' level has shortcomings. Although adjuncts of VPs can be generated in X'-theory, adjunction to the X' level is not desirable for TPs.

3. Old Structure
   In the morning, he ate the sandwich

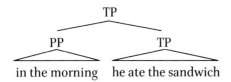

4. X-Theory Structure
   In the morning, he ate the sandwich

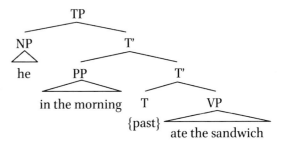

In (3), adjuncts are successfully added by our old grammar rules, without any problems. However, in (4), adjunction of PP to the T' level violates precedence, and does not generate the desired sentence. Sentence (4) structurally reads as: *he in the morning ate the sandwich*. This is because the NP *he* occupies the specifier position, and there is no T' position above the specifier where the PP can be adjoined unless we propose an unnecessary XP above TP for adjuncts. Thus, we will keep our old adjunction proposal in (3) because it is more practical, not to mention the fact that X'-theory remains silent about adjuncts. In Unit 113, we will develop a better transformation-based analysis for adjuncts within X'-theory.

UNIT 74

Determiner Phrase 1

Determiner Phrases

X′-Theory leads to a new view of noun phrases. Consider the following examples.

1. I received *the* books.
2. I received books.

To generate the noun phrases above, we proposed the old PSR in (3).

3. NP → (D) (AP) N (PP)

Rule (3) suggests that nouns like *books* can be preceded by a specifier, which is an optional determiner (D) such as *the*. D is sometimes present as in (1), or absent as in (2). Optionality means that if we remove the optional element, the phrase remains grammatical. This is the case with plural NPs as in (2). However, when it comes to singular NPs, rule (3) is proven wrong. Consider the following examples.

4. I received *the* book.
5. *I received book.

The determiner *the* that precedes a singular noun in (4) is not optional at all. If it is removed, the sentence becomes ungrammatical as in (5). Rule (3) wrongfully predicts that the noun phrase *book* in (5) is correct because the determiner is always optional. This is a flaw in the old PSR in (3); it starts to generate ungrammatical noun phrases as in (5). Thus, rule (3) must be revised. The missing determiner in (5) seems obligatory. Obligatoriness suggests that the determiner is not an optional specifier as in (3), but a head because heads are always obligatory. Given that heads select complements, we expect D (if it is really a head) to select complements. D indeed selects certain complements as shown in the examples below.

6. I receive **a** [NP *good book*].
7. *I received **a** [NP *good books*].
8. I received **many** [NP *good books*].
9. *I received **many** [NP *good book*].

In (6), the D *a* selects only a singular NP, but it does not select a plural NP as in (7). Although the D *many* selects a plural NP in (8), it does not select a singular NP in (9). Complement selection also suggests that D is not a specifier but a head that selects NPs. Thus, we will revise our view of determiners, and consider them heads (Ds). Given that every head projects its own phrase, the head D should project a **DETERMINER PHRASE** (DP). Based on these new revisions, rule (3) is wrong and should be revised as in (10). After the removal of D from rule (3), the remainder is given in (11).

10. DP → D NP   A new rule
11. NP → (AP) N (PP)   The residual rule of (3) after the removal of D

UNIT 75

Determiner Phrase II

Determiner Phrases

Based on empirical facts, determiners such as *a, the, many* etc are now heads (Ds) that select certain complements as in the subcategorization frames below.

1. *a*, D [___ NP$_{[singular]}$]   example: **a** [$_{NP}$ *good book*].
2. *many*, D [___ NP$_{[plural]}$]   example: **many** [$_{NP}$ *good books*]
3. *the*, D [___ NP]   example: **the** [$_{NP}$ *good book/books*]

In (1) through (3), the head D selects NP with specific properties. The head D *a* in (1) only selects a singular NP. The same subcategorization frame is given to all other determiners that select singular NP such as *an, one, each, every* etc. In (2), the head D *many* selects a plural NP only. The same applies to other determiners such as *several, some, few* etc. As for the determiner *the* in (3), it selects an NP unspecified in number (i.e. singular or plural). Under certain circumstances, however, it seems that we do not have D at all as in (4) and (5). Does this mean that D should be treated again as a specifier?

4. I received ___ **good books**.
5. I invited ___ **Ahmed**

In these cases, D is still a head. Yet, this D is not *the/a/may* etc but a null and unpronounced determiner ∅. The head D ∅ selects only a plural NP as in (6), or a proper noun as in (7).

6. I received ∅ [$_{NP}$ good books].
7. I received ∅ [$_{NP}$ Ahmed].

Thus, the subcategorization frame of the head D ∅ will be as follows.

8. ∅, D [___ NP$_{[plural/proper]}$]   for examples (6) and (7)

In light of these revisions, we conclude that the PSR rule in (9) should be revised as in (10).

9. OLD RULE   OLD REPRESENTATION

    NP → (D) (AP) N (PP)   NP
                                                     D AP N PP

10. NEW RULES   X'-THEORY REPRESENTATION

    DP → D NP   DP
    NP → (AP) N (PP) |
                                            D'
                                     D   NP
                                     AP NP PP

UNIT 76

Determiner Phrase III

Determiner Phrases

All the previous noun phrases (NPs) are now determiner phrases (DPs). D is a head that selects NP as shown in rule (1).

1. DP → D NP

The complement NP in (1) conforms to rule (2), which is the old PSR but without D.

2. NP → (AP) N (PP)

Rule (2), however, needs to be revised as well as it does not generate the NPs below.

3. a beautiful dog.   one adjective
4. a beautiful big dog.   two adjectives
5. a beautiful big white dog.   three adjectives
6. a beautiful big white German dog.   four adjectives

The number of adjectives increases, moving from (3) towards (6). Our old PSR (2) cannot generate noun phrases with more than one adjective. Rather than adding more APs to rule (2), we can simply treat APs as adjuncts because iterativity is a property of adjunction (see Unit 22). Since adjectives iterate in (3) through (6), they are adjuncts. Thus, we will delete AP from rule (2), and assign an adjunction rule for adjectives as in (7) represented in (8).

7. NP → AP NP

8. Representation of Rule (7)

```
      NP
     /  \
    AP   NP
```

Adjunction rule (7) can now generate a long noun phrase such as (6) as shown in (9).

9. Tree for (6)

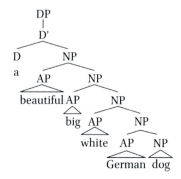

UNIT 77

Determiner Phrase IV

Determiner Phrases

As a provisional summary, our old PSR for NP was as laid out in (1). After removing the head D from it, it became as in (2). Following the removal of the AP from it, it is now like (3). The removed elements D and AP are given separate rules in (4) and (5) respectively.

1. NP → **(D)** (AP) N (PP)   before removing (D)
2. NP → **(AP)** N (PP)   before removing (AP)
3. NP → N (PP)   Final, after removing (D) and (AP)

4. DP → D NP   Determiner phrase
5. NP → AP NP   Adjunction rule for adjectives

The residual NP rule in (3) is important. Nouns can be followed by an optional PP, which is sometimes present as in (6), and sometimes absent as in (7).

6. The destruction [$_{PP}$ of the city].   Complement
7. The destruction.

Given that the PP in (6) is an optional complement, it can be generated by rule (3). Thus, rule (3) cannot be removed from our grammar. However, we need a new rule to account for the following data where the PP is an adjunct iterating more than once.

8. Every project [$_{PP}$ in Paris] [$_{PP}$ during the weekend] was cancelled.

The PPs in (8) cannot be generated by rule (3), which only shows a single PP, not more. Given that all the PPs in (8) are adjuncts, they need to be treated like adjectives. Thus, the adjunction rule in (9) should be proposed for these PPs.

9. NP → NP PP

10. Representation of Rule (9)

    NP
    ╱╲
    NP PP

The adjunction rule in (9) can now generate the long NP in (8) as shown in (11).

11. Tree for (8)

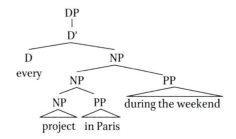

UNIT 78

Determiner Phrase V

Determiner Phrases

To sum up, the PSRs rules that we developed after the introduction of DP are as follows:

Complementation Rules
1. DP → D NP   This rule generates [$_D$ a [$_{NP}$ book]]; [$_D$ many [$_{NP}$ books]]
                                     [$_D$ ∅ [$_{NP}$ books]]; [$_D$ ∅ [$_{NP}$ Ahmed]]
2. NP → N PP   This rule generates [$_N$ destruction [$_{PP}$ of the city]]

Adjunction Rules
3. NP → AP NP This rule generates [$_{AP}$ nice] [$_{AP}$ big] [$_{AP}$ red] [$_{NP}$ dog]
4. NP → NP PP This rule generates [$_{NP}$ events [$_{PP}$ in NY][$_{PP}$ in weekdays]

Using X'-Theory principles and the rules above, we can generate the following long noun phrase in (5). Note that all NPs are now headed by D, which projects as DP.

5. The horrible   complete   destruction   of the city   at night
    D   AP-$_{Adjunct}$ AP-$_{Adjunct}$ N   PP-$_{complement}$ PP-$_{Adjunct}$

6.

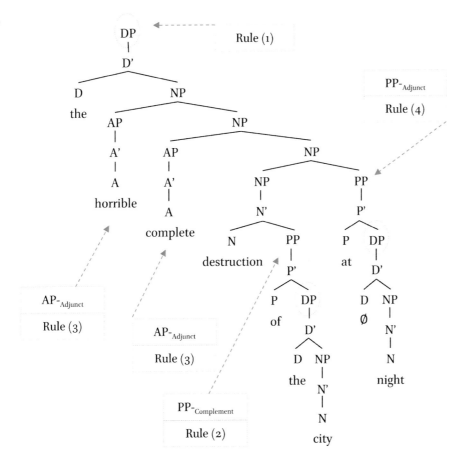

UNIT 79

Determiner Phrase VI

Pronouns

One advantage of the DP-hypothesis (Abney, 1987) is that it accounts for pronouns as well. Remember that pronouns were presented in the following old PSR.

1.   NP → Pron

PSR (1) is theoretically wrong because Pron seems to be a head, but this head does not project **PRONOUN PHRASE** (PronP) similar to other PSRs. Another problem is that pronouns are NPs in (1); thus, we expect them to be modified by nominal modifiers such as adjectives. However, adjectives cannot modify pronouns as in (2).

2.   *Small he came.

Thus, in light of the DP hypothesis, syntacticians propose that pronouns appear in the head D position. In certain cases, pronouns are followed by an NP as in (3); yet, in most cases, they are not followed by any NP as in (4).

3.   We students acknowledged that ...   4.   We acknowledged that ....

Thus, we can argue that the NP that follows D should be optional as in (5).

5.   DP → D (NP)

Consider the representation of (3) and (4) in (6) and (7) respectively.

6.   Tree for (3)   7.   Tree for (4)

This proposal does not contradict our earlier findings because NP after D can also be removed as shown in (9) in contrast to (8). In (9), the determiner *some* stands alone.

8.   [_D Some [_NP good books]] arrived.   9.   [_D Some] [_NP ~~good books~~]] arrived.

The NP in (9), drawn in (11), is elided due to a syntactic operation called **NOUN ELLIPSIS**.

10.   Tree for (8)   11.   Tree for (9)

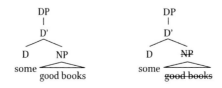

UNIT 80

Determiner Phrase VII

PSRs

In light of the DP-hypothesis, all NPs in the old PSRs should be changed into DPs. These PSRs also need to be converted into the X′ theory scheme.

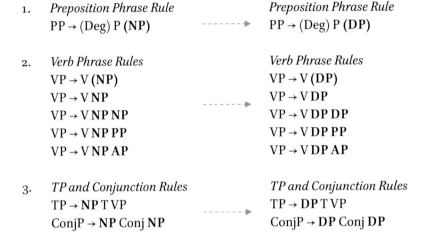

1. *Preposition Phrase Rule*   *Preposition Phrase Rule*
   PP → (Deg) P (**NP**)   PP → (Deg) P (**DP**)

2. *Verb Phrase Rules*   *Verb Phrase Rules*
   VP → V (**NP**)   VP → V (**DP**)
   VP → V **NP**   VP → V **DP**
   VP → V **NP NP**   VP → V **DP DP**
   VP → V **NP** PP   VP → V **DP** PP
   VP → V **NP** AP   VP → V **DP** AP

3. *TP and Conjunction Rules*   *TP and Conjunction Rules*
   TP → **NP** T VP   TP → **DP** T VP
   ConjP → **NP** Conj **NP**   ConjP → **DP** Conj **DP**

Genitive 's

Based on the X′-theory scheme in (4), DP can take the following scheme in (5).

4. **X′-Theory Scheme**   5. **DP Rules**
   XP → Specifier, X′   DP → Spec, D′
   X′ → X, complement   D′ → D, NP

Recall that the head D in (5) can host a determiner or a pronoun whereas the complement position is filled by a noun phrase (NP). Yet, it is not clear what may occupy the specifier position of DP. One advantage of the DP-hypothesis and X′-theory is that it can generate possessive phrases such as *my brother's car* by putting the possessor DP *my brother* in the specifier position while treating the possessed NP as a complement. The head D will be filled with the possessive suffix ('s). The phrase *my brother's car* will be structured as in (6).

6.
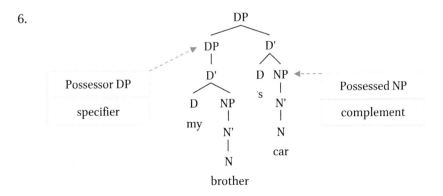

UNIT 81

Complementizer Phrase 1

Complementizer Phrase

Let us revise complementizer phrases (CPs). We have learned that all CPs are complements of verbs such as *believe, wonder* and *ask* as shown in the following examples.

1. I **believe** *that* Ahmed wrote a letter.
2. I **wonder** *whether* Ahmed has been writing a letter.
3. I **ask** *if* Ahmed will write a letter.

In (1) through (3), the verbs *believe, wonder* and *ask* are followed by CPs: *that/whether/if*-clauses. These complementizers (*that, whether, if*) introduce subordinate clauses which have verbs with different tenses: *wrote* (past), *has been writing* (continuous perfect) and *will write* (future). The inflected verbs are called **FINITE VERBS**, and they inflect (= change in morphology) for tense, number, gender and person as in (4). **NON-FINITE VERBS**, as in (5), appear in bare form and do not inflect for tense, number, gender and person.

4. Ahmed writ**es**/wrote/**has** writt**en**/**is** writ**ing** a letter.
5. Ahmed wants to **write** a letter.

The non-finite verb *write* in (5) remains in bare form with no tense specifications such as past, present, etc. Thus, we can say that the complementizers *that/if/whether* in (1) through (3) are followed by **FINITE CLAUSES** (i.e. clauses with tensed verbs) whereas a new complementizer, such as *for* in (6) and (7), is followed by a **NON-FINITE CLAUSE** (i.e. clauses with a verb in bare form).

6. They **need** *for* their son to win. 7. I **hope** *for* you to succeed.

To generate syntactic trees for (6) and (7), we should treat the blue phrases as CPs. The word *for* is a complementizer followed by TP whose head hosts the infinitive *to*. Compare the CP followed by a finite clause in (8) with the CP followed by a non-finite one in (9).

8. Tree for sentence (1)

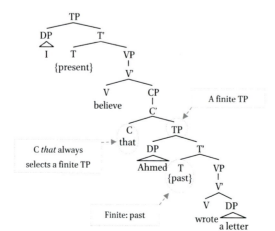

9. Tree for sentence (7)

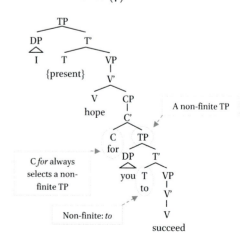

UNIT 82

Complementizer Phrase II

Complementizer Phrase

We have learned that the complementizers *that/whether/if* can be followed by finite clauses as in (1) through (3), while the complementizer *for* is followed by non-finite clauses as in (4).

1. I **believe** *that* Ahmed wrote a letter.
2. I **wonder** *whether* Ahmed has been writing a letter.
3. I **ask** *if* Ahmed will write a letter.
4. They **need** *for* their son to win.

Note that every verb selects a special complementizer as shown below.

5. I **believe** *that* Ahmed wrote a letter.
6. *I **believe** *whether/if* Ahmed wrote a letter.
7. *I **believe** *for* Ahmed to write a letter.
8. I **wonder** *whether/if* Ahmed has been writing a letter.
9. *I **wonder** *that* Ahmed has been writing a letter.
10. *I **wonder** *for* Ahmed to write a letter.
11. They **need** *for* their son to win.
12. *They **need** *that* their son wins.
13. *They **need** *whether/if* their son wins.

In (5), the verb *believe* selects only a CP headed by the head C *that*, but not *whether/if* as in (6) or *for* with a non-finite clause as in (7). In contrast, the verb *wonder* in (8) selects only a CP headed by *whether/if*, but not *that* as in (9) or *for* as in (10). As for the verb *need*, it selects only a CP headed by *for* followed by a non-finite clause as in (11), but not *that* or *whether/if* with finite clauses as in (12) and (13) respectively. To ensure that every verb takes CP with the appropriate head, we should insert this information into the subcategorization frames of these verbs as shown in (14).

14. Subcategorization frames   other similar verbs:
    a. *believe*, V [___ CP$_{[that]}$]   *claim, say, notice, declare, etc.*
    b. *wonder*, V [___ CP$_{[whether/if]}$]   *ask, inquire, question, etc.*
    c. *need*, V [___ CP$_{[for]}$]   *hope, want, wish, etc.*

These subcategorization frames feed syntax with appropriate CP-complements. Given that the non-finite verb *win* in (11) is in bare form after the infinitive *to*, we can also add this information as a selectional property in the subcategorization frame of the infinitival word *to*.

15. *to*, T$_{[nonfinite]}$ [___ VP$_{[bare]}$]

UNIT 83

Complementizer Phrase III

Complementizer Phrase

One important fact about CPs is that the complementizer *that* is optional: compare (1) to (2). However, other complementizers, such as *whether/if/for*, are obligatory as in (3) through (5). The notation *(word) means that the starred bracketed word is not optional. Should a word between such brackets be removed, the sentence would become ungrammatical.

1. I **believe** *that* Ahmed wrote a letter.
2. I **believe** Ahmed wrote a letter.
3. I **wonder** *(whether)* Ahmed has been writing a letter.
4. I **ask** *(if)* Ahmed will write a letter.
5. They **need** *(for)* their son to win.

Because C is a head that cannot be optional, we will assume that the complementizer in (2) is null -∅. Thus, the tree for (2) will be identical to the tree given for (1) (see Unit 81, e.g. 8). The only difference is that C head will be filled with -∅ for (2) rather than *that* for (1).

Another important fact about CPs is that they can be complements of adjectives, nouns or even prepositions. Consider the following examples.

6. He is **afraid/aware/sure/certain** *that* Ahmed wrote a letter.
7. We have (a) **belief/feeling/proof/evidence** *that* Ahmed wrote a letter.
8. We argued **about/over** *whether* Ahmed wrote a letter.

In (6), the adjectives *afraid/aware/sure/certain* are followed by a CP. The same CP-selection applies to the nouns *belief/feeling/proof/evidence* in (7) and the prepositions *about/over* in (8). The AP, NP and PP in (6) through (8) can be illustrated as follows.

9. Tree for (6) 10. Tree for (7) 11. Tree for (8)

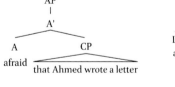 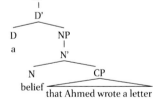 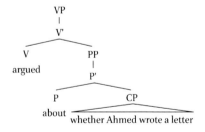

UNIT 84

Auxiliaries and Modals 1

Auxiliaries and Modals

Auxiliaries (*is, am, are, was, were, has, have, had* etc.) and modals (*shall, should, will, would, may, might*, etc.) occupy the head T in every sentence. Although all the modals are followed by a verb in bare form, auxiliaries (*is, am, are* etc.) are followed by different VPs.

Present
1. He is *coming*.   (auxiliary + continuous form: verb + *ing*)
2. He is *beaten*.   (auxiliary + passive form: verb+*en*)
3. He is *a student*.   (auxiliary + a noun phrase)
4. He is *angry*.   (auxiliary + an adjective phrase)

Past
5. They were *coming*.   (auxiliary + continuous form: verb + *ing*)
6. They were *beaten*.   (auxiliary + passive form: verb+ *en*)
7. They were *students*.   (auxiliary + a noun phrase)
8. They were *angry*.   (auxiliary + an adjective phrase)

In light of the examples above, the auxiliary *be* can be in a present form as in (1) through (4), or in a past form as in (5) through (8). In both tenses, the auxiliary is followed by one of the following: a verb in a continuous form (+ing) as in (1) and (5); a verb in a passive form (+en) as in (2) and (6); a noun phrase as in (3) and (7); or an adjective phrase as in (4) and (8). Thus, we can conclude that the auxiliary *be* selects different complements as illustrated in the following subcategorization frames.

9. *be*, T [___ VP$_{[ing]}$]   for (1), (5)
10. *be*, T [___ VP$_{[en]}$]   for (2), (6)
11. *be*, T [___ DP]   for (3), (7)
12. *be*, T [___ AP]   for (4), (8)

The syntactic tree structures for sentences (1) through (4) will be as follows:

13. Sentence (1)   14. Sentence (2)   15. Sentence (3)   16. Sentence (4)

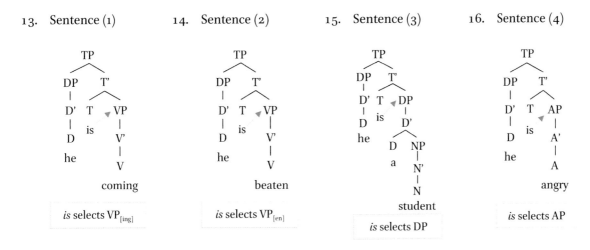

UNIT 85

Auxiliaries and Modals 11

Auxiliaries and Modals

In the past unit, we discussed sentences with only one auxiliary in their predicates. We assume that auxiliaries and modals occupy the head T. In certain cases, however, more than one auxiliary or modal may appear in one sentence. Thus, we need to investigate whether all these auxiliaries and modals appear in the head T. Consider the following examples.

1. He should study. (modal + verb in bare form)
2. He should be studying. (modal + be + Verb$_{[ing]}$)
3. He should be beaten. (modal + be + Verb$_{[en]}$)
4. He should have been studying. (modal + have + Verb$_{[en]}$ + Verb$_{[ing]}$)
5. He should have been beaten. (modal + have + Verb$_{[en]}$ + Verb$_{[en]}$)

In (1), a modal such as *should* is followed by a verb in bare form. Thus, all modals such as *shall, should, will, would, may* and *might* select a verb in bare form. As discussed in Unit 84, the auxiliary *be* selects VP in a continuous form as in (2), or VP in a passive form as in (3). In (4), however, the auxiliary *have* is followed by a perfect VP[en]. Thus, we will claim that the auxiliary *have* selects a VP[en] as a complement. Finally, the auxiliary *been* (which is a form of *be*) is followed by a verb in a continuous form as in (4), or a passive form as in (5). These selectional properties are summarized as follows.

6. *should*, T [__ VP$_{[bare]}$] for 1–5 8. *be/been*, V [__ VP$_{[en]}$] for 3/5
7. *be/been*, V [__ VP$_{[ing]}$] for 2/4 9. *have*, V [__ VP$_{[en]}$] for 4/5

In (7) through (9), the auxiliaries *be/been* and *have* are categorized as verbs (V), whereas the modal *should* in (8) is treated as a tense word (T). Thus, in (10) and (11), the modal *should* occupies the head T while the auxiliaries *have* or *been* function as verbs selecting other VPs.

10. Tree for sentence (4) 11. Tree for sentence (5)

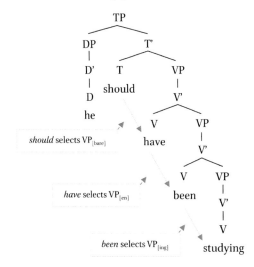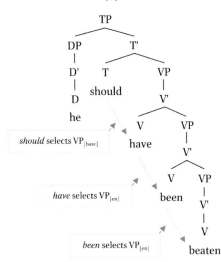

SECTION 6

Transformations

∴

UNIT 86

Yes/No Questions 1

Transformational Grammar

In the past units, we have shown that the X'-theory scheme in (1) can generate an infinite number of phrases and sentences.

1. **X-bar Theory Scheme**
   XP → Specifier, X'
   X' → X, complement

Let us now see how the scheme in (1) generates constructions such as **YES/NO QUESTIONS**. A yes/no question is derived from its relevant sentence through the inversion of auxiliaries/modals and the subject. Questions (3) and (5) are derived from sentences (2) and (4) respectively, and they are yes/no questions because their answers are either 'yes' or 'no'.

2. The police **have** *arrested the criminals.* (Subject + **Auxiliary** + *VP*)
3. **Have** the police .... *arrested the criminals?* (**Auxiliary** + Subject + *VP*)
4. The police **should** *arrest the criminals.* (Subject + **Modal** + *VP*)
5. **Should** the police .... *arrest the criminals?* (**Modal** + Subject + *VP*)

Notice that the auxiliaries/modals in the yes/no questions in (3) and (5) move from the position indicated by dots (....) to the front of their relevant sentences. These auxiliaries/modals cannot be repeated as in the ungrammatical questions (6) and (7).

6. ***Have** the police **have** *arrested the criminals?*
7. ***Should** the police **should** *arrest the criminals?*

The non-repetition of auxiliaries/modals indicates that these auxiliaries/modals in yes/no questions are the same elements in their relevant sentences. Since auxiliaries/modals occupy the head T, they must structurally move from T to a higher projection above TP so that they precede the subject in spec,TP. Thus, one may propose that there be a **QUESTION PHRASE** (QP) above TP, and that auxiliaries/modals move from head T to head Q as in (8) and (9).

8. Tree for (3)   9. Tree for (5)

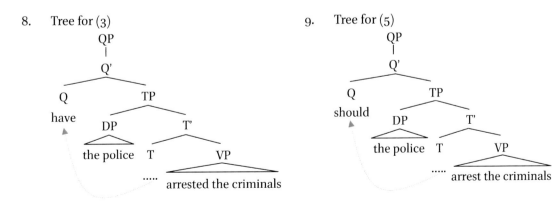

UNIT 87

Yes/No Questions II

Transformational Grammar

The tentative proposal for yes/no question formations assumes that auxiliaries/modals move from head T to head Q. This proposal of a **QUESTION PHRASE** (QP), however, is unnecessary because there is another XP (above TP) that may function as a landing site for auxiliaries/modals in yes/no questions: the Complementizer Phrase as in (1) and (2).

1. I believe [$_{CP}$ that [$_{TP}$ the police should arrest the criminals].

2. Tree for (1)

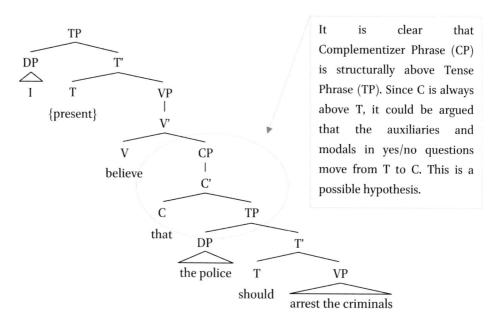

It is clear that Complementizer Phrase (CP) is structurally above Tense Phrase (TP). Since C is always above T, it could be argued that the auxiliaries and modals in yes/no questions move from T to C. This is a possible hypothesis.

Thus, there are two possible positions for auxiliaries/modals to move to in yes-no questions, either head Q as in (4), or head C as in (5). Which one is the better option?

3. **Should** the police .... *arrest the criminals*? (**Modal** + Subject + ... + *VP*)

4. Tree for (3)

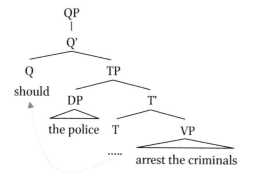

5. Tree for (3)

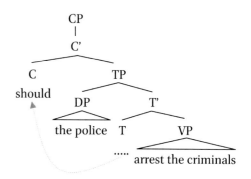

UNIT 88

Yes/No Questions III

Transformational Grammar

Evaluating the proposals of CP or QP, it seems that CP is more appropriate for questions than QP. We have evidence that there is CP above TP, and this C is sometimes filled with *that/if/whether/for*. However, we do not have evidence for the presence of QP; we simply invented it as a landing site for auxiliaries/modals. Further evidence that auxiliaries/modals move from T to C in question formation follows from the examples below.

1. The police **should** arrest them. (A sentence)
2. **Should** the police .... arrest them? (main question: inversion)
3. I wonder if the police **should** arrest them. (embedded question: No inversion)
4. *I wonder if **should** the police ... arrest them. (embedded question: No inversion)

Question (2) is derived from sentence (1), where the modal *should* inverts with the subject *the police*. However, in an embedded question like (3), the modal *should* cannot invert with the subject *the police*. Should the modal *should* invert with the subject in an embedded question as in (4), the sentence would become ungrammatical. Why? In (5), the head C is filled with the complementizer *if*. Thus, when the modal *should* attempts to move from T to C to form an embedded question, it finds the position of C filled with the complementizer *if*, and it is thus blocked from landing on C. These examples provide evidence for the fact that that auxiliaries/modals indeed move from T to C in question formations. If auxiliaries/modals, on the other hand, were to move from T to Q, it would be possible in English to have an embedded question as in (4) above, because Q would always be an empty site. Consider structure (5) for the embedded question in (3).

5. Tree for (3)

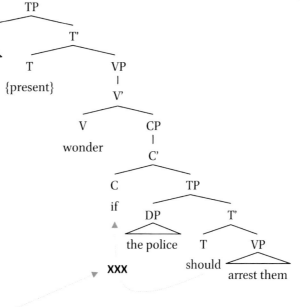

The modal *should* cannot move from T to C because C is filled with the complementizer *if* and blocks the movement of the modal. Thus, *should* remains in the head T. This shows that auxiliaries/modals sometimes move from T to C, but cannot in certain cases, because of the presence of other complementizers such as *if*. In short, CP is a better landing site for yes/no questions than QP.

UNIT 89

Yes/No Questions IV

Transformational Grammar

In conclusion, yes/no questions are derived from their respective sentences through the inversion of auxiliaries/modals and subjects. The auxiliaries/modals are first base-generated in the head T and then moved from T to C as shown in (2) and (3) respectively.

1. **Should** the police .... *arrest the criminals?*   (**Modal** + Subject + ... + *VP*)

2. Tree for (1) before movement   3. Tree for (1) after movement

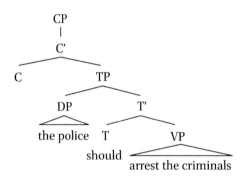   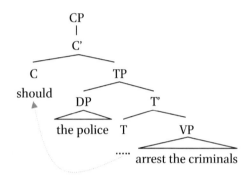

The trees in (2) and (3) are related. In theory, tree (2) is known as **DEEP STRUCTURE** (d-structure or DS). D-structure represents how the question was before it was formed, i.e. what it looked like deeply. Tree (3) is known as **SURFACE STRUCTURE** (s-structure, or SS) and represents what the question looks like after it is finally formed, i.e. how it surfaces.

The movement of auxiliaries/modals from T to C as shown in (3) is accomplished via a **TRANSFORMATIONAL RULE**. A transformational rule is a rule that moves a syntactic constituent from one position to another position known as **LANDING SITE**, e.g. position C in (3) is a landing site because the element *should* lands there. Since auxiliaries/modals move from **the head T** to **the head C**, this transformation rule moves a syntactic constituent from one head position to another head position, and is theoretically known as **HEAD-TO-HEAD MOVEMENT**. Consider the transformational rule for yes/no questions formulated in (4).

4. Move T to C   Head-to-Head Movement   Yes/No Question

Rule (4) above is the first transformational rule we have developed. It is specific to yes/no questions, and it transforms elements from T to C in a head-to-head movement operation. This transformational rule is part of what is known as **TRANSFORMATIONAL GRAMMAR** (TG) (Chomsky, 1965). Transformational grammar has a set of transformational rules that move elements from their original positions to different landing sites.

UNIT 90

Yes/No Questions V

Transformational Grammar

To form yes/no questions, one might propose that we do not need to move auxiliaries/modals from T to C. We could simply put auxiliaries/modals in C head from the outset. However, this proposal is problematic because, if auxiliaries/modals did not start in the head T, the head T would be empty and could be filled by another auxiliary/modal as in (2).

1. **Should** the police .... *arrest the criminals*?   (**Modal** + Subject + ... + *VP*)

2. Tree for (1)

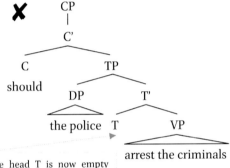

Notice here that the modal *should* starts in C right away. This proposal is problematic because the head T is now empty, and it can be filled with any auxiliary/modal. This will generate undesirable sentences such as the one in (3).

3. *should the police *should arrest the criminals*?

To overcome this problem, we should generate the auxiliaries/modals in T first to ensure that T is not filled by anything else. In this way, we will have only one auxiliary/modal to move for yes/no questions.

The head T is now empty and can be filled by any auxiliary/modal! This is problematic.

To ensure that T cannot be filled with anything else after the movement of auxiliaries/modals from T to C, we should base-generate the auxiliaries/modals in T first. However, note that after the auxiliaries/modals move from T and C, T does not become empty. **TRACE THEORY** suggests that, after the movement of an element to a landing site, the moved element leaves a **TRACE** in its original position. This trace does not allow any element to take the former position of the moved element. The trace is written with a small letter (t) and it indicates that there used to be an element in this position, but it has moved to another site. Thus, we should abandon our representation in (3) and adopt the representation in (4).

3. Tree for (1) after movement   4. Tree for (1) after movement

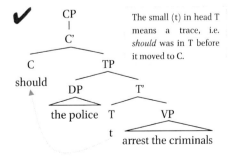

The dotted line (....) in head T is now wrong.

The small (t) in head T means a trace, i.e. *should* was in T before it moved to C.

UNIT 91

Yes/No Questions VI

Transformational Grammar

In certain cases, sentences do not have auxiliaries or modals that are moved from T to C to form yes/no questions. Rather, *do/does/did* are used to form their yes/no questions.

1. They play soccer. (sentence: present, plural)
2. He plays soccer. (sentence: present, singular)
3. He played soccer. (sentence: past, singular)
4. Do they play soccer? (question: present, plural, *do*)
5. Does he play soccer? (question: present, singular, *does*)
6. Did he play soccer? (question: past, singular, *did*)

In (1) through (3), there are no auxiliaries or modals for movement. However, the respective forms *do/does/did* are used instead for question formation as in (4) through (6). To solve this problem, syntacticians propose that *do*-forms (such as *do/does/did*) be inserted in the head T and then moved from T to C. This process is known as **DO-SUPPORT** or **DO-INSERTION**.

7. **Do-Support/Insertion** is an operation that occurs at the d-structure, where a dummy *do* (or its other forms *does* and *did*) inserts in T based on its tense status.

With the help of do-insertion, the structure of sentence (5) will be derived as follows.

8. Deep Structure (DS)   9. After Do-insertion   10. Surface Structure (SS)

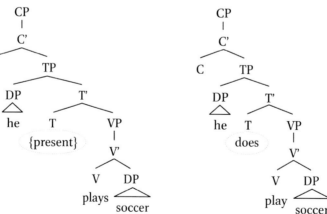
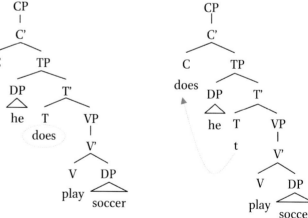

Do-insertion replaces the word {present} in the head T in (8) with the present form *does* as shown in (9). Subsequently, the word *does* moves from T to C in a head-to-head movement to form a question as in (10). The same operation applies to (4) and (6), where the respective forms *do* and *did* are inserted instead, i.e. based on their tense. As a final step, these do-forms move from T to C.

UNIT 92

Principles I

Transformational Grammar

In syntactic theory, any grammar in any language consists of two basic components: (i) the **LEXICON** and (ii) the **PHRASE STRUCTURE RULES** (PSRs). The lexicon provides syntax with words. The syntax, which is the computational component of the grammar, takes these words and arranges them in a well-formed structure (i.e. a well-formed phrase or sentence). Since language is the connection between sound and meaning, this syntactic structure/phrase/sentence is spelled out phonologically and semantically. At a point known as **SPELL OUT**, the structure diverges into two interfaces: **ARTICULATORY-PERCEPTUAL** (**PHONETIC FORM**, PF: for phonology) and **CONCEPTUAL-INTENTIONAL** (**LOGICAL FORM**, LF: for semantics). Consider the grammar architecture in (1) below.

1. Grammar Architecture

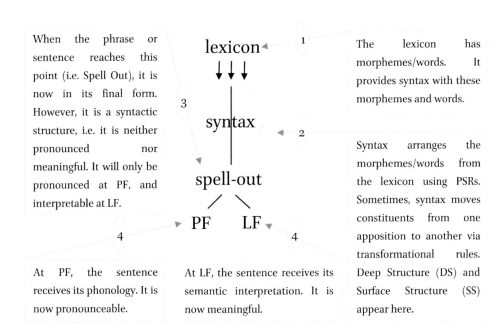

In the syntactic computation, where words are arranged via PSRs, the constituents of the structure may not remain in their original positions. Many transformational rules may change the distribution of the constituents in the structure. We may have many transformational rules; thus, we may need to represent each transformation in a separate tree or derivation. The first tree structure that the syntax builds is known as the **DEEP STRUCTURE** (**DS, OR D-STRUCTURE**). This d-structure is also known as the **BASE REPRESENTATION**. After the structure undergoes all the transformations, we call the final tree the **SURFACE STRUCTURE** (**SS, OR S-STRUCTURE**). The s-structure is the final pronounced and interpreted output, and it is also called the **SURFACE REPRESENTATION**.

UNIT 93

Principles 11

Transformational Grammar

Suppose the syntactic component aims to generate the following question.

1. What does Ahmed speak?

Sentence (1) will not be structured as it stands all at once, but it will pass through multiple stages of derivation. First, the syntax will generate the *deep structure* or the *base representation* of sentence (1); that is, it will generate (1) as a statement before transforming it into a question. Therefore, it will arrange the words in (1) as '*Ahmed speaks what*'. This is the first structure, i.e. the d-structure. The same d-structure will introduce *does* via a do-insertion operation, and the structure will become '*Ahmed does speak what*'. This is the second stage. Third, the syntax will move *does* to the front of the sentence. The d-structure will become '*Does Ahmed speak what*'. Finally, the wh-word *what* will be displaced to the front of the do-form *does*. The structure will eventually become '*what does Ahmed speak*', which is the same structure as in (1). Since no other transformations will be applied, the final output is called the *surface structure* or the *surface representation*. The stages above are illustrated below.

2. Generation of Sentence (1)

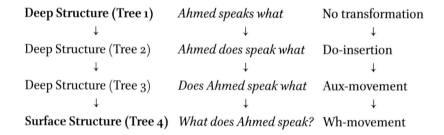

The trees in (2), i.e. trees 1, 2, 3 and 4, are related to each other. Tree 2 and Tree 3 in (2) do not have any special importance to us as syntacticians. The most important trees are tree (1) and tree (4) as they represent the first d-structure and the final s-structure respectively. In all the sentential derivations, the deep structure must respect the phrase structure rules and the X'-theory scheme discussed earlier. Furthermore, the phrase structure rules must be preserved in all subsequent trees. This principle is known as the **STRUCTURE PRESERVATION PRINCIPLE**, and it was first proposed by Emonds (1970). The structure preservation principle states that all the derived structures that follow the d-structure must be largely identical to the d-structure. The structure and the PSRs should not be radically altered; rather, the structure should always be preserved.

3. **Structure Preservation Principle:** All derived structures must be identical to the base/d-structure. No movements should alter the X-theory scheme. The X'-Theory scheme must always be preserved.

UNIT 94

Principles III

Structure Preservation Principle

The Structure Preservation Principle states that the structure at the base (i.e. d-structure) must be identical to the structure in its final output (i.e. s-structure). It must preserve the X'-theory scheme.

1. **Structure Preservation Principle**: All derived structures must be identical to the base/d-structure. No movements should alter the X-theory scheme. The X'-Theory scheme must always be preserved.

Consider the following examples that show violations of the Structure Preservation Principle.

2. Ahmed played football.
3. Football, Ahmed played.

One might draw inaccurate syntactic trees for (3) such as the following.

4. DS for (3)   5. SS for (3)

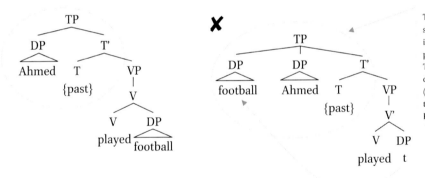

The circled portion in s-structure (5) is not identical to the circled portion in d-structure (4). The d-structure in (4) is dramatically jumbled in (5). This is a violation of the Structure Preservation Principle.

As shown above, it is assumed that the d-structure and the s-structure of (3) are the trees in (4) and (5) respectively. In s-structure (5), the DP *football* is attached to the left of the DP *Ahmed*. However, s-structure (5) is structurally incorrect because it does not maintain the binary branches of d-structure (4), i.e. it violates the Structure Preservation Principle. In X'-theory scheme (6), there is only one spec,TP where the subject DP *Ahmed* can appear. The DP *football* in (5) moves and lands on another non-existing spec,TP, which is not desirable.

6. a. TP → DP, T'
   b. T' → T, VP

We will learn in Units 113 and 114 how to derive (3) and preserve its d-structure. The proper derivation of (3) will be accomplished via adjunction transformational rules.

UNIT 95

Principles IV

Projection Principle

Another important principle in transformational grammar is the **PROJECTION PRINCIPLE**. This principle, as formulated by Chomsky (1986) in "Knowledge of Language: its Nature, Origin and Use", states that 'lexical structure must be represented categorically at every syntactic level' (Chomsky 1986:84). It is also known as the **PRINCIPLE OF LEXICAL SATISFACTION**. In other words, the complement selection shown in the subcategorization frames must be respected at both the d-structure and s-structure.

1. **Projection Principle**: lexical properties and complement selection must be respected at both the d-structure and s-structure.

Consider the subcategorization frame of the auxiliary *has* that selects VP[en].

2. *has*, T [___ VP$_{[en]}$]

3. Ahmed has driven the car.
4. Has Ahmed driven the car?

One may wrongly draw the trees of (4) as below, thereby violating the Projection Principle.

5. DS for (4) 6. SS for (4) 7. SS for (4)

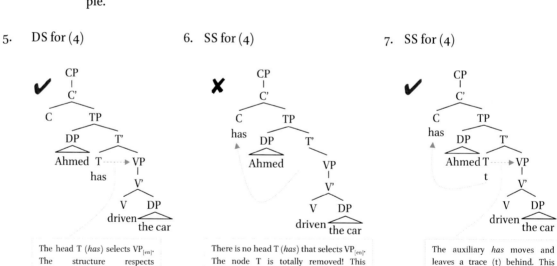

The head T (*has*) selects VP$_{[en]}$. The structure respects subcategorization frame (2).

There is no head T (*has*) that selects VP$_{[en]}$. The node T is totally removed! This violates the Projection Principle.

The auxiliary *has* moves and leaves a trace (t) behind. This trace of *has* in T selects VP$_{[en]}$.

It is clear from subcategorization frame (2) that the auxiliary *has* selects VP$_{[en]}$. This selection is satisfied at the d-structure in (5). However, after the movement of the auxiliary *has* in (6), the T node is totally removed. Now, there is no auxiliary that selects VP$_{[en]}$, and this violates the Projection Principle, which requires that the auxiliary *has* select VP$_{[en]}$ at every level, i.e. both the d-structure and s-structure. However, the s-structure (7) is correct because the trace of *has* (t) still selects VP$_{[en]}$. Thus, traces play a key role in preserving the Projection Principle.

UNIT 96

Principles v

Inclusiveness Principle

Another important principle in transformational grammar is the **INCLUSIVENESS PRINCIPLE**. This principle states that no new information is introduced during the derivation. All the information (i.e. words) introduced at the d-structure of a sentence should be the same at the s-structure. We do not expect new words to appear all of a sudden at the s-structure.

1. **Inclusiveness Principle**: No new information/words should be introduced by transformations during the derivation of a sentence.

This principle excludes *do/does/did* that are inserted at the d-structure in questions lacking auxiliaries or modals, perhaps because these do-forms are functional and dummy. Expletives such as *it* are also an exception because they have no semantic content as in the sentence: *It is likely that they will win* (see Units 123 through 131). However, meaningful words are not expected to be introduced during the derivation. Consider the examples below.

2. They come.
3. Have they come?

One may wrongly draw the tree of (3) as in (4) and (5), violating the Inclusiveness Principle.

4. DS for (3) 5. SS for (3)

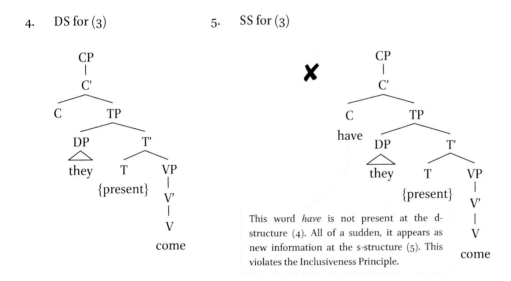

This word *have* is not present at the d-structure (4). All of a sudden, it appears as new information at the s-structure (5). This violates the Inclusiveness Principle.

In (4), the d-structure does not include the auxiliary *have* at all. The only available words at the d-structure are *they* and *come*. In (5), however, the derivational structure introduces *have* as a new element to form a question. This new element *have* violates the Inclusiveness Principle because it appears all of a sudden in the head C at the s-structure. It should first be available in the head T in the d-structure in (4) before it moves to the head C.

UNIT 97

Principles VI

Recoverability Principle

Another important principle in transformational grammar is the **RECOVERABILITY PRINCIPLE**. This principle states that no information is lost during the derivation. All the information (i.e. words) introduced at the d-structure should be the same at the s-structure. It means that transformations should not lead to loss of information. It is the opposite of the Inclusiveness Principle, which states that no new information should be introduced.

1. **Recoverability Principle:** no information should be lost from the d-structure during the derivation.

Consider the following examples.

2. Ahmed kicked the ball. (active)
3. The ball was kicked. (passive)

In most grammar books, the passive form is widely assumed to be derived from its active form. Under this assumption, one might wrongly assume that the DS and the SS of (3) are given in (4) and (5) respectively.

4. DS for (3)   5. SS for (3)

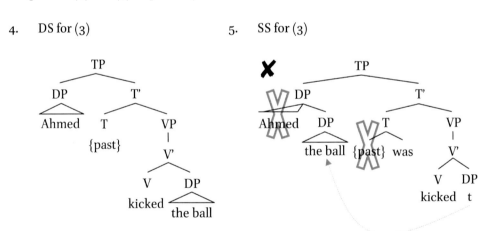

Under this wrong assumption, (4) is the d-structure of the passive in (3). As illustrated in (5), to derive the passive from the active, the object *the ball* is moved to spec,TP, where the subject *Ahmed* is located. However, because the subject *Ahmed* is not available in (3), it is removed from the s-structure (5). This removal of *Ahmed* violates the Recoverability Principle, which states that all the words at the d-structure should be preserved at the s-structure. Another problem in (5) follows from the removal of the head T {past}, which is another violation of the Recoverability Principle. A third problem stems from the presence of the auxiliary *was* in the s-structure (5) although it was not available at the d-structure (4). This is a violation of the Inclusiveness Principle, which disallows the introduction of new words. The proper derivation of the passive will be discussed in detail in Units 132–134.

UNIT 98

Negation Movement 1

Negation

Sentences can be positive or negative. To negate positive sentences, we add the negation word *not* after their modals, auxiliaries or do-forms as shown below.

1. He *may* come.
2. He *is* sleeping.
3. He speaks English.
4. He *may* **not** come.
5. He *is* **not** sleeping.
6. He *does* **not** speak.
7. *He **not** *may* come.
8. *He **not** *is* sleeping.
9. *He **not** *does* speak.
10. *He *may* come **not**.
11. *He *is* sleeping **not**.
12. *He *does* speak **not**.

Sentences (1) through (3) are positive. We made these sentences negative by adding the word *not* after the modal *may* as in (4), the auxiliary *is* as in (5) or the dummy *do*-form *does* as in (6). The negation word *not* cannot precede the auxiliaries/modals/do-forms as shown in (7) through (9), neither can it follow the main verbs, i.e. *come, sleeping*, and *speak* as shown in (10) through (12). Thus, we can conclude that the word *not* must appear after the auxiliaries/modals/do-forms, but before the main verbs. These observations suggest that sentences must include a **NEGATION PROJECTION** (NegP) with a Neg head in their structures. This NegP appears between TP (which hosts auxiliaries/modals/do-forms) and VP (which hosts main verbs). The PSRs of TP and NegP will therefore be revised as follows.

13. PSRs of Negative Sentences

    TP → DP, T'
    T' → T, NegP

14. PSRs of Negation Word *Not*

    NegP → spec, Neg'
    Neg' → Neg, VP

15. Representations of Rules (13) & (14)

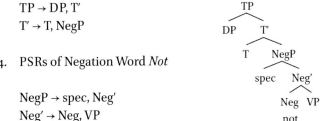

Thus, the representations of (4), (5) and (6) will be as in (16), (17) and (18) respectively.

16.   17.   18.

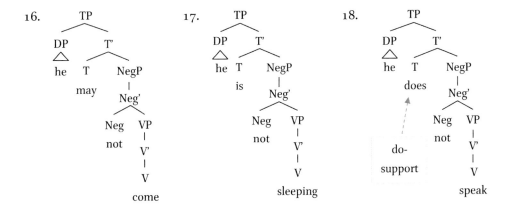

UNIT 99

Negation Movement II

Negation

Questions can be derived from negative sentences as well.

1. He *may* **not** come.
2. He *is* **not** sleeping.
3. He *does* **not** speak.
4. *May* **not** he come?
5. *Is* **not** he sleeping?
6. *Does* **not** he speak?
7. **May* he **not** come?
8. **Is* he **not** sleeping?
9. **Does* he **not** speak?

Recall that, in negative sentences such as (1), (2) and (3), the negation word *not* is inserted between the auxiliaries/modals/do-forms and the main verb. To derive yes/no questions from negative sentences, both the auxiliaries/modals/do-forms and the negation word *not* move to a position before the subject as in (4) through (6). The auxiliaries/modals/do-forms cannot move alone leaving the word *not* behind, as shown in the ungrammatical questions (7) through (9). In light of these observations, we can conclude that the negation word *not* first moves from the head Neg to the head T as in (10), and both move from T to C as in (11).

10. Move Neg to T   Head-to-Head Movement   Neg-Movement
11. Move T to C   Head-to-Head Movement   Yes/No Question

Rule (11) is an old transformation rule proposed for yes-no questions, but (10) is a new one. Rule (10) states that the negation word *not* moves from the head Neg to the head T, and merges with the auxiliaries/modals/do-forms. Then, the newly merged words (auxiliaries/modals/do-forms + NOT, such as *may-not, is-not*, and *does-not*) move together from T to C to form yes/no questions. This is known as **CYCLIC HEAD-TO-HEAD MOVEMENTS**. The structure for question (5) is given below.

12. DS for (5)   13. DS for (5)   14. SS for (5)

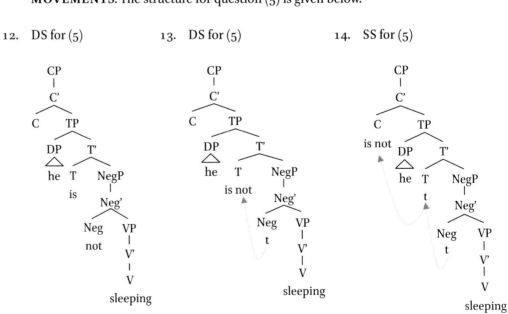

Verb Movement 1

Verb Movement in Early Modern English

Thus far, we have two transformational rules:

1. Move T to C   Head-to-Head Movement   Yes/No Question
2. Move Neg to T   Head-to-Head Movement   Negation

Let us now consider a new rule that operated only in **EARLY MODERN ENGLISH** (EME). EME is the version of English spoken from 1500 CE to 1700 CE before it developed into **MODERN ENGLISH** (ME), which is roughly the current version of English. Study the following examples from EME (cf. Shakespeare's plays).

3. You **heard** this.
4. **Heard** you ___ this?   (Alonso, The Tempest, II.i)
5. You **came** from the church.
6. **Came** you ___ from the church?   (Tranio, Taming of the Shrew, IV.ii)

Examples (4) and (6) are yes/no questions derived from sentences (3) and (5). In EME, do-forms are not inserted to derive yes/no questions from sentences lacking auxiliaries/modals. To form yes/no questions in EME, the main verb moves in front of the subject. Thus, in questions (4) and (6), it seems that the main verb first moves from the head V to the head T, and then from the head T to the head C. The T-to-C movement is an old transformational rule as shown in (1). However, we need a new rule such as the one in (7), to relocate the verb from the head V to the head T.

7. Move V to T   Head-to-Head Movement   Verb Movement (EME)

According to this rule, the generation of question (4) will proceed as in (8) through (10).

8. DS for (4)   9. DS for (4): move V to T   10. SS for (4): move T to C

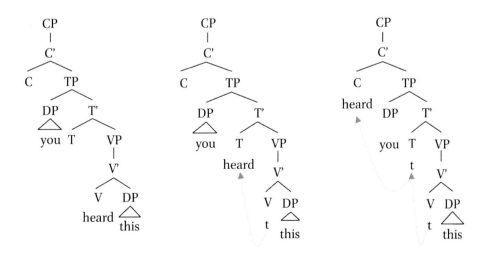

UNIT 101

Verb Movement II

Verb Movement in Early Modern English

We have proposed three transformational rules up to now:

1. Move T to C — Head-to-Head Movement — Yes/No Question
2. Move Neg to T — Head-to-Head Movement — Negation
3. Move V to T — Head-to-Head Movement — Verb Movement (EME)

Rule (3), however, is specific to Early Modern English (EME). With this in mind, one may wonder whether the main verb also moves from V to T in Modern English (ME). In fact, it does not, and the evidence follows from the inability of verbs in ME to move beyond certain adverbs such as *hardly* and *almost*. Consider the following examples.

4. He hardly passed the exam.
5. *He passed hardly the exam.
6. He almost passed the exam.
7. *He passed almost the exam.

As shown in (4) and (6), adverbs such as *hardly* and *almost* must precede the main verb *passed*. If the verb precedes these adverbs, the sentences become ungrammatical as shown in (5) and (7). Sentences (4)/(6) and (5)/(7) can be drawn as in (8) and (9) respectively.

8. Tree for (4)/(6)   9. Tree for (5)/(7)

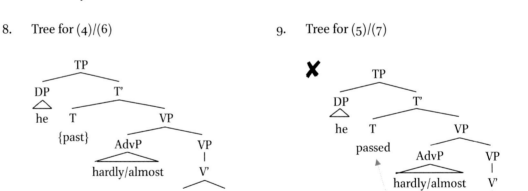

It is obvious from tree (8) that the adverbs *hardly* and *almost* occur between the verb (V) and the head T. If the rule of EME in (3) equally applied to ME, we would expect that the verb may move from the head V to the head T as shown in (9). Yet, the verb cannot move in (9) because this movement would yield ungrammatical sentences such as (5) and (7). In light of these observations, we conclude that the V-to-T movement is operative only in EME.

UNIT 102

Tense Markers 1

Verb Movement

At this point, it is important to revisit some problematic proposals in our old grammar. Recall that we have generated sentences (1) through (3) as shown in (4) through (6) respectively.

1. They play soccer.   (sentence: present, plural)
2. He plays soccer.   (sentence: present, singular)
3. He played soccer.   (sentence: past, singular)

4. Tree for (1)   5. Tree for (2)   6. Tree for (3)

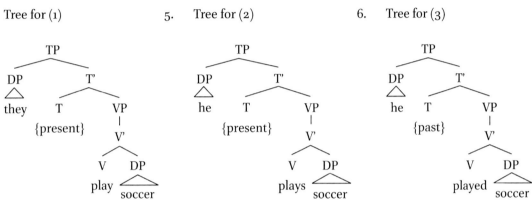

The structures in (4) through (6) are theoretically problematic. One obvious problem in these structures follows from the unpronounced words {present} and {past} in the head T. These words are redundant tense notations, and they need to be removed from the structures. As a solution, and since the head T stands for tense, syntacticians have proposed that T bear the morphological tense markers attached to the main verbs such as *play, play-s, play-ed*. In (1), it is assumed that the verb *play* bears a null marker -∅ (for present/plural). In (2) and (3), the verb *play* takes -s (for present/singular) and -ed (for past) respectively. Thus, it is proposed that these markers (-∅, -s, and -ed) should rather occupy the position of the head T. Structures (4), (5) and (6) will therefore be revised as in (7), (8) and (9) respectively. Notice that the verb *play* in (7) through (9) is in bare form.

7. Tree for (1)   8. Tree for (2)   9. Tree for (3)

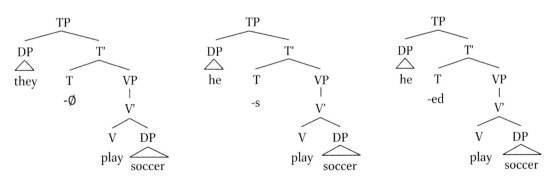

UNIT 103

Tense Markers II

Verb Movement and Morphological Markers

We have argued that tense markers such as -∅, -s, and -ed should occupy the head T rather than the words {present} and {past}. This proposal is advantageous for do-support/insertion. Consider examples (1) through (3).

1. They **do** *play* soccer.   (do-insertion: present, plural)
2. He **does** *play* soccer.   (do-insertion: present, singular)
3. He **did** *play* soccer.   (do-insertion: past)

In the old structure, we inserted *do*-forms in the position of {present} and {past} as shown in (4) through (6).

4. Tree for (1)   5. Tree for (2)   6. Tree for (3)

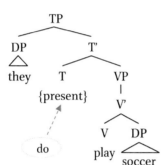 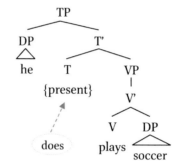 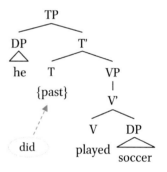

Do-insertion as represented in (4) through (6) is problematic. The verb *play* in the above structures is morphologically marked with -∅, -s, and -ed although *do/does/did* occupy the head T. The do-forms *do/does/did* do not co-occur with tensed verbs as this co-occurrence would yield ungrammatical sentences such as *he does plays soccer* in (5), or *he did played soccer* in (6). Verbs that follow *do*-forms must be in bare form as in (1) through (3). We can now solve this problem by putting tense markers -∅, -s, and -ed in the head T. When the form *do* inserts into T, it bears these markers and yields the forms *do-∅*, *do-s* (= does), and *do-ed* (= did) as in (7) through (9). The verb *play* is also in bare form, which is desirable.

7. Tree for (1)   8. Tree for (2)   9. Tree for (4)

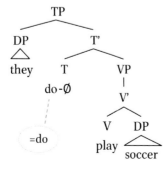 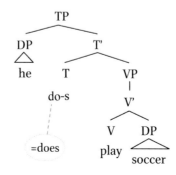 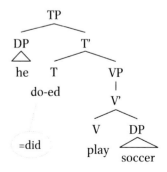

UNIT 104

Affix Hopping 1

Affix Hopping

By now, the head T bears the tense markers -∅, -s, and -ed. Under this account, it is expected that these markers will precede the main verb because T structurally precedes V.

1. They *play*-∅ soccer.   (wrongly structured in (4) as: They -∅ *play* soccer.)
2. He *play*-s soccer.   (wrongly structured in (5) as: He -s *play* soccer.)
3. He *play*-ed soccer.   (wrongly structured in (6) as: He -ed *play* soccer.)

4. Tree for (1)   5. Tree for (2)   6. Tree for (3)

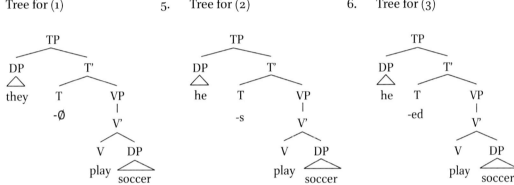

As shown in structures (4) through (6), the tense markers -∅, -s, and -ed precede the verbs although they are suffixes by nature. To attach these markers to the end of the verb, one might propose that the verb *play* move from V to T. However, this movement is not operative in ME, as discussed in Unit 101. Alternatively, Lansik (1994) proposed that these tense markers (-∅, -s, and -ed) move downwards from the head T to the head V in an operation known as **AFFIX HOPPING** or **AFFIX LOWERING**. This transformational rule is given in (7).

7. Move T to V   Head-to-Head Movement   Affix Hopping

Thus the structures in (4) through (6) should be revised as in (8) through (10). For the purpose of simplicity, however, we will keep these markers attached to the verb in the coming units.

8. Tree for (1)   9. Tree for (2)   10. Tree for (3)

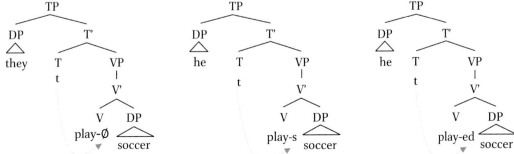

UNIT 105

Affix Hopping II

Affix Hopping

To recap, we have developed the following transformational rules:

1. Move T to C   Head-to-Head Movement   Yes/No Question
2. Move Neg to T Head-to-Head Movement   Negation
3. Move V to T   Head-to-Head Movement   Verb Movement (EME)
4. Move T to V   Head-to-Head Movement   Affix Hopping

All the rules above are head-to-head movements. The first rule moves auxiliaries/modals/do-forms from T to C to form yes/no questions as in (5) below. The second rule is specific to negation, where the negation word *not* moves from Neg to T, and both move from T to C to form a yes/no negative question such as the one in (6). As for rule (3), it occurs only in EME (not in ME); it transforms the verb from V to T, and then from T to C as in (7). Rule (4) is a morphological rule that moves the morphological tense markers -∅, -s, and -ed from T to V as shown in (8).

5. *Can* you ___ stay?

6. *Is not* he ___ ___ sleeping?

7. *Heard* you ___ this?

8. He ___ play -s soccer.

The structures assigned to (5) through (8) are given below.

9. Tree for (5)   10. Tree for (6)   11. Tree for (7)   12. Tree for (8)

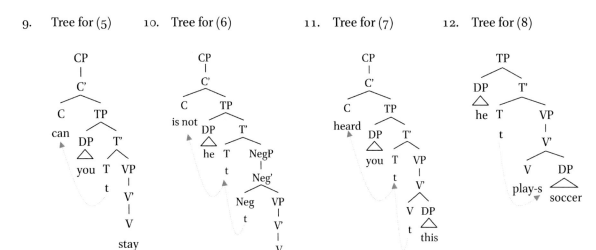

UNIT 106

Wh-Questions I

Wh-Questions

Unlike yes/no questions, there are questions whose answers are words or phrases. We call them **WH-QUESTIONS** because they start with wh-words such as *what, where, when, whose* and *how*. Consider the following examples.

1. You are driving a car.
2. You are driving which car?
3. Which car are you driving? (Wh-question)

4. You are driving a car (or a bike).
5. You are driving which?
6. Which are you driving? (Wh-question)

7. The teacher might raise some questions.
8. The teacher might raise what questions?
9. What questions might the teacher raise? (Wh-question)

10. The teacher might raise some questions.
11. The teacher might raise what?
12. What might the teacher raise? (Wh-question)

In wh-questions, the words that are potential answers are wholly or partially replaced with wh-words. Wh-words can replace determiners only. In (1) and (2), the phrase *a car* becomes *which car*; that is, only the determiner *a* is replaced with the word *which*. In the phrase *some questions* in (7) and (8), the determiner *some* is substituted with *what*, yielding *what questions*. Since wh-words replace determiners, it is proposed that wh-words occupy the head D. In other cases, however, the phrase in question is wholly replaced by a wh-word. In (4) and (5), for instance, the word *which* replaces the whole phrase *a car*. In (10) and (11), the whole phrase *some questions* is replaced with the wh-word *what*. In light of these observations, we conclude that *which* and *what* are determiners (Ds) that select optional NPs. The structures for *which car* and *what questions* are illustrated in (13) and (14) respectively, whereas the structures for *which* and *what* are given in (15) and (16) respectively. The most important conclusion from this unit is that wh-words are DPs.

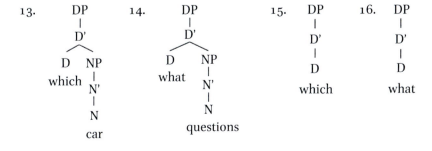

UNIT 107

Wh-Questions II

Wh-Questions

Consider the following wh-questions.

1. You *are* driving which car?
2. Which car *are* you driving? (Wh-question)

3. You *are* driving which?
4. Which *are* you driving? (Wh-question)

5. The teacher *might* raise what questions?
6. What questions *might* the teacher raise? (Wh-question)

7. The teacher *might* raise what?
8. What *might* the teacher raise? (Wh-question)

9. You found what?
10. What *did* you find? (Wh-question)

To form a wh-question, wh-words move to the front of the sentence. Also, the auxiliaries/modals/do-form invert with the subject (as discussed in yes/no questions in Units 86 through 91). The movement of auxiliaries/modals/do-form is accomplished via transformation rule (11), where auxiliaries/modals/do-form move from T to C.

11. Move T to C   Head-to-Head Movement   Yes/No Question

To derive the correct word order, the wh-words (i.e. DP) must move in front of the auxiliaries/modals/do-form. Given that auxiliaries/modals/do-form move from T to C, as in (12), the wh-word must move higher than the head C. The only available landing site is the specifier of CP as in (13). Thus, the *wh*-word (DP) is assumed to move to spec,CP.

12. Yes/No Question   13. Wh-Questions

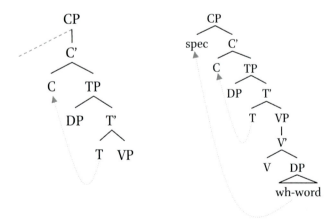

Wh-Questions III

UNIT 108

Wh-Questions

To form wh-questions, we need two transformational rules.

1. Move T to C   Head-to-Head Movement   Yes/No Question
2. Move DP to spec,CP   Phrasal Movement   Wh-Question

Rule (1) constitutes a head-to-head movement because we move elements from the head T to the head C. Though we have claimed that this rule is specific to yes/no questions, it is also needed for wh-questions. Rule (2) is exclusive to wh-questions, and it is not a head-to-head movement, but rather a **PHRASAL MOVEMENT**, because we move the phrase DP (i.e. wh-word) to spec,CP. The specifier position is a landing site for phrases, not heads. Phrases move to specifiers while heads move to head positions. Let us derive (3) and (4) below.

3. You *are* driving which car?
4. Which car *are* you driving?   (Wh-question)

The structural derivations of example (4) proceed as follows.

5. DS for (4)   6. DS for (4)   7. SS for (4)

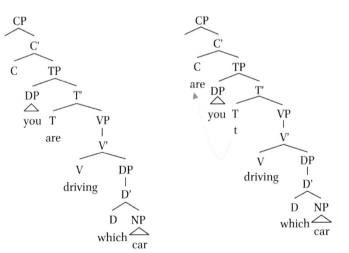
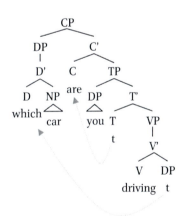

In wh-questions, both rules (1) and (2) are applied. As in (5), the d-structure of example (4) is base-generated with the auxiliary *are* in the head T, and the wh-word *which car* as a complement of the verb *driving*. In (6), rule (1) transposes the auxiliary *are* from the head T to the head C in a head-to-head movement operation. In (7), rule (2) moves the DP *which car* from the complement of the verb *driving* to spec,CP in a phrasal movement operation.

UNIT 109

Wh-Questions IV

Wh-Questions

Rules (1) and (2) are also applied to wh-questions with wh-words as determiners.

1. Move T to C   Head-to-Head Movement   Yes/No Question
2. Move DP to spec,CP Phrasal Movement   Wh-Question

Consider the following sentences, where wh-words appear without NP-complements.

3. The teacher *might* announce some questions.
4. The teacher *might* raise what?
5. What *might* the teacher raise?   (Wh-question)

The structural derivations of question (5) will proceed as follows.

6. DS for (5)   7. DS for (5)   8. SS for (5)

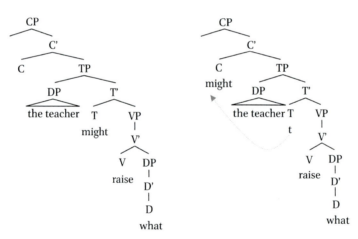
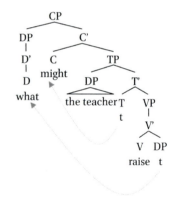

As shown in (7), the auxiliary *might* moves from T to C, while the wh-word *what* moves from its original position to spec,CP. In certain cases, however, wh-words do not seem to be DPs. It depends on what role a wh-word plays in questions. There are wh-questions whose answers are PPs or AdvPs as shown in the examples below.

9. Where did he find this pen?   AdvP: nearby; PP: at the fence.
10. When did the judge pass the verdict? AdvP: recently; PP: in the morning.
11. How does the student behave?   AdvP: politely; PP: in a polite way.

UNIT 110

Wh-Questions V

Wh-Questions

Wh-questions can be raised to elicit information about place, time or manner. Under these circumstances, wh-words may project as PPs or AdvPs.

1. He found this pen [$_{AdvP}$ nearby]/[$_{PP}$ at the store].
2. He found this pen where?
3. Where did he find this pen?   (Wh-question)

4. The judge passed the verdict [$_{AdvP}$ recently]/[$_{PP}$ in the morning].
5. The judge did pass the verdict when?
6. When did the judge pass the verdict?   (Wh-question)

7. The student behaves [$_{AdvP}$ politely]/[$_{PP}$ in a polite way].
8. The student does behave how?
9. How does the student behave?   (Wh-question)

Based on the expected answer, be it PP or AdvP, wh-words in the wh-questions above must occupy the head position of PP or AdvP: either P or Adv. Thus, the structural representations of the wh-words *where, when* and *how* can be either PP or AdvP as shown below.

10. *where*

    AdvP   PP
    | |
    Adv'   P'
    | |
    Adv   P
    where   where

11. *when*

    AdvP   PP
    | |
    Adv'   P'
    | |
    Adv   P
    when   when

12. *how*

    AdvP   PP
    | |
    Adv'   P'
    | |
    Adv   P
    how   how

Because the wh-words *where, when* and *how* are addressed to elicit information about place, time or manner, they are adjuncts. Adjuncts are not essential to complete the meaning of verbs. In the previous units, we moved the DP from the complement of the verb to spec,CP. Now, we will simply move the adjuncts PP/AdvP from their adjoined position to spec,CP.

13. Wh-complements   14. Wh-adjuncts

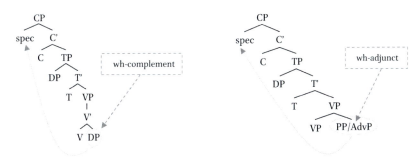

UNIT 111

Wh-Questions VI

Wh-Questions

If questions aim to elicit information about place, time or manner, wh-words are PP or AdvP.

1. He should sit nearby.
2. He should sit where?
3. Where should he sit?   (Wh-question)

4. He will come in the morning.
5. He will come when?
6. When will he come?   (Wh-question)

The structure of (3) will be as illustrated below, where the adjunct AdvP moves to spec,CP.

7. DS for (3)   8. DS for (3)   9. SS for (3)

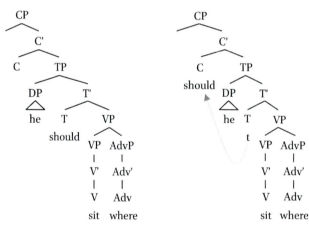
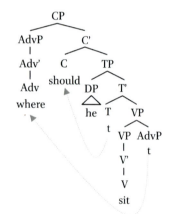

As for (6), it will be derived as shown below, where the adjunct PP moves to spec,CP.

10. DS for (6)   11. DS for (6)   12. SS for (6)

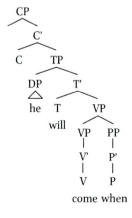
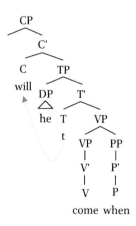
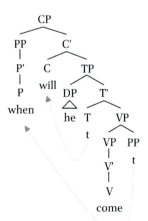

UNIT 112

Wh-Questions VII

Wh-Questions

Some wh-questions begin with a preposition followed by a wh-word as shown in the examples below.

1. He is talking about this topic.
2. He is talking about which topic?
3. About which topic is he talking? (Wh-question)

4. They will meet at this time.
5. They will meet at what time?
6. At what time will they meet? (Wh-question)

The wh-words *which* and *what* are preceded by a preposition such as *about* or *at* as shown in (3) and (6) respectively. In these cases, the head P *about* or *at* selects a DP (i.e. a wh-word) as its complement. Then, the whole PP moves from its original position to spec,CP in a phrasal movement operation as represented in the following trees for question (3).

7. DS for (3)   8. DS for (3)   9. SS for (3)

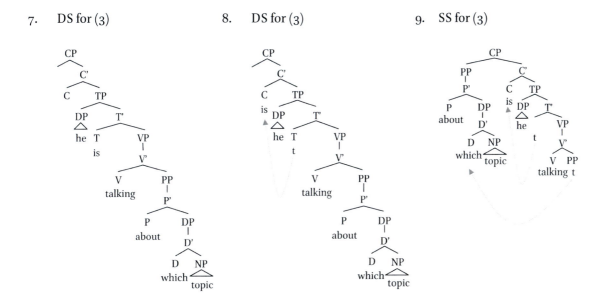

In (9), the whole PP *about which topic* is transposed from the complement of the verb *talking* to spec,CP in a phrasal movement operation, whereas the auxiliary *is* moves from the head T to the head C in a head-to-head movement operation. Question (6) will be derived similarly to question (3). The auxiliary *will* moves from the head T to the head C, while the adjunct PP *at what time* moves to spec,CP.

UNIT 113

Adjunction Revisited 1

Adjunction

In our old grammar, it was suggested that the blue phrases (AdvP or PP) in (1) through (8) are adjuncts. These adjuncts are placed to the right or left of VP or TP.

1. The girl has *devoured a sandwich* recently.   VP → VP   AdvP
2. The girl has recently *devoured a sandwich*.   VP → AdvP VP
3. The girl *reads the books* in the room.   VP → VP   PP
4. The girl, in the room, *reads the books*.   VP → PP   VP

5. *The girl has devoured a sandwich* recently.   TP → TP   AdvP
6. Recently, *the girl has devoured a sandwich*.   TP → AdvP TP
7. *The girl reads the book* in the room.   TP → TP   PP
8. In the room, *the girl reads the books*.   TP → PP   TP

For each sentence in (1) through (8), we proposed a single PSR. Upon closer inspection, though, some of these PSRs—such as the ones in (5) through (8)—seem unnecessary and redundant. Notice that sentence (1) is like (5) while (3) is like (7). Thus, PSR (1) can function as PSR (5) because the AdvP in (1) is the same AdvP as in (5). We can propose that AdvP be attached to the VP not the TP, thus eliminating the need for PSR (5). PSR (3) can also function as PSR (7) because the PP in (3) is the same as the PP in (7). Similarly, it can be argued that the PP should be attached to the VP not the TP, thus eliminating the need for PSR (7). By now, PSRs (5) and (7) are dispensed with by attaching the AdvP and PP to VP instead of TP. After removing (5) and (7), the only remaining PSRs to be disregarded are (6) and (8). Transformational grammar suggests that PSRs (6) and (8) are also redundant as the sentences in (6) and (8) can be derived through rules. We can propose that the AdvP in (1) simply move from the VP to the front of the TP to generate (6), while the PP in (3) move from the VP to the front of the TP to generate (8). This movement is known as **PREPOSING** or **TOPICALIZATION**. The transformational rules that move these phrases (AdvP/PP) to the front of sentences are known as **ADJUNCTION RULES**.

9. Move XP to adjoin TP   Phrasal Movement   Adjunction Rule
   XP = AdvP or PP

Thus, the generation of (6) and (8) can be derived from (1) and (3) as shown in (10) and (11).

10. ___ [TP The girl has [VP *devoured a sandwich* recently]] ◄-- VP → VP AdvP
                                                                ◄------ Adjunction Rule (9)

11. ___ [TP The girl [VP *read the books* in the room]] ◄------ VP → VP PP
                                                          ◄------------ Adjunction Rule (9)

UNIT 114

Adjunction Revisited II

Adjunction

Consider (1) through (4).

1. The girl has *devoured a sandwich recently*.   VP → VP AdvP
2. *Recently, the girl has devoured a sandwich*.   By Adjunction Rule
3. The girl *read the books in the room*.   VP → VP PP
4. *In the room, the girl read the books*.   By Adjunction Rule

We proposed earlier that the AdvP *recently* in (1) is base-generated within the VP. The AdvP in (2) is the same AdvP as in (1), but in (2) it moves from the VP via an adjunction rule to the clause periphery. The same applies to the PP *in the room*. In (3) it originates in the VP, but it moves to the front of TP in (4) via an adjunction rule. This adjunction rule is devised in (5).

5.   Move XP to adjoin TP   Phrasal Movement   Adjunction Rule
     XP = AdvP or PP

Applying rule (5), the derivation of (1) and (2) will proceed as follows.

6.   DS for (2)   7.   SS for (2)

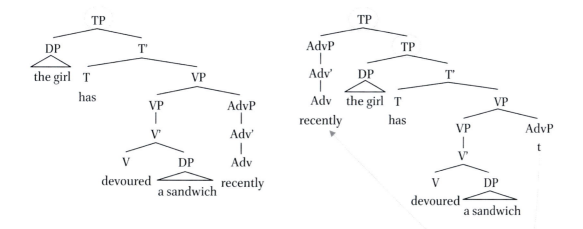

In (6), the AdvP *recently* is first adjoined to the VP. Then, it moves from its position as in (7) and adjoins the TP via rule (5). Observe how the AdvP is adjoined to TP in (7), and compare it with (6); note that adjunction means adding a new node TP above the main TP. The same rule in (5) applies to (4); like the AdvP in (7), the PP *in the room* moves and adjoins the TP.

UNIT 115

Topicalization 1

Topicalization

TOPICALIZATION is a syntactic process where a phrase is moved to the front of sentences. In the previous units, we noticed that some adjuncts, such as AdvP and PP, are moved to the front of sentences via an adjunction rule. Like adjuncts, complements can move to the clause periphery as well. Consider the following examples.

1. The student has bought a car.
2. A car, the student has bought ___.   (DP topicalization)
3. They bought a car for the boy.
4. For the boy, they bought a car ___.   (PP topicalization)
5. Ali will never be happy.
6. Happy, Ali will never be ___.   (AP topicalization)

In (1), the DP *a car* is the complement of the verb *bought*. It moves to the front of the sentence in (2). In (3), the PP *for the boy* is a complement of the verb *bought*, and it is moved clause-initially as in (4). The same applies to the AP complement *happy* in (5), which is topicalized as shown in (6). These topicalized complements can be derived via the same adjunction rule presented earlier for the adjuncts, which is now revised in (7).

7. Move XP to adjoin TP   Phrasal Movement   Adjunction Rule
   XP = AdvP, PP, DP, AP etc.

Thus, sentence (2) will be represented as follows.

8. DS for (2)   9. SS for (2)

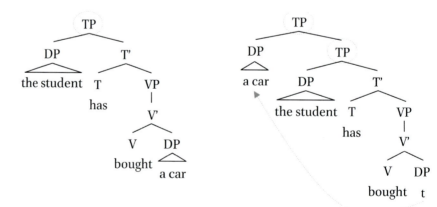

The same applies to the complements PP *for the boy* and AP *happy*. They move from their complement positions and adjoin the TP in the same way the DP *a car* moves in (9).

UNIT 116

Topicalization II

Topicalization

Topicalization is not limited to a single phrase; two phrases (complements or adjuncts) can be topicalized to the front of the clause. This is manifested in the following examples.

1. We have given [DP *a present*] [PP to the student].
2. [DP *a present*], we have given [PP to the student].   (topicalization of one phrase)
3. [PP To the student], [DP *a present*], we have given.   (topicalization of two phrases)

To generate sentence (3), we can apply adjunction rule (4) twice.

4. Move XP to adjoin TP   Phrasal Movement   Adjunction Rule
   XP = AdvP, PP, NP, AP etc.

Thus, the derivation of sentence (3) will proceed as follows.

5. DS for (3)   6. DS for (3)

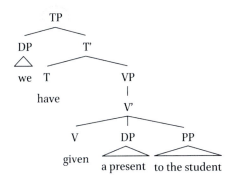 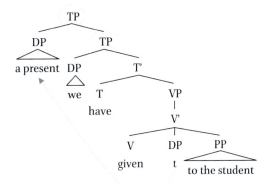

7. SS for (3)

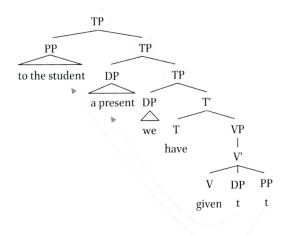

SECTION 7

Theta Theory

∴

Thematic Roles 1

Thematic Relations

Consider sentences (1) through (5).

1. [NP Jack] plays football.
2. [NP Jack] feels well.
3. John hit [NP Jack].
4. The university gave [NP Jack] a certificate.
5. They bought a car for [NP Jack]

In (1) through (5), the word *Jack* is a noun phrase (NP). This NP occurs in different syntactic positions: sometimes as a subject, and other times as an object. Although *Jack* refers to the same person in all the sentences above, it plays a different role in each one. In (1), *Jack* is the subject, i.e. he is the one who does, performs or initiates the action *playing*. Although *Jack* is the subject in (2) as well, he does not do, perform or initiate anything. He simply feels and experiences something, i.e. *wellness*. In (3), *Jack* is the object, i.e. he undergoes the action of *hitting*. In (4), *Jack* is still the object, but with a different role from that of the object in (3); he is now the recipient of a certificate. In (5), *Jack* is the object of a preposition; he benefits from those who bought a car for him. He is a beneficiary.

In short, *Jack* plays a different role in every sentence above: he is a doer in (1), an experiencer in (2), a sufferer in (3), a recipient in (4) and a beneficiary in (5). In theory, these roles are known as **SEMANTIC** or **THEMATIC ROLES**. Every phrase in a sentence plays a semantic/thematic role, contributing to the meaning of the whole sentence. It is important to note that the verb in each of the sentences above informs us about its participants. The verb *plays* in (1) tells us that *Jack* is in action; he is doing something. The verb *hits* in (3) reveals that *Jack* suffers from being hit, whereas the verb *bought for* shows the purpose of the transaction—the car is bought for *Jack*, making him a beneficiary. Thus, the relationships between the NP *Jack* and these verbs are known as **THEMATIC RELATIONS**.

Consider the verbs in examples (6) through (12), and try to figure out what semantic/thematic roles the blue phrases (i.e. participants) may play in the sentence. Assign a term to each participant whenever possible.

6. [NP Ahmed] plays [NP the guitar].
7. [NP We] bought [NP books].
8. [NP The boss] listened to [NP the complaint].
9. [NP The university] gave [NP the student] [NP a certificate].
10. [NP The tailor] cut [NP the fabric] [PP with scissors].
11. [NP They] bought [NP a toy] [PP for their son].
12. [NP This singer] came [PP from Germany].

UNIT 118

Thematic Roles II

Thematic Relations

Consider example (1).

1. [NP The university]   gave   [NP the student]   [NP a certificate].
    ARGUMENT   PREDICATE   ARGUMENT   ARGUMENT

In (1), all the participants (NPs) in the event *gave* are called **ARGUMENTS**: the giver, the recipient, and the thing given. We call the event/verb *gave* and the elements that follows it a **PREDICATE**. **PREDICATE-ARGUMENT STRUCTURE** is the structure where the PREDICATE (i.e. the main verb with its own auxiliaries and modals) selects certain ARGUMENTS (i.e. expressions such as NP, PP etc.) to complete the meaning of the whole sentence. Since the predicate needs one or more arguments (subject, object etc.) to complete its meaning, all the complements appearing to its right are arguments because they complete the meaning of the verb. These arguments are called **INTERNAL ARGUMENTS** because they are inside the predicate. In (1), the NP *the student* and the NP *a certificate* are complements of the verb *gave*. Thus, they are called internal arguments. The subject that precedes the predicate also participates in completing the meaning. We call this subject (e.g. NP *the university*) an **EXTERNAL ARGUMENT** because it is outside the predicate. **THEMATIC RELATION** is the relation between the predicate (i.e. the verb) and its arguments (NP, PP etc.). For any event (i.e. verb), we need to know the participants/arguments that are involved. For example, the verb *eat* has a thematic relation with its arguments. We have two arguments for the verb *eat*: the subject NP (the eater) and the object NP (the eaten). Consider the following examples.

Sentence		Thematic roles
2.	[NP Jack] plays football.	**Agent**
3.	We bought [NP books].	**Theme** (sometimes **Patient**)
4.	[NP The boss] listened to the complaint.	**Experiencer**
5.	The university gave [NP the student] a certificate.	**Recipient**

In (2) through (5), every blue NP plays a thematic role in the sentence. The doer, performer, initiator of an act is called the **AGENT**. In (2), *Jack* is an **agent** because he initiates the act of *playing*. A **THEME** (sometimes known as **PATIENT**) is the one that is performed upon or undergoes an action. In (3), *books* is a **theme** because they underwent the action of *buying*. An **EXPERIENCER** differs from an agent in that it receives sensory or emotional input, and does not initiate or perform an action. Thus, *the boss* in (4) is an **experiencer** because he did not initiate the act of *listening*, yet he experienced this sensory activity. All the arguments that precede verbs such as *feel, see, hear, cry* etc. are experiencers. A **RECIPIENT** is the one who receives something. This occurs in cases where a switch in ownership or possession occurs. In (5), *the student* is a **recipient** because he received a certificate.

UNIT 119

Thematic Roles III

Thematic Relations

More thematic roles are illustrated in the examples below.

Sentence		Thematic roles
1.	This singer came [PP from Germany].	**Source**
2.	The player flew [PP to the US].	**Goal**
3.	The workers met [PP at the station].	**Location**
4.	The tailor cut the fabric [PP with scissors].	**Instrument**
5.	They bought a toy [PP for their son].	**Beneficiary**

Given that all the PPs in the examples above are complements, they are arguments as well, so they must play a thematic role. A **SOURCE** is the argument from which things move, while a **GOAL** is the argument to which things move. In (1), the PP *from Germany* functions as a **source** for the singer, whereas the PP *to the US* functions as a **goal** for the player. A **LOCATOIN** is the argument referring to the location of an action. In (3), the PP *at the station* is the **location** of the meeting. An **INSTRUMENT** is a means by which an action is accomplished. In (4), the PP *with scissors* is the **instrument** that cuts the fabric. As for **BENEFICIARY**, he/she/it is the one who/which benefits from an action. In (5), the PP *for their son* functions as a **beneficiary** because *the son* benefits from the action of *buying*. In certain cases, however, it is hard to tell what thematic role an argument plays as in (6) and (7).

6. The president deemed these steps [AP necessary].
7. Boeing planes weigh [PP around 445 kg].

The blue phrases in (6) and (7) are complements for the verbs *deemed* and *weigh* respectively. They are arguments, but their thematic roles are unclear. What thematic roles do the arguments *necessary* and *around 445 kg* play in the above sentences? They surely play thematic roles, but we do not know what those are. We do not have terms for them. In certain cases, an argument does not have any thematic role at all as in (8).

8. [NP It] seems that Ahmed came.

The argument *it* in (8) is not easy to describe. It is neither an agent that initiates an action nor an experiencer that undergoes the act of *seeming*. In English, a pronoun such as *it* in (8) is called **EXPLETIVE**. An expletive is a word (usually a dummy pronoun) that plays a syntactic role but does not have a thematic role, i.e. *it* makes no contribution to the meaning of the whole sentence. It is there for syntactic purposes, i.e. to make the sentence grammatical, because sentences cannot stand without a subject as in (9).

9. *seems that Ahmed came.

UNIT 120

Thematic Roles IV

Thematic Roles

To sum up, **thematic roles** (agent, theme, experiencer, recipient, source, goal, location, instrument and beneficiary) are collectively termed **THETA ROLES** or, more conventionally, **θ-ROLES**. These **θ-ROLES** need to be represented in syntax. Since complements are arguments that play thematic roles, and complements are listed in the subcategorization frames of verbs, we will simply need to add these theta roles to subcategorization frames as shown below.

Sentences		Subcategorization frames
1.	John often *collects* many stamps.	*collects*, V [_____ NP] AGENT THEME
2.	Jack *gave* a prize to the student.	*gave*, V [_____ NP PP] AGENT THEME RECIPIENT
3.	They *bought* flowers for the sick.	*bought*, V [_____ NP (PP$_{[for]}$)] AGENT THEME BENEFICIARY
4.	I *travelled* from Italy to France.	*travelled*, V [_____ PP$_{[from]}$ PP$_{[to]}$] AGENT SOURCE GOAL
5.	He *opened* the door with a key.	*opened*, V [_____ NP (PP$_{[with]}$)] AGENT THEME INSTRUMENT
6.	The worker *left*.	*left*, V [_____] AGENT
7.	He *cried*.	*cried*, P [_____] EXPERIENCER
8.	It *seems* that Ahmed came.	*seems*, V [__ CP] THEME

In (1) through (8), all the subcategorization frames include the arguments and their theta roles. Because subjects are not added to subcategorization frames in the first place, we simply put their theta roles under the empty position (___) where the verb occurs. In (8), the verb *seems* assigns a theta role to its complement (CP) only, not to the subject *it*. This is because the pronoun *it* is an expletive, i.e. it plays no thematic role, neither that of an agent or an experiencer.

Note that in (1), the AdvP *often* plays no thematic role either. This is because *often* is not a complement that completes the meaning of the sentence. The AdvP *often* is an adjunct, and adjuncts, such as *often, in the morning* etc., are not included in subcategorization frames in the first place. Only complements are included; thus, only complements (plus the subject) are assigned theta roles.

UNIT 121

Thematic Roles V

Thematic Roles

One problem with our earlier characterization is that thematic roles are added to subcategorization frames as complete words: AGENT, EXPERIENCER, THEME etc. We need to shorten these words to be appropriate when we insert them in such frames. For this purpose, we will use the theta symbol (θ) and insert it in subcategorization frames to represent all the thematic roles assigned by a verb. Consider the revised subcategorization frames below.

Sentences / Subcategorization frames

1. John often *collects* many stamps.   *collects*, V [__ NP]
       θ̲   θ

2. Jack *gave* a prize to the student.   *gave*, V [__ NP PP]
       θ̲   θ   θ

3. They *bought* flowers for the sick.   *bought*, V [__ NP (PP$_{[for]}$)]
       θ̲   θ   θ

4. I *travelled* from Italy to France.   *travelled*, V [__ PP$_{[from]}$ PP$_{[to]}$]
       θ̲   θ   θ

5. He *opened* the door with a key.   *opened*, V [__ NP (PP$_{[with]}$)]
       θ̲   θ   θ

6. The worker *left*.   *left*, V [__]
       θ̲

7. He *cried*.   *cried*, P [__]
       θ̲

8. It *seems* that Ahmed came.   *seems*, V [__ CP]
       θ

All the words (AGENT, EXPERIENCER, THEME etc.) have now been replaced by the symbol (θ). To differentiate between theta roles assigned to internal arguments and those assigned to external arguments, we simply underlined the θ-roles assigned to external arguments (i.e. subjects). In syntax, every argument must receive one θ-role. Having substituted the thematic role words (AGENT, EXPERIENCER etc.) with the symbol (θ), we do not know which particular role the symbol (θ) refers to. However, syntax does not need to know. This unidentified symbol (θ) is advantageous because there are arguments that we cannot characterize such as *necessary* and *around 445 kg* in Unit 119. Syntax cares about how many arguments a verb requires, and how many theta roles (θ-roles) it assigns. In short, syntax stipulates that 'every argument that participates in the event in the structure must receive one and only one θ-role'.

UNIT 122

Thematic Roles VI

Thematic Roles

Let us now consider how every argument (i.e. NP, PP etc.) is assigned a θ-role in syntax. This is accomplished according to the **PRINCIPLES OF THETA ROLE ASSIGNMENT** in (1).

1. Principles of Theta Role Assignment
    i. Assign one θ-role to every complement (i.e. internal arguments)
    ii. Assign one θ-role to the subject (i.e. the external argument).

According to the principles above, an argument cannot receive more than one θ-role. Two θ-roles cannot be assigned to one argument either, even if the argument seems to play two distinct thematic roles at the same time. Consider the sentence in (2) and the subcategorization frame of the verb *gives* in (3).

2. [NP Jack] often gives [NP a prize] [PP to the students].

3. *gives*, V [__ NP PP]
    θ θ θ

Sentence (2) has three arguments, each of which should be assigned one θ-role. According to the Principles of Theta Role Assignment in (1), sentence (2) is structurally drawn in (4). Notice how θ-roles are assigned to the arguments from the verb in (4).

4. Tree for (2)

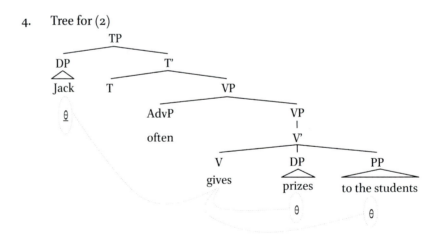

In (3), the subcategorization frame of the verb *gives* distributes three θ-roles, and we have three θ-roles in the structure (4) as well: one for the subject *Jack*, another for the first complement (the object *prizes*) and the third for the second complement (the prepositional object *to the students*). The adverb *often* is an adjunct; thus it is not assigned any θ-role.

UNIT 123

Thematic Roles VII

Thematic Roles

Consider the following examples.

1. *It* seems that Ahmed came.
2. *It* is raining.

We claimed before that the argument *it* in (1) is the expletive *it*. Expletives do not play any thematic role. In (1), the argument *it* is neither an agent that initiates the action *seeming*, nor an experiencer that experiences it. We come across similar expletives in constructions such as *it seems that, it appears that, it is possible that, it is likely that* etc. The same applies to the argument *it* in (2), which does not refer to the sky nor the clouds or the weather. It does not play any thematic role. The expletive *it* in (2) is sometimes called 'the weather *it*' because it appears in weather constructions like *it is snowing, it is sunny* etc. The expletive *it* in (1) and (2) is there to fulfill syntactic purposes, i.e. to make sentences grammatical because every sentence requires a subject. Consider the subcategorization frames for the verbs *seems* and *raining* below.

3. *seems*, V [___ CP]
                    θ

4. *raining*, V [___]

In (3) and (4), the verbs *seems* and *raining* do not assign any external θ-role to the subject *it* because *it* does not play any thematic role. Because the verb *seems* selects CP [*that Ahmed came*] as a complement as shown in (1), it assigns an internal θ-role to CP in (3). The verb *rain* in (4) does not assign any internal θ-role because it does not select a complement in (2).

It is important to note that the pronoun *it* is not always an expletive, i.e. a dummy pronoun.

5. Look at that cat. *It* is staring at us.

The pronoun *it* in (5) refers to a cat. The pronoun *it* functions as an agent that initiates the action *staring*. Thus, the subcategorization frame of the verb *staring* in (6) assigns an external θ-role (of agent) to the subject *it*, and an internal θ-role to the complement PP [*at us*].

6. *starting*, V [___ PP]
                  θ   θ

In short, a verb assigns an external θ-role iff the subject plays a thematic role, e.g. that of agent or experiencer. Otherwise, it assigns no θ-roles as is the case in expletive constructions.

UNIT 124

Thematic Roles VIII

Thematic Roles

In the previous unit, we discussed the pronoun *it* as a subject as shown below.

1. *It* seems that Ahmed came.   *seems*, V [__ CP]
                                                                          θ

2. *It* is raining.   *raining*, V [__]

3. Look at that cat. *It* is staring at us.   *starting*, V [__ PP]
                                                                                               θ   θ

We concluded that the pronoun *it* in (1) and (2) are expletives because they do not play any thematic role. Thus, they are not assigned any external θ-role as shown in their sub-categorization frames. However, the pronoun *it* in (3) is not an expletive because it plays the role of agent. Thus, its subcategorization frames includes an external θ-role.

To illustrate how θ-roles are assigned in (1) through (3), we need to revise the Principles of Theta Role Assignment that we developed earlier, and add a condition that bans any external θ-role assignment to expletives. The revised principles will therefore be as in (4).

4. Principles of Theta Role Assignment
   i. Assign one θ-role to every complement (i.e. internal arguments)
   ii. Assign one θ-role to the subject (i.e. the external argument), unless it is an expletive.

The structures for (1) through (3) in accordance with the principles in (4) are given below.

5. Tree for (1)   6. Tree for (3)   7. Tree for (2)

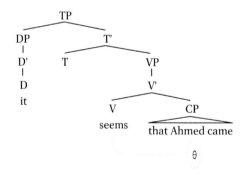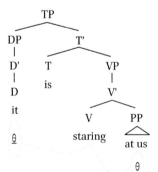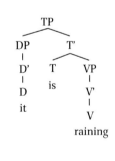

This tree has no θ-roles, because the verb *raining* does not assign any θ-roles at all, as indicated in its subcategorization frame in (2).

UNIT 125

Subject Condition 1

Subject Condition

Consider the following examples.

1. *Ahmed* is **afraid** that they will win.
2. *Ahmed* **claims** that they will win.
3. **It* is **afraid** that they will win.   (Here, *it* is an expletive, not *a cat*)
4. **It* **claims** that they will win.   (Here, *it* is an expletive, not *a cat*)

In (1) through (4), the adjective *afraid* and the verb *claims* select CP, i.e. *that they will win*. Sentences (1) and (2) are grammatical and they have *Ahmed* as a subject. However, sentences (3) and (4) are ungrammatical and their subjects are the expletive *it*. The ungrammaticality of (3) and (4) follows from the fact that the adjective *afraid* and the verb *claims* require a thematic subject (that plays a θ-role), whereas the expletive *it* does not.

In (1), *Ahmed* experiences and feels the fear that they will win; thus, he is an experiencer. In (2), *Ahmed* is an agent that initiates a claim. For this reason, it is proposed that the adjective *afraid* and the verb *claim* assign an external θ-role to their subjects, and an internal θ-role to their complements (CP) as shown in their subcategorization frames below.

5. *afraid*, A [__ CP]
           θ̲ θ

6. *claim*, V [__ CP]
          θ̲ θ

The assignment of an external θ-role by the adjective *afraid* and the verb *claim* indicates that these events require thematic subjects. Expletives fail in these contexts because they are non-thematic. The expletive *it* does feel the fear nor does it initiate a claim. Besides *afraid* and *claim*, there are many other adjectives and verbs that require thematic subjects as in (7) and (8); these adjectives and verbs do not allow expletive subjects either as shown in (9) and (10).

7. *Ahmed* is **sure/certain** that they will win.
8. *Ahmed* **believes/thinks** that they will win.
9. **It* is **sure/certain** that they will win.   (Here, *it* is an expletive, not *a cat*)
10. **It* **believes/thinks** that they will win.   (Here, *it* is an expletive, not *a cat*)

The subcategorization frames of the adjectives and verbs in (7) and (8) are given below.

11. *sure/certain*, A [__ CP]
                 θ̲ θ

12. *believes/thinks*, V [__ CP]
                    θ̲ θ

UNIT 126

Subject Condition II

Subject Condition

In contrast to the cases in the previous unit, consider the following examples.

1. *It* is **likely** that they will win. (Here, *it* is an expletive, not *a cat*)
2. *It* **seems** that they will win. (Here, *it* is an expletive, not *a cat*)
3. **Ahmed* is **likely** that they will win.
4. **Ahmed* **seems** that they will win.

In (1) through (4), the adjective *likely* and the verb *seems* select the CP *that they will win*. Sentences (1) and (2) are grammatical because the expletive *it* functions as a subject. Sentences (3) and (4), in contrast, are ungrammatical because the subjects are *Ahmed*. The ungrammaticality of (3) and (4) follows from the fact that the adjective *likely* and the verb *seem* do not allow thematic subjects at all; they only need an expletive subject such as *it*.

For this reason, it is submitted that the adjective *likely* and the verb *seem* do not assign an external θ-role (to their subjects), but that they assign only an internal theta role to their complements (CP) as shown in their subcategorization frames below.

5. *likely*, A [__ CP]
                    θ

6. *seem*, V [__ CP]
                   θ

The non-assignment of an external θ-role by the adjective *likely* and the verb *seem* indicates that they require non-thematic external arguments. The non-thematic expletive *it* is therefore the best choice to complete their predicates. Besides *likely* and *seem*, there are many other adjectives and verbs that do not assign external θ-roles and require only expletives as in (7) and (8); these adjectives and verbs do not allow thematic subjects such as *Ahmed* as shown in (9) and (10).

7. *It* is **clear/possible** that they will win. (Here, *it* is an expletive, not *a cat*)
8. *It* **appears/looks** that they won. (Here, *it* is an expletive, not *a cat*)
9. **Ahmed* is **clear/possible** that they will win.
10. **Ahmed* **appears/looks** that they won.

To recap, there are adjectives (such as *afraid, sure, certain* etc.) and verbs (such as *claim, believe, think* etc.) that assign an external θ-role to their subjects. These words only take thematic subjects such as *Ahmed*, and do not allow the non-thematic expletive *it* in their constructions. On the other hand, there are adjectives and verbs that do not assign external θ-roles to their subjects, such as the adjectives *likely, clear, possible* etc. and the verbs *seem, appear, look* etc. These allow non-thematic expletives, but ban the occurrence of thematic subjects such as *Ahmed* in their constructions.

UNIT 127

Subject Condition III

Subject Condition

In conclusion, consider the table below that summarizes whether a word assigns an external θ-role or not.

	A: afraid, sure, certain V: claim, believe, think *They assign an external θ-role*	A: likely, clear, possible V: seem, appear, look *They don't assign an external θ-role*
Expletive subject e.g. *it*	✗	✓
Thematic subject e.g. *Ahmed*	✓	✗

The derivation of sentences (1) and (2) is given in (3) and (4) respectively.

1. *He* **claims** that they will win.   *claim*, V [__ CP]
                                                                    θ   θ

2. *It* **seems** that they will win.   *seems*, V [__ CP]
                                                                         θ

3. Tree for (1)   4. Tree for (2)

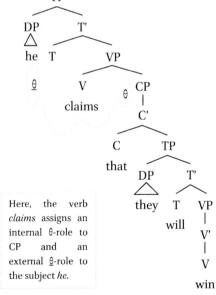
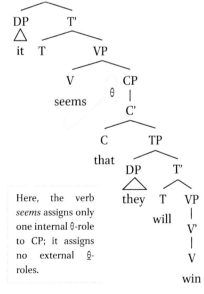

Here, the verb *claims* assigns an internal θ-role to CP and an external θ-role to the subject *he*.

Here, the verb *seems* assigns only one internal θ-role to CP; it assigns no external θ-roles.

UNIT 128

Subject Condition IV

Subject Condition

Consider the following adjectives and verbs that allow the expletive *it* as a subject.

1. *It* is **likely/clear/possible** that they will win.
2. *It* **seems/appears/looks** that they won.

We have pointed out that these words do not assign an external θ-role as shown in their subcategorization frames in (3) and (4).

3. *likely/clear/possible*, A [___ CP]
   θ

4. *seems/appears/looks*, V [___ CP]
   θ

Given that the subcategorization frames above do not show any external θ-role symbol, one might assume that these words do not require subjects in their sentences because their subjects have no semantic content. In other words, the sentences in (1) and (2) can be semantically interpreted without any subject involved. However, from a syntactic perspective, sentences (1) and (2) cannot be grammatical without subjects as in (5) and (6).

5. *is **likely/clear/possible** that they will win.
6. ***seems/appears/looks** that they won.

Subject-less sentences (5) and (6) are ungrammatical, even though the meaning of the whole sentence can be derived without subjects. In syntactic theory, every sentence must contain a subject; this condition is known as the **SUBJECT CONDITION** or **EXTENDED PROJECTION PRINCIPLE (EPP)** (Chomsky, 1982). The EPP is formulated in (7).

7. **Extended Projection Principle (EPP):** every sentence must have a subject.

Given that the EPP requires that all sentences take subjects, it is required from the adjectives and verbs that assign no external θ-role that they insert the expletive *it* as an external argument in their spec,TP. For the EPP, there is an obligatory process known as **EXPLETIVE INSERTION** that inserts the expletive *it* into any empty spec,TP. The expletive insertion rule is defined in (8)

8. **Expletive insertion:** an operation that inserts the expletive *it* as a subject in sentences including adjectives or verbs that do not assign external θ-roles.

To conclude, some words do not assign external θ-roles, and their spec,TP remains empty at the d-structure. The EPP, however, requires that sentences should have subjects. Thus, a process known as expletive insertion adds the non-thematic expletive *it* in the empty spec,TP at the d-structure. This expletive appears at the s-structure.

THETA THEORY

UNIT 129

Subject Condition v

Subject Condition

In light of the EPP, every sentence must have a subject. Thus, (1) and (2) are ungrammatical, but they become grammatical once the expletive *it* is added to them.

1. *is likely that they will win → It is likely that they will win.
2. *seems that they will win. → It seems that they will win.

Thus, it is submitted that the structures for (1) and (2) start at the d-structure without a subject as shown in (3) and (4).

3. DS for (1)   4. DS for (2)

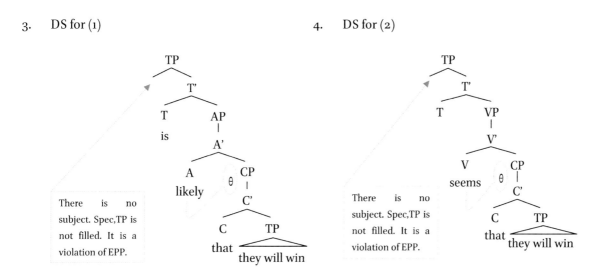

Given that the structures in (3) and (4) violate the EPP, the expletive insertion rule is activated, and it inserts the expletive *it* in spec,TP as shown in (5) and (6) below. Because of the Inclusiveness Principle, that does not allow the addition of new information, it is assumed that the expletive *it* is present and inserted at the d-structure.

5. DS for (1)   6. DS for (2)

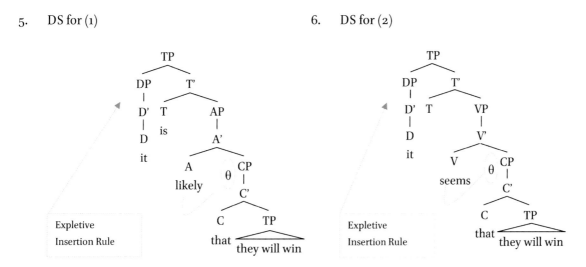

UNIT 130

Subject Condition VI

Subject Condition

It is important to know that when sentences involve adjectives or verbs that do not assign external θ-roles, the EPP can be satisfied in two ways: (i) through expletive insertion in spec,TP or (ii) through the movement of the whole CP to spec,TP.

1. *is likely/clear/possible* that they will win.   (violation of EPP)
2. It *is likely/clear/possible* that they will win.   (expletive insertion)
3. That they will win *is likely/clear/possible*.   (movement of CP)

The d-structure of sentences (2) and (3) has no subjects as in (1) represented in (4), i.e. there is no element in spec,TP. Since this is a violation of the EPP, spec,TP can be filled with the expletive *it* as in (2) (represented in (5) in Unit 129), or the whole CP can be moved to spec,TP as in the derivation of (3) in (5).

4. DS for (3)   5. SS for (3)

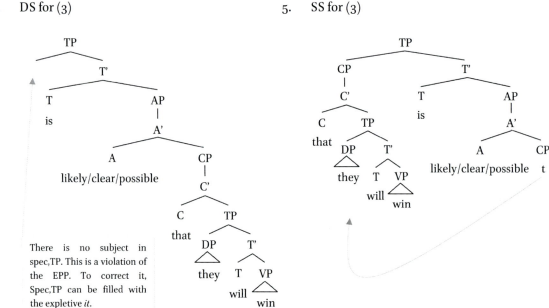

To summarize, the d-structure of sentences involving adjectives and verbs that do not assign external θ-roles violate the EPP. Thus, empty spec,TP can be filled in two ways:

6. Expletive Insertion: the insertion of the expletive *it* in spec,TP.

For the Inclusiveness Principle that disallows the addition of new information, it is assumed that the expletive "it" is present and inserted at the d-structure.

7. Move CP to spec,TP   Phrasal movement   For EPP

UNIT 131

Subject Condition VII

Subject Condition

Note that the subject of sentences that involve adjectives or verbs with no external θ-role is not always the expletive *it* or a *that*-clause (i.e. CP). Consider the following examples.

1. *exist many solutions.   *exist*, V [__ DP]
2. There *exist* many solutions.   θ
3. Many solutions *exist*.

Sentence (1) is ungrammatical because it violates the EPP. Thus, the EPP is satisfied either by (i) the insertion of the expletive *there* (which is DP with no semantic content) as in (2), or (ii) the movement of DP to spec,TP as in (3). Consider the derivations of (2) and (3) below.

4.   DS for (2) and (3)   5.   DS and SS for (2)   6.   DS and SS for (3)

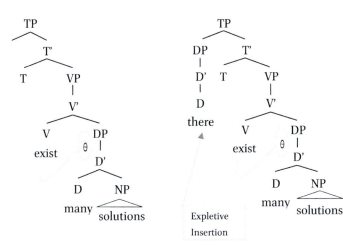
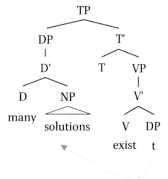

In (4), the structure is lacking an important element in spec,TP, which is the subject. To satisfy the EPP, this spec,TP must be filled by the expletive DP *there* as in (5). If the expletive *there* is not inserted, the other approach would be to move the DP *many solution* from its original position to spec,TP as in (6).
  Thus, the two operations that satisfy the EPP are revised as follows.

7.   Expletive Insertion: insert the expletive *it* or *there* in spec,TP.

For the Inclusiveness Principle that does not allow for the addition of new information, it is assumed that the expletives "it" and "there" are present and inserted at the DS.

8.   Move CP/DP to spec,TP   Phrasal movement   For EPP

UNIT 132

Passive 1

Passive

Every sentence can take an active form as in (1), or a passive form as in (2).

1. *The man* **drove** *the car.* (active)
2. *The car* **was driven** by *the man.* (passive)

Due to the semantic similarity between (1) and (2), traditional grammarians assume that the passive sentence (2) is derived from the active one, i.e. (1). The object *the car* and the subject *the man* in (1) switch positions as shown in (2). The object *the car* is promoted (i.e. moved forwards) to the subject position, whereas the subject *the man* is demoted (i.e. moved backwards) to the end of the sentence, preceded by the preposition *by*. Also, the verb *drove* in (1) inflects as *driven* in (2) and is preceded by the auxiliary *was*. This traditional description cannot be implemented theoretically, however. Consider the wrong derivation of (2), which assumes that a passive form adopts the d-structure of an active form.

3. DS for (2)   4. SS for (2)

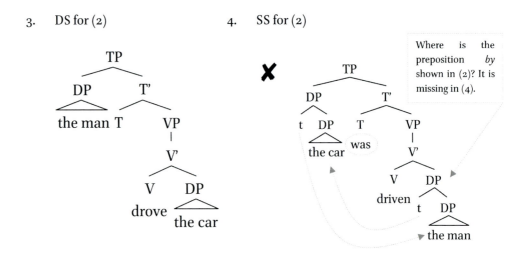

To derive the passive sentence in (2) from the active sentence in (1), the object *the car* must move to the subject position as shown in (4), even though the subject *the man* still occupies spec,TP. Also, the subject *the man* must move downwards to the complement of the verb *driven*, although the object *the car* is still in that position. These kinds of movement are problematic because they must assume that XP can move to positions filled by YP; XP then removes YP or its trace, and occupies its position. In syntax, such a movement violates the recoverability principle which states that 'no information should be lost from the d-structure during the derivation'. In other words, an element cannot be removed from its position in order for another element to land in its position.

Another problem with the derivation in (4) is that we do not know how to add the preposition *by* before the subject *the man* after its downward movement. Also, the auxiliary *was* is added to the s-structure in (4) although it was not present in the d-structure in (3). This violates the inclusiveness principle, which prevents the addition of new elements to the d-structure.

THETA THEORY

UNIT 133

Passive II

Passive

We pointed out that every sentence can take an active or a passive form as in (1) and (2).

1. *The man* **drove** the car. (active)
2. *The car* **was driven** by *the man*. (passive)

Because of the recoverability and inclusiveness principles, we concluded that passive forms cannot be derived from their active counterparts.

As an alternative proposal, syntacticians propose that the passive be derived from a different d-structure than that of the active form. We should assume that the active verb *drove* in (1) and the passive verb *driven* in (2) are different lexical entries with different subcategorization frames as shown below.

3. *drove* [active], V [__ DP] (for active, e.g. 1)

4. *driven* [passive], V [__ DP (PP[by])] (for passive, e.g. 2)
5. *be* [passive], T [__ VP[en]]

In (3), the active verb *drove* selects a DP, namely *the car* in (1). However, the passive verb *driven* selects two complements: an obligatory DP and an optional PP. As shown in (2), the obligatory DP is the object *the car*, while the optional PP is *by the man*. The PP *by the man* is optional in (4) because it can be removed from (2). In addition to the subcategorization frame of the passive verb *driven*, the auxiliary *be* in (5) selects a verb that bears the passive marker [en]. This suffix [en] is symbolic and appears as [ed] in regular verbs. The auxiliary *be* must be present in the d-structure of the passive so that it does not violate the inclusiveness principle. Under these assumptions, the d-structure of the passive sentence (2) represented in (7) will be different from that of the active sentence (1) in (6).

6. DS for active (1)
7. DS for passive (2)

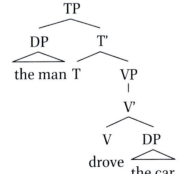

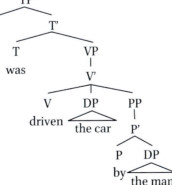

UNIT 134

Passive III

Passive

In light of the earlier discussion, the lexical entries in passive sentence (1) take the subcategorization frames in (2) and (3).

1. The car **was driven** by *the man*.   (passive)

2. *driven* [passive], V [___ DP (PP[by])]   (for passive, e.g. 1)
3. *be* [passive], T [___ VP[en]]

It has been argued that the passive takes the d-structure in (4).

4. DS for (1)   5. SS for (1)

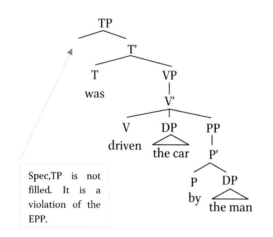
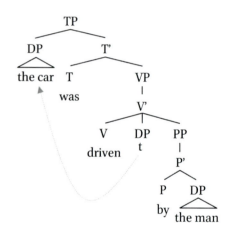

Spec,TP is not filled. It is a violation of the EPP.

The passive d-structure in (4) is generated with an empty spec,TP and this is a violation of the EPP. Furthermore, the d-structure in (4) produces the wrong word order for passive sentence (1), yielding sentences like the one in (6).

6. *was driven the car by the man.

To solve these problems, it is proposed that the obligatory DP *the car* move from its original position to spec,TP as shown in (5). This movement satisfies the EPP and generates the correct word order in (1). Thus, a new transformational rule should be proposed for passive constructions. Consider this new rule in (7).

7. Move DP to spec,TP   Phrasal Movement   Passive Structure

This is a preliminary derivation of the passive. In Units 168–170, we will learn that Case, besides EPP, motivates the DP-movement to spec,TP in passive structures.

THETA THEORY

UNIT 135

A- and A′-Movement I

A-Movement vs. A′-Movement

In syntactic theory, a distinction has been made between two types of movement: **A-MOVEMENT** and **A′-MOVEMENT** (pronounced as "A-bar movement"). The distinction is based on whether the landing site on which a moved element lands is a potential θ-role position. In a tree structure, a **θ-POSITION** is a position to which a θ-role is potentially assigned, whereas a **θ′ (θ-BAR) POSITION** is a position to which no θ-role is potentially assigned. Consider the subcategorization frame of the verb *destroy* in (2), taken from the sentence in (1).

1. The army will *destroy* the city.

2. *destroy*, V [__ DP]
              θ   θ

The verb *destroy* in (2) assigns two θ-roles: an external θ-role to the subject *the army* and an internal θ-role to the complement *the city* as shown in (3).

3. Tree for (1)

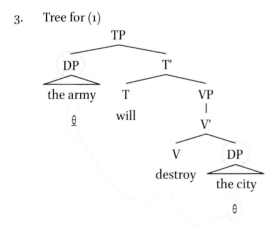

Given that any structural position that is possibly assigned a θ-role is considered a θ-position, spec,TP and the complement of the verb (i.e. circled in the structure in (3)) are called θ-positions.

In light of these observations, the movement of any element to spec,TP or the complement(s) of the verb is termed **A-MOVEMENT** (pronounced as "Ay Movement"). A-movement is defined in (4).

4. **A-movement:** a movement that transposes an element from any position to a potential θ-position such as spec,TP or the complement(s) of a verb.

UNIT 136

A- and A'-Movement II

A-Movement vs. A'-Movement

In contrast, any position other than the two θ-positions (spec,TP or the verb's complement(s)) is known as a θ' ("θ-bar") position. This includes spec,CP, head C, adjoined positions and any position above TP/CP. Consider the derivation of question (1) given in (2) and (3).

1. What will the army destroy?

2. DS for (1)   3. SS for (1)

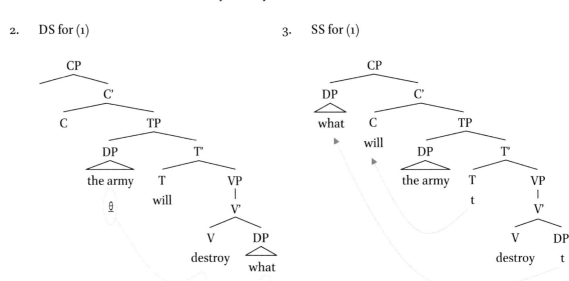

As shown in (2), the only positions that may be assigned θ-roles are spec,TP and the verb's complement. Spec,CP and C are not assigned any θ-role; thus, they are known as θ'-positions. In light of these observations, the movement of *will* from T to C and the movement of *what* from the complement of the verb *destroy* to spec,CP are termed **A'-MOVEMENTS** (pronounced as "Ay Bar Movements"). A'-movement is defined in (4).

4. **A'-movement:** a movement that transposes an element from any position to a position that is not potentially assigned a θ-role such as spec,CP, head C, adjoined positions and many others.

Adjoined positions (above TP) are also potential θ'-positions because they are not assigned θ-roles. Consider the NP, PP and AP that are adjoined above TP as bracketed in (5) through (7).

5. [TP [NP *football*] [TP [NP the player] [T' [T will [VP play [NP *t*]]]]]].

6. [TP [AP *very necessary*] [TP [NP he] [T' [T [VP deemed [NP these steps] [AP *t*]]]]]].

7. [TP [PP *in the morning*] [TP [NP the students] [T' [T will [VP [VP come] [PP *t*]]]]]].

UNIT 137

Summary

Summary of Movements

Most of the movements that we have covered thus far are A'-movements because their landing sites are θ'-positions. A-movements only occur in (8) and (9) in the sentences below because θ-roles are potentially assigned to spec,TP.

1. Move T to C   Head-to-Head Movement   Yes/No Question
   Can you ___ stay?

2. Move Neg to T   Head-to-Head Movement   Negation Movement
   Is not he ___ ___ sleeping?

3. Move V to T   Head-to-Head Movement   Verb Movement (EME)
   Heard you ___ this?

4. Move T to V   Head-to-Head Movement   Affix Hopping
   He ___ play -*s* soccer.

5. Move DP to spec,CP   Phrasal Movement   Wh-Question
   Which car *are* you ___ driving ___?

6. Move XP to adjoin TP   Phrasal Movement   Adjunction Rule
   (XP = AdvP/PP/DP/AP)
   To the student, *a present*, we have given ___ ___.

7. Move CP/DP to spec,TP   Phrasal movement   For EPP
   That they will win is likely ___.

   Many solutions exist ___.

8. Expletive Insertion: insert the expletive *it* or *there* in spec,TP for EPP.
   ___*It*___ is likely that they will win.   OR   ___*There*___ exist many solutions.

9. Move DP to spec,TP   Phrasal Movement   Passive Structure
   The car was driven ___ by the man.

SECTION 8

Constraints on Movements

∵

UNIT 138

PBC 1

Constraints on Movements

Recall that we define movement as a process where an element moves from one position to another. These movements are either **head-to-head movements** or **phrasal movements**.

1.	Move T to C	Head-to-Head Movement	Yes/No Question
2.	Move Neg to T	Head-to-Head Movement	Negation Movement
3.	Move V to T	Head-to-Head Movement	Verb Movement (EME)
4.	Move DP to spec,CP	Phrasal Movement	Wh-Question
5.	Move XP to adjoin TP	Phrasal Movement	Adjunction Rule
6.	Move DP/CP to Spec,TP	Phrasal Movement	For EPP
7.	Move DP to Spec,TP	Phrasal Movement	Passive Structure

We have found that all the movements in (1) through (7) move from a lower position to a higher landing site. That is, the moved elements move 'upwards' not 'downwards'. This direction is a constraint, technically known as the **Proper Binding Condition** (PBC).

8. **Proper Binding Condition (PBC):** Traces must be bound. (Fiengo 1977, Saito 1985)

PBC requires that a trace must be bound by its moved element. Binding is held via a c-command relationship. If A binds B, A c-commands B. C-command is defined as follows.

9. C-command relationship
   A c-commands B iff
   i. A does not dominate B, and B does not dominate A
   ii. The first node that dominates A dominates B

Note that c-command is based on dominance (see Unit 45). Dominance is defined in (10).

10. Dominance: A dominates B iff A appears above B in the tree.

To better remember dominance and c-command, consider the following representations.

11. Dominance   12. C-command

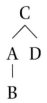

In tree (11), A dominates B because A is right above B. C dominates D, A and B because C is above them all. Because A is not above D, and D is not above A, A and D do not dominate each other. As for B, it dominates nothing.

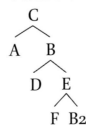

As shown in tree (12), because A is not above B, and B is not above A, A and B c-command each other. Also, we can say that A c-commands B2 because: (i) A does not dominate B2, and B2 does not dominate A (as required in (9i)); and (ii) C, that dominates A, also dominates B2 (as required in (9ii)).

UNIT 139

PBC II

Proper Binding Condition

We argued in the previous unit that **binding** is defined by **c-command** relationship in (1).

1. C-command relationship
   A c-commands B iff
   i. A does not dominate B, and B does not dominate A
   ii. The first node that dominates A dominates B

Consider the following tree structure.

2.
```
        X
       / \
      A   B
         / \
        C   D
           / \
          E   F
```
A c-commands B (note: X, that dominates A, also dominates B)
B c-commands A (note: X, that dominates B, also dominates A)
A c-commands B, C, D, E, F
C c-commands D, and D c-commands C (= mutual c-command)
C c-commands D, E, F
E c-commands F and F c-commands E (= mutual c-command).
B does not c-command C, D, E, F because it dominates them.

PBC states that when an element moves, it must c-command its trace in its original position.

3. **Proper Binding Condition (PBC):** Traces must be bound. (Fiengo 1977, Saito 1985)

In other words, a moved element must bind/c-command its trace.

In fact, all the movements we have covered respect PBC because traces are always bound/c-commanded by the moved elements. Let us examine the following sentence, where both head-to-head movement and phrasal movement occur. Traces are always bound/c-commanded by the moved elements. C-command is illustrated with a dotted line in (5) below.

4. Which car are you driving?

5.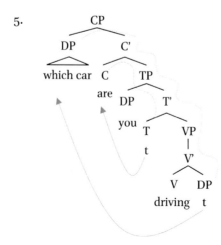

- T (t) is bound/c-commanded by C (*are*). PBC is respected.
- DP (t) is bound/c-commanded by DP (*which car*). PBC is also respected.
- Both (T to C) and (DP to spec,CP) respect PBC.
- As long as an element moves 'upwards', PBC will be respected. However, if an element moves 'downwards', there will be a violation of PBC because the trace will be above the moved element. Traces will not be bound/c-commanded by their related elements. The reverse will be true.

CONSTRAINTS ON MOVEMENTS

UNIT 140

PBC III

Proper Binding Condition

One of the movements that we covered in the previous units does not seem to respect PBC in (1). This movement is the affix hopping given in (2).

1. **Proper Binding Condition (PBC):** Traces must be bound. (Fiengo 1977, Saito 1985)
   In other words, a moved element must bind/c-command its trace.

2. Move T to V   Head-to-Head Movement   Affix Hopping

3. He play-s soccer.

4. Tree for (3)

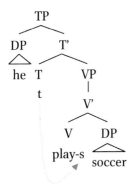

In (4), it is assumed that the morphological tense marker -s moves downwards to V, and attaches to it as a suffix. Obviously, this movement does not respect PBC because the trace (t) on T is not bound by the morpheme -s on V. The trace (t) on T is above the suffix -s and c-commands it, although we want the morpheme -s to c-command the trace instead. To overcome this problem, it has been suggested that affix lowering is not syntactic; thus, it does not need to respect PBC. Because it is related to morphology (i.e. tense morphological affixes), it occurs at PF and not in the syntactic component as shown in (5). At PF, the tense morpheme is merged with the main verb via a process known as **MORPHOLOGICAL MERGER** (Marantz, 1984; Bobljik, 1994). Other movements occur in syntax and must respect PBC.

5. Grammar Architecture

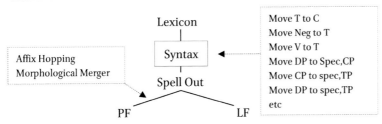

UNIT 141

Locality 1

Locality

In theory, **LOCALITY** is a constraint that limits the span over which an element moves from its position to a landing site. It requires a movement to be short and local. **HEAD MOVEMENT CONSTRAINT (HMC)** in (1) is a constraint formulated in light of locality.

1. **Head Movement Constraint (HMC):** Head X moves to head Y but cannot skip an intervening head Z between X and Y (Travis, 1984).

In short, the landing site to which a head moves must be the closest c-commanding head.

2. Allowed Head Movement   3. Disallowed Head Movement

In (2), the head X first moves to the head Z, and then to the head Y. In (3), however, X moves to Y directly, skipping the intervening Z, which is a violation of HMC in (1). Because the head-to-head movement is an adjunction rule, another constraint stipulates that, if X moves to Z, X must adjoin Z, and both heads X^Z must move together and adjoin Y as shown below.

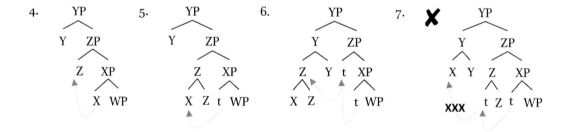

As shown in (4) and (5), X first moves to Z and adjoins it. The newly merged heads X^Z move together and adjoin Y as in (6). The head-to-head movement in (7) is disallowed because X adjoins Z, and then X moves to Y alone. The movement in (7) is banned because it violates a constraint known as **NO EXTRACTION CONSTRAINT**.

8. **No Extraction Constraint:** If X moves to Z, then X cannot be extracted, i.e. move alone to the higher head Y without Z. X^Z must move together to a higher head position.

UNIT 142

Locality 11

Locality

In the last unit, we covered two constraints related to locality: (i) **HEAD MOVEMENT CONSTRAINT (HMC)** in (1) and (ii) **NO EXTRACTION CONSTRAINT** in (2).

1. **Head Movement Constraint (HMC):** Head X moves to head Y but cannot skip an intervening head Z between X and Y (Travis, 1984).

2. **No Extraction Constraint:** If X moves to Z, then X cannot be extracted, i.e. move alone to the higher head Y without Z. X^Z must move together to a higher head position.

All the head-to-head movements that we covered earlier respect HMC and No Extraction Constraint. Let us discuss the negation movement in questions.

3. He is not sleeping.
4. Is not he sleeping?

To derive (4), the head Neg moves to T, and then both T^Neg move to C to form a question.

5. DS for (4)　　　6. DS for (4)　　　7. SS for (4)

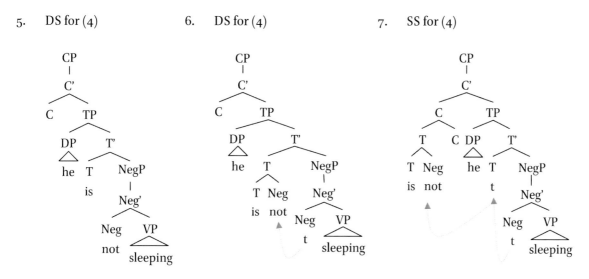

As shown in (6), the head Neg (*not*) first moves and adjoins T (*is*). Then, the complex of the adjoined heads T^Neg (*is not*) moves together and adjoins C as in (7). If extraction is allowed, the head Neg (*not*) can first move to T, and then move alone to C without T. However, this solo movement of Neg from T to C violates the **No Extraction Constraint** in (2). If allowed, it yields an ungrammatical sentence as in (8).

8. **Not* he is ___ sleeping?

UNIT 143

Subjacency 1

Subjacency

SUBJACENCY is another locality constraint on movements. It restricts movements to be short and local, and dictates that elements cannot move out of certain phrases (XPs). These XPs are called **BOUNDING NODES**. In English, bounding nodes are DP and TP.

1. **Subjacency**: elements cannot move beyond two bounding nodes like two DPs or TPs.

In other words, an element can move beyond one DP or one TP, but not more. These bounding nodes (DP and TP) are also called **ISLANDS** (Ross, 1967). In theory, elements cannot move out of islands. Consider the following examples.

2. [TP Ahmed *is* coming]. (one TP)
3. [CP *is* [TP Ahmed ___ coming? (possible question)

In (2), there is only one TP, and question (3) is derived from it. The auxiliary *is* moves across one bounding node, i.e. one TP. Now consider the following examples.

4. [TP They *are* saying] [CP that [TP Ahmed *is* coming]. (two TPs)
5. [CP are [TP they ___ saying] [CP that [TP Ahmed is coming]? (possible question)
6. *[CP is [TP they are saying] [CP that [TP Ahmed ___ coming]? (impossible ques.)
    xxx

In (4), there are two TPs; thus, syntax can only generate question (5) out of statement (4) because the auxiliary *are* crosses one bounding node (one TP). However, it is not possible for the auxiliary *is*, as in (6), to move across two bounding nodes (two TPs) as this violates subjacency in (1). Consider the syntactic tree structures for (5) and (6) below.

7. Tree for (5)   8. Tree for (6)

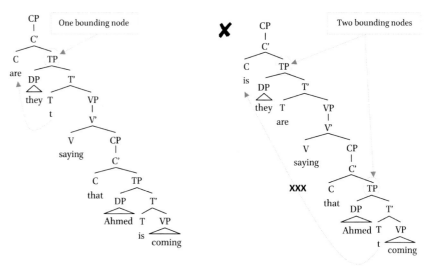

UNIT 144

Subjacency II

Subjacency

In the previous unit, we argued that **SUBJACENCY** is a locality constraint which precludes elements from moving across two **BOUNDING NODES**.

1. **Subjacency**: elements cannot move beyond two bounding nodes like two DPs or TPs.

Let us consider how subjacency restricts the movement of elements out of two DPs, especially when these DPs occur in a subject position.

2. The name of the street will change to Broadway.
3. What will change to Broadway?   Answer: the name of the street.
4. The name of the street will change to Broadway.
5. *What will the name of ___ change to Broadway?   Answer: the street.

In (2), the subject is a complex noun phrase consisting of two DPs: (i) the DP *the name* and (ii) the DP *the street*. According to subjacency, it is possible to ask about the complex phrase *the name of the street* as a whole as shown in (3). However, it is not possible to ask only about the embedded DP *the street* as in (5) because the complex DP functions as an island in the subject position. This island is known as **SUBJECT ISLAND CONSTRAINT**.

6. **Subject Island Constraint**: no element that occurs in a subject position can be moved out of the complex DP.

Consider the following tree structures for questions (3) and (5). In (8), the circled DP is an island out of which the lower DP cannot move.

7. Tree for (3)   8. Tree for (5)

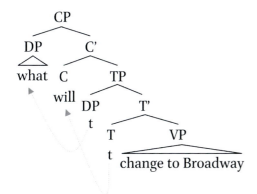
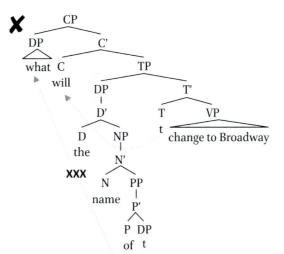

UNIT 145

Islands 1

Subject Island Constraint

In Subject Island Constraint in (1), the higher DPs that dominate lower DPs are islands, i.e. they block the movement of any embedded DP out of them.

1. **Subject Island Constraint:** no element that occurs in a subject position can be moved out of the complex DP.

However, note that Subject Island Constraint is by nature confined to the complex DP occurring in a **subject** position. The same complex DP that occurs in an object position allows the movement of the embedded DPs out of it. Consider the examples below.

2. We will change [$_{DP}$ the name of the street].
3. What will we change? Answer: the name of the street.
4. We will change [$_{DP}$ the name of the street].
5. What will we change the name of___? Answer: the street.

As shown in (2) and (3), it is allowed to ask about the complex DP *the name of the street* as a whole. Because the DP occurs in an object position, it does not function as an island; therefore, it is also possible to ask about the embedded DP *the street* in (4) as shown in (5). Consider the following tree structures for questions (3) and (5).

6. Tree for (3)

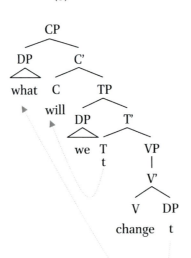

7. Tree for (5)

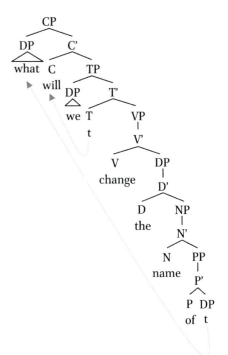

UNIT 146

Islands 11

Islands

In addition to Subject Island Constraint, there are several more islands as shown below.

1. Left Branch Island
2. Coordinate Structure Island
3. Complex Noun Phrase Island
4. Wh-Island
5. Adverbial Clausal Island

Left Branch Island

LEFT BRANCH ISLAND states that the left-hand elements within the DP spine (such as possessors or adjectives) cannot be extracted from, or moved out of, the DP.

6. We are reading [DP Ahmed's book].
7. *Whose are we reading [DP ___ book]?   Answer: Ahmed's.
8. We are reading [DP a very insightful book].
9. *How insightful are we reading [DP a ___ book]?   Answer: very insightful.

In (6), the left-hand word in the DP *Ahmed's book* is the possessor *Ahmed's*. This left-hand element cannot be moved and asked about as in (7). In (8), the left-hand element in the DP *very insightful book* is the adjective *very insightful*, which cannot be moved and asked about in (9). These left-hand elements are not allowed to move out of the DP because of the Left Branch Island. Consider the tree structures given to questions (7) and (9).

10. Tree for (7)

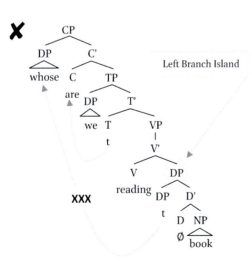

11. Tree for (9)

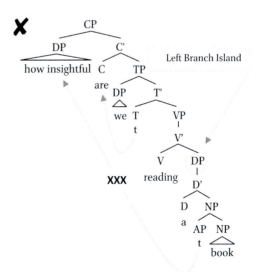

UNIT 147

Islands III

Coordinate Structure Island

COORDINATE STRUCTURE ISLAND stipulates that no elements in the coordinated DP can be moved out of the complex DP and asked about. In every conjunct phrase, there are two elements conjoined with a coordinator such as *and, but* and *or*. Neither of the two conjuncts can be moved alone due to Coordinate Structure Island.

1. He is reading [ConjP [DP a poem] and [DP a novel]].
2. What is he reading [ConjP ___]?   Answer: a poem & a novel
3. *What is he reading [ConjP [DP ___] and [DP a novel]]?   Answer: a poem.
4. *What is he reading [ConjP [DP a poem] and [DP ___]?   Answer: a novel.

In (1), there is a conjunct phrase, namely *a poem and a novel*. We can ask about the whole conjunct phrase as in (2). However, it is not possible to ask about only one element of this coordinate structure, be it the left-hand conjunct as in (3), or the right-hand one as in (4). Consider the tree structures given to (3) and (4).

5. Tree for (3)

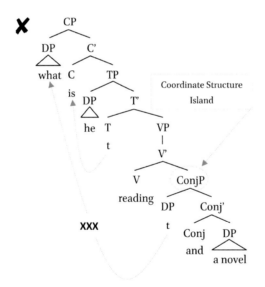

6. Tree for (4)

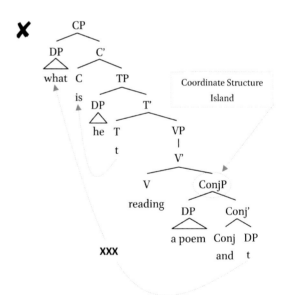

In certain cases, it is possible for both conjuncts to be asked about together as in (7) and (8).

7. Ahmed [VP took money from you] and [VP gave a present to him]
8. What did Ahmed take ___ from you and gave ___ to him?

UNIT 148

Islands IV

Complex Noun Phrase Island

COMPLEX NOUN PHRASE ISLAND dictates that no element can be moved from complex noun phrases. Complex noun phrases are of two types:

1. Noun + complementizer phrase (*that*-clause)
2. Noun + relative clause (*that/wh*-clause)

Complex Noun Phrase Island prevents any element from moving across the two types in (1) and (2). Consider the following examples.

3. The kids deny [DP the idea that their parents may die].
4. *Who do the kids deny [DP the idea that ___ may die]?   Answer: their parents.
5. He met [DP the person who had bought the car].
6. *What did he meet [DP the person who had bought ___]?   Answer: the car.

In (3), there is a complex noun phrase (Noun + CP), namely *the idea that their parents may die*. Thus, we cannot ask about the DP *their parents* within this complex NP as in (4). The same applies to the relative clause in (5): *the person who had bought the car*. We cannot move *the car* out of this complex NP as in (6). In the previous units, we did not cover how the relative clauses are structurally drawn but we will assign a preliminary structure to them for illustration in (8). Consider the trees for questions (4) and (6) in (7) and (8) respectively.

7. Tree for (4)

8. Tree for (6)

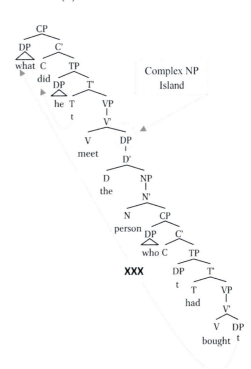

UNIT 149

Islands V

Wh-Island

WH-ISLAND is an island related to wh-questions, particularly embedded ones. Wh-island stipulates that no elements can be moved out of an embedded question. Embedded questions are CPs that follow verbs such as *ask, inquire, know, believe* etc.

1. Ahmed asks [CP why Saeed has taken the book].
2. *What does Ahmed ask [CP why Saeed has taken ___]?   Answer: the book.
3. He knows [CP what Ahmed has said].
4. *Who does he know [CP what ___ has said]?   Answer: Ahmed.

In (1) and (3), the verbs *asks* and *knows* are followed by an embedded question (CP). According to Wh-islands, it is not possible to move an element from an embedded question as in (2) and (4). In (2), the object *the book* is not allowed to move out of the embedded question *why Saeed has taken the book*, and the same applies to the subject *Ahmed* that occurs in the embedded question *what Ahmed has said* in (4). These movements are disallowed because the moved elements are within embedded questions, i.e. Wh-islands. Consider the tree structures given to (2) and (4) below.

5. Tree for (2)   6. Tree for (4)

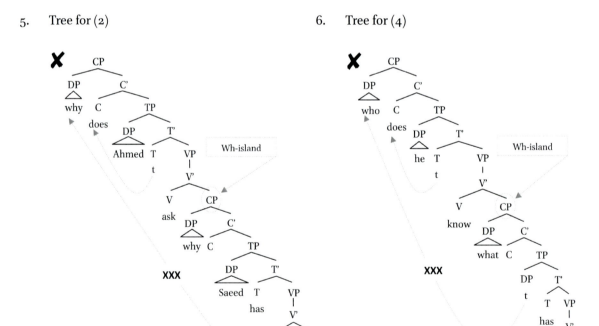

UNIT 150

Islands VI

Adverbial Clause Island

ADVERBIAL CLAUSE ISLAND is an island related to adjuncts and requires that no elements can be moved out of adverbial clauses. These adverbial clauses are CP-adjuncts that start with words such as *because, if* and *when*. Consider the following examples.

1. The kid cried [CP because his friend had broken the toy].
2. *What did the kid cry [CP because his friend had broken ___]?   Answer: the toy.
3. I will come [CP if he accepts my offer].
4. *What will I come [CP if he accepts ___]?   Answer: my offer.

In (1) and (3), the verbs *cried* and *come* are followed by an adverbial clause (CP). In (2), the DP *the toy* cannot be asked about and moved out of the adverbial clause *because his friend had broken the toy*. The same applies to the DP *my offer* that cannot be extracted out of the adverbial clause *if he accepts my offer*. Consider the tree structures given to (2) and (4).

5. Tree for (2)   6. Tree for (4)

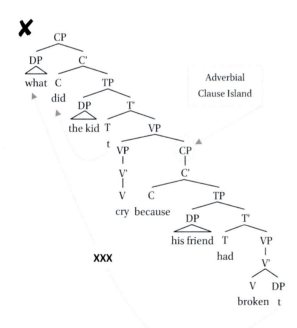
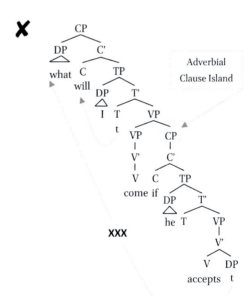

As shown above and in all the islands discussed earlier, it is clear that CP is an island that blocks the movement of any element out of it. This includes (i) complex NP islands (i.e. nouns followed by a *that*-clause [CP]) or a relative clause [CP]); (ii) wh-islands (i.e. verbs followed by embedded questions [CP]) and (iii) adverbial clauses (i.e. CPs headed by *because, if* or *when*).

UNIT 151

Summary

Summary

To recap, we covered the following six islands. An island is a domain out of which an element cannot be extracted or moved.

1. **Subject Island Constraint**
   *What will the name of __ change to Broadway? Answer: the street.

2. **Left Branch Island**
   *Whose are we reading [DP __ book]? Answer: Ahmed's.

   *How insightful are we reading [DP a __ book]? Answer: very insightful.

3. **Coordinate Structure Island**
   *What is he reading [ConjP [DP __] and [DP a novel]]? Answer: a poem.

   *What is he reading [ConjP [DP a poem] and [DP __]]? Answer: a novel.

4. **Complex Noun Phrase Island**
   *Who do the kids deny [DP the idea that __ may die]? Answer: parents.

   *What did he meet [DP the person who had bought __]? Answer: the car.

5. **Wh-island**
   *What does Ahmed ask [CP why Saeed has taken __]? Answer: the book.

   *Who does he know [CP what __ has said]? Answer: Ahmed.

6. **Adverbial Clause Island**
   *What did the kid cry [CP because his friend had broken __]? Answer: the toy.

   *What will I come [CP if he accepts __]? Answer: my offer.

   *What did I read the book [CP when __ rang] Answer: the phone

SECTION 9

Government and Binding Theory

∴

UNIT 152

Case Markers 1

Government and Binding Theory

GOVERNMENT AND BINDING THEORY is a theory developed by Noam Chomsky (1981) within transformational grammar. Government and Binding (GB) refer to two grammatical concepts: **GOVERNMENT**, which is an abstract syntactic principle for case assignment, and **BINDING**, which is a syntactic relationship between anaphoric elements (anaphors and pronouns) and the referring expressions. We will discuss each concept separately.

Case and Government

CASE is a grammatical category that indicates the syntactic role of each DP in a sentence. For example, case can tell us whether a DP functions as a subject or an object.

1. Did Ali meet Ahmed? Yes, he met him.
2. Did Ali meet Ahmed? Yes, *him met he.

In (1), the third person singular pronoun appears in different forms (*he* or *him*) based on its position in the sentence: (*he*) refers to the subject *Ali*, and (*him*) refers to the object *Ahmed*. Sentence (2) is ungrammatical because *him* cannot function as a subject, and *he* cannot appear in an object position. In English, pronouns are all case-marked, i.e. they appear in a special morphological form based on their syntactic roles in the sentence. The **NOMINATIVE** case is assigned to pronouns in a subject position (yielding *he, she, they, we* etc.), whereas the **ACCUSATIVE** case is assigned to pronouns in an object position (yielding *him, her, them, us* etc.). These cases are morphological, i.e. we can see that the same word inflects differently and has a special form, based on its syntactic position. Although the accusative case is assigned to the object of verbs in (1), it can also be assigned to the object of prepositions.

3. Is Ali angry at Ahmed? Yes, he is angry at him.
4. Is Ali angry at Ahmed? Yes, *he is angry at he.

In (3), the pronoun that follows the preposition *at* takes the accusative form *him*. After prepositions, the pronoun cannot take the nominative form *he* as in (4). In short, the nominative case is assigned to DP in a subject position, whereas the accusative one is assigned to DP in (i) an object position of verbs, or (ii) an object position of prepositions. In addition to the nominative and accusative, the third morphological case marking in English is the **GENITIVE**. The genitive case appears in possessive structures, referring to possessors.

5. Is this Ahmed's book? Yes, this is his book.
6. Is this Ahmed's book? Yes, *this is he/him book.

In possessive construction (5), the pronoun inflects for the genitive case taking a special form, namely *his*. It does not take the nominative form *he* or the accusative form *him* as in (6).

UNIT 153

Case Markers II

Case and Government

We claimed that case determines the syntactic roles of DPs in a sentence. In English, three cases exist: **nominative** (for subjects, e.g. *he*), **accusative** (for objects after verbs or prepositions, e.g. *him*) and **genitive** (for possessors, e.g. *his*). Because pronouns (= DPs) are morphologically case-marked, we say that they take **MORPHOLOGICAL CASE**. The table below shows how English pronouns inflect for case based on their syntactic roles.

Subject/nominative	Object/accusative	Possessor/genitive
I	*Me*	*My*
You	*You*	*Your*
They	*Them*	*Their*
We	*Us*	*Our*
He	*Him*	*His*
She	*Her*	*Her*
It	*It*	*Its*

Although some pronouns inflect differently based on their position/case (like *I, me, my*), some others do not change their forms. Consider *you* and *it*, which take the same forms for the nominative and accusative, or *her*, which remains uninflected for the accusative and genitive. Despite these similarities, it is still assumed that the nominative *you/it* are different from the accusative *you/it*, and the accusative *her* is totally different from the genitive *her*. We assume that they are differently case-marked but their markings are abstract or covert. That is, we do not see any morphology that displays case distinctions. In light of these facts, it is suggested that other English DPs (like proper nouns or common nouns) are also case-marked but their cases are covert. Covert case is called **ABSTRACT CASE**. In other words, all English DPs are case-marked with a null marker -∅ based on their positions in the sentences, but we cannot see this marking morphologically because it is neither pronounced nor written.

1. **Ali**-∅$_{NOM}$ met **Fatima**-∅$_{ACC}$.
2. The **boy**-∅$_{NOM}$ kicked the **ball**-∅$_{ACC}$.
3. The librarian put the **book**-∅$_{ACC}$ back on the **table**-∅$_{ACC}$.

In (1), the proper noun *Ali* is assumed to be morphologically marked with a null **nominative** marker -∅ as subject, whereas *Fatima* is marked with a null **accusative** marker as object. The same applies to common nouns such as *the man* and *the ball* in (2). In (3), **accusative** is assigned to both the object of the verb (*book*) and the object of the preposition (*table*). As for the **genitive** case, it is morphological on common and proper nouns. In (4), the proper noun *Ahmed* bears the apostrophe (-'s), which is supposed to be the genitive marker in English.

4. **Ahmed's** car arrived.

UNIT 154

Case Markers III

Case and Government

In summary, English has three cases: **nominative**, **accusative** and **genitive**. These markers can be (i) **morphological** as in pronouns or possessors (i.e. -'s), or (ii) **abstract** as in proper or common noun phrases. The table below illustrates these facts.

Case	Syntactic positions	Examples
NOMINATIVE	subject of the sentence	✓ *Ahmed*-$\varnothing_{NOM}$ came.
		✓ *He.*$_{NOM}$ came.
		✗ **Him.*$_{ACC}$/*His.*$_{GEN}$ came.
ACCUSATIVE	object of the verb	✓ *I met Ahmed*-$\varnothing_{ACC}$.
	object of the preposition	✓ *He is angry at Ahmed*-$\varnothing_{ACC}$.
		✓ *I met him.*$_{ACC}$.
		✓ *He is angry at him.*$_{ACC}$.
		✗ **I met he.*$_{NOM}$/*his.*$_{GEN}$
		✗ **He is angry at he.*$_{NOM}$/*his.*$_{GEN}$
GENITIVE	possessor	✓ *Ahmed's car.*
		✓ *My.*$_{GEN}$ *car.*
		✗ **I.*$_{NOM}$/*Me.*$_{ACC}$ *car.*

A Special Remark on the Nominative Case

An important point to bear in mind is that the nominative case (*he, she, it, we* etc.) is assigned only to subjects of finite/tensed clauses, not to subjects of non-finite/non-tensed ones.

1. I hope that *he played football*.   (finite clause)
2. I want *him to play football*.   (non-finite clause)
3. *I want *he to play football*.   (non-finite clause)

In (1) and (2), the subject in the embedded clauses is the pronoun *he/him*, and it functions as the agent of the action *playing*. In (1), however, the verb *played* is tensed, bearing the suffix *-ed*. Thus, the embedded clause *he played football* is described as **FINITE/TENSED**. In finite clauses, the pronoun in the subject position takes the nominative form (*he*). In contrast, the verb *play* in (2), following the infinitival *to*, appears in bare form. The embedded clause *him to play football* is known as **NON-FINITE/NON-TENSED**. In non-finite clauses, the pronoun does not take the nominative form (*he*, e.g. (3)) but the accusative form (*him*, e.g. (2)). In light of these facts, the nominative case is confined to subjects of finite clauses as in (4).

4. Case in English
   Nominative   *Subjects of Finite Clauses*
   Accusative   *Objects of Verbs/Preposition; Subjects of Non-Finite Clauses*
   Genitive   *Possessors*

UNIT 155

Case Assignment I

Case Filter

In syntactic theory, there is a condition that every DP (whether pronouns, proper or common noun phrases) must be case-marked, either morphologically or abstractly. This condition is known as **CASE FILTER**.

1. **Case Filter:** Every pronounced DP must be case-marked, either morphologically or abstractly.

The Case Filter condition is satisfied by two approaches: (i) case assignment or (ii) case checking. Case assignment is an old mechanism in the syntactic literature. It stipulates that a head X assigns (i.e. gives) a case to the closest DP in its structural domain. In other words, every DP receives (i.e. is assigned) case (nominative, accusative or genitive) from a head X. This head X can be T, V, P or D. Consider the following case assigners in English.

2. Case assigners in English
    i. **The head T** assigns the **nominative** case to the DP that occurs in its specifier, i.e. spec,TP. (*The subject of the sentence*, e.g. **He** came).
    ii. **The head V** assigns the **accusative** case to the DP occurring in its complement. (*The object of the verb*, e.g. She met **him**).
    iii. **The head P** assigns the **accusative** case to the DP that occurs in its complement, i.e. complement of the preposition. (*The object of the preposition*, e.g. She is angry at **him**).
    iv. **The head D** assigns the **genitive** case to the DP that occurs in its specifier, i.e. spec,DP (*the possessor DP*, e.g. **Ahmed's** book, or **his** book)

Structurally speaking, the case assigners assign their cases to the closest DP in their projection or configuration. Thus, every head gives a case to the closest DP as shown below.

3. NOM Assigner (T) 4. ACC Assigner (V) 5. ACC Assigner (P) 6. GEN Assigner (D)

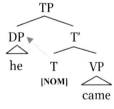 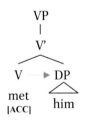 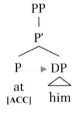 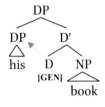

UNIT 156

Case Assignment II

Case Assignment

In case assignment, the head X assigns a case to the closest DP in its structural configuration. Case-assigning heads are T (assigning nominative to DP in its spec,TP), V (assigning accusative to its DP-complement), P (assigning accusative to its DP-complement) and D (assigning genitive to DP in its spec,DP). In short, the case assigners are heads that assign case to DP either in (i) their specifiers (as in T and D), or (ii) their complements (as in V and P). Case assignment is accomplished by **GOVERNMENT** (dominance + m-command). The heads must govern the DP. The principles of government are stated as follows.

1. **Principles of Government**
   X governs Y iff
   i. X *m-commands* Y, and
   ii. No barrier (WP) intervenes between X and Y

To understand government, we need to understand **M-COMMAND**. M-command is a syntactic relationship between two elements in the tree structure. It is defined as follows.

2. M-command relationship
       X *m-commands* Y iff
   i. X does not dominate Y, and Y does not dominate X
   ii. The maximal projection of X (i.e. XP) dominates Y

The following tree demonstrates the m-command relationship between X and Y.

3. Demonstration of the M-command Relationship

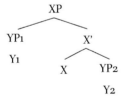

In light of the definition of m-command in (2), it is now clear that X in (3) m-commands Y (both Y1 and Y2). The condition (2i) stipulates that X should not dominate Y, and Y should not dominate X. This is true in (3); X does not dominate Y1 or Y2, and Y1 and Y2 do not dominate X either. Condition (2ii) requires that the maximal projection of X, i.e. XP, dominate Y. In (3), the XP dominates both Y1 and Y2. Therefore, we can conclude that X m-commands Y1 and Y2 in (3).

UNIT 157

Case Assignment III

Case Assignment

In the previous units, we showed that case-assigning heads must govern the case-assigned DP. We claimed that the heads T and D assign case to the DPs in their specifiers (spec,TP/spec,DP), and the heads V and P assign case to their DP-complements. Case assignment has been demonstrated to respect government (i.e. *m-command* relationship).

1. Principles of Government
   X governs Y iff
   i. X *m-commands* Y, and
   ii. No barrier (WP) intervenes between X and Y

2. M-command relationship
   X *m-commands* Y iff
   i. X does not dominate Y, and Y does not dominate X
   ii. The maximal projection of X (i.e. XP) dominates Y

We showed that the following structure in (3) demonstrates that the head X *m-commands* the specifier (Y1) and the complement (Y2).

3. Demonstration of M-command   4. Barrier between X and YP2

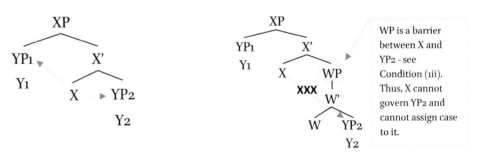

Since x *m-commands* Y1 and Y2 in (3), it governs both, and can assign case to the specifier YP1 and the complement YP2. The government relationship now explains why X (= T/D) assigns the nominative/genitive case respectively to DP in its specifiers (spec,TP/spec, DP), and why X (= V/P) assigns the accusative case to its DP-complements.

Until now, we have not discussed the second condition in the government principles in (1), namely "No barrier (WP) intervenes between X and Y". For case assignment to be accomplished, condition (1ii) requires that no barrier (WP) should intervene between X and Y. Otherwise, X does not govern Y and cannot assign case to it. In representation (4) above, WP functions as a barrier between X and Y2; thus, it is assumed in (4) that X cannot govern YP2 and cannot assign case to it.

Case Assignment IV

Case Assignment

To sum up, head X assigns case to Y iff X governs Y, i.e. if X m-commands Y, and there is no intervening barrier (WP) between X and Y. In light of these conditions, we can confirm the following conclusions about the structural configurations where case-assigning heads assign case to their DPs.

1. Case Assigner x   2. NOM (T)   3. ACC (V)   4. ACC (P)   5. GEN (D)

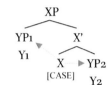

In short, we can formulate the following **CASE ASSIGNMENT RULE**.

6. **Case Assignment Rule:** Head X assigns case to DP iff the DP is in its specifier or in its complement position.

Thus, English case-assigning heads only assign case to their specifiers or their complements.

7. Case assigners in English
   i. **The head T** assigns the **nominative** case to the DP that occurs in its specifier, i.e. spec,TP. (*The subject of the sentence*, e.g. **He** came).
   ii. **The head D** assigns the **genitive** case to the DP that occurs in its specifier, i.e. spec,DP (*the possessor DP*, e.g. **Ahmed's** book, or **his** book)
   iii. **The head V** assigns the **accusative** case to the DP that occurs in its complement, i.e. the verb's complement (*The object of the verb*, she met **him**).
   iv. **The head P** assigns the **accusative** case to the DP that occurs in its complement, i.e. the complement of the preposition. (*The object of the preposition*, e.g. She is angry at **him**).

In brief, case can be assigned in two local configurations: (i) spec-head configuration as in (8), and (ii) head-complement configuration as in (9).

8. **Spec-Head Configuration**   9. **Head-Complement Configuration**

UNIT 159

Case Checking 1

Case Checking

CASE CHECKING is a new approach to meet the Case Filter condition. In case assignment, the head X assigns/provides/gives case to the DP in its specifier or complement. In other words, the DP has no case in and of itself, but receives it from the head X. Case checking has a different view. It stipulates that both the DP and the head X have similar case features. These features are checked against each other if they appear in the same configurations (head-specifier configuration for T and D, or head-complement configuration for V and P). These are the same configurations for case assignment discussed in the previous unit. Under this view, Case Filter requires a different definition as set out in (1).

1. **Case Filter:** Every pronounced DP must have a case that is checked by another case feature in an appropriate configuration.

It is assumed that DP enters the syntactic computation bearing a case feature (nominative, accusative or genitive). For case checking to be accomplished, the same case feature (nominative, accusative and genitive) must be available on the head X. If these features match up with each other—i.e. nominative on DP matches nominative on T, accusative on the DP matches accusative feature on V/P, or genitive on the DP matches genitive on D—case checking takes place. Put differently, case checking is a matching operation.

2. Case-checker X   3. NOM (T)   4. ACC (V)   5. ACC (P)   6. GEN (D)

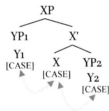 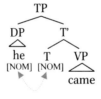 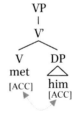 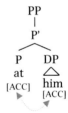 

As shown in (2), case checking is still subject to a government relationship. However, it fails iff case features do not match up. For instance, if a DP enters the syntax with an accusative feature and occupies a possessor position (spec,DP), this accusative feature will not match the genitive feature associated with the head D. This mismatch impedes case checking, and the phrase becomes ungrammatical as in (7) represented in (8).

7. *Him book   8. Tree for (7)

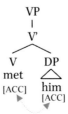

UNIT 160

Case Checking II

Case Checking

To summarize our discussion of Case, English pronouns (= DPs) show different forms for case based on their syntactic positions: **nominative** (for subjects of finite clauses), **accusative** (for object of verbs/prepositions) and **genitive** (for possessors). These differences in form show **morphological case**. Proper or common nouns (= DP) also receive case, but theirs is an **abstract case** because it is not morphologically realized.

We assume that there is an abstract case because case theory stipulates that every DP must be case-marked, i.e. meet the **Case Filter** condition. This requirement can be accomplished via (i) **case assignment** or (ii) **case checking**. Both approaches respect government, i.e. a head X governs the DP on which the morphological/abstract case appears. Government requires a local configuration: (i) *spec-head configuration* and (ii) *head-complement configuration*. In case assignment, a head X directly assigns case to a DP that has no case feature. In case checking, both the DP and the head X must bear matching case features. Consider (1).

1. Ahmed's driver has parked the car under the tree.

In (1), all the blue DPs must be abstractly case-marked. The DP *Ahmed* is case-marked in the genitive case because it is in a possessor position, whereas the NP *driver* takes the nominative case because it is the subject of the whole sentence. Both the DPs *the car* and *the tree* are marked in the accusative case because they are the objects of the verb *parked* and the preposition *under* respectively. The syntactic tree structure for (1) is given in (2), where all the DPs are case-checked by the appropriate case-checking heads. An important observation about (2) is that, after the DP *Ahmed* checks its genitive case against the genitive case associated with the head D, the nominative feature on the whole DP (which will be marked on the NP *driver*) in spec,TP is checked against the nominative feature of the head T.

2. Tree for (1)

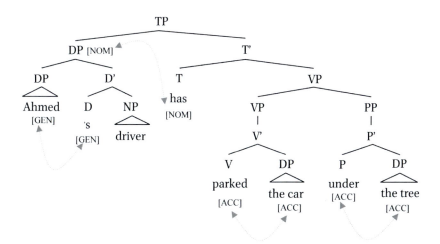

UNIT 161

Exceptional Case Marking 1

Exceptional Case Marking

EXCEPTIONAL CASE MARKING is a phenomenon where the subject of a non-finite clause is marked in the accusative case rather than the nominative one. Consider (1) and (2).

1. She believes that he wins.
2. She needs for him to win.

In the above examples, the verbs *believes* and *needs* are followed by CP: *that*-clause as in (1) or *for*-clause as in (2). In (1), the CP is finite because the verb *wins* is tensed. In (2), the CP is non-finite because the verb *win* follows the infinitive word *to* and appears in bare form. Consider the tree structures given to the blue CPs in (1) and (2).

3. Tree for CP in (1)   4. Tree for CP in (2)

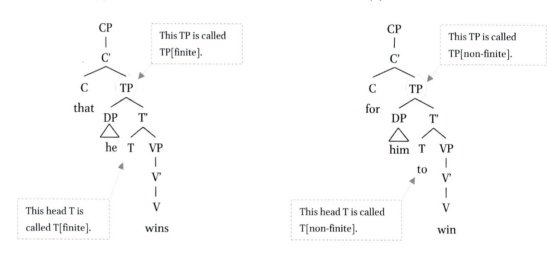

In (3), the CP *that he wins* has a TP[finite] with a head T[finite] because the verb *wins* is tensed. The present marker -s was originally on T but it has been lowered to V (see Unit 104). In contrast, the CP *for him to win* in (4) has a TP[non-finite] with a head T[non-finite] because the verb *win* appears in bare form, and the infinitive *to* occupies the head T[non-finite]. Note that the pronominal subject inside both CPs is the same. Although the pronoun in (3) and (4) occupies the same position, i.e. spec,TP, it takes the nominative form (*he*) in (3), but the accusative form (*him*) in (4). Given that the pronoun *he* occupies spec,TP in (3), it comes as no surprise that it takes the nominative form; but, why does the same pronoun take the accusative form *him* in (4) in the same spec,TP (where the nominative case is checked)? The answer lies in the fact that the nominative case is disallowed in non-finite CPs, e.g. (5).

5. *She needs for he to win.

UNIT 162

Exceptional Case Marking II

Exceptional Case Marking

Consider the exceptional case marking constructions in (1) through (3).

1. She believes [CP that [TP[finite] **he** wins]. [Finite Clause]
2. She needs [CP for [TP[non-finite] **him** to win]. [Non-Finite Clause]
3. *She needs [CP for [TP[non-finite] **he** to win]. [Non-Finite Clause]

As discussed earlier, the subject in spec,TP[finite] takes the nominative form *he* as in (1). Yet, the subject in spec,TP[non-finite] takes the accusative form *him* in (2) rather than the nominative one *he* as in (3). Consider the structures (4) and (5) for (1) and (2) respectively.

4. Tree for (1) 5. Tree for (2)

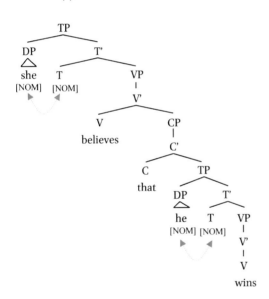 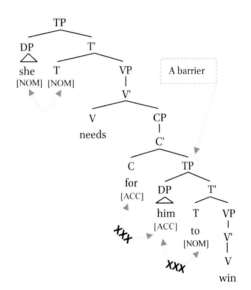

The structure in (4) is straightforward because both subjects in both spec,TPs (*she/he*) take the nominative form. Their nominative is checked against the nominative case associated with the head T[finite]. An interesting question arises from structure (5): which head checks the accusative case of the pronoun *him* that occurs in spec,TP[non-finite]? If it is assumed that T[non-finite] in (5) checks the nominative, it is reasonable to expect the DP to take the nominative form (i.e. *he*); however, the nominative case is disallowed in (3). We may then conclude that the head T[non-finite] is not a nominative case-checker in English, assuming instead that the head C (*for*) in (5) is in charge of checking the accusative of the DP *him*. However, this assumption violates the principles of government. It should be remembered that the DP *him* is not a direct complement of the head C. The circled TP is a barrier that prevents the head C from checking the accusative case of the DP *him*.

UNIT 163

Exceptional Case Marking III

Exceptional Case Marking

To solve the problems related to exceptional case marking constructions, it is important to revise our view of government. Recall that we argued that head X checks its case against the case of DP only if X governs DP. The government principles are illustrated in (1) below.

1. Principles of Government
   X governs Y iff
   i. X *m-commands* Y, and
   ii. No barrier (WP) intervenes between X and Y

Condition (1i) states that X can check its case against that of the DP iff the DP appears in its specifier or complement position as in (YP1) and (YP2) respectively in (2). Condition (1ii) requires that there be no barrier between the head and its complement as in (3).

2. Demonstration of the M-command   3. Barrier between X and YP2

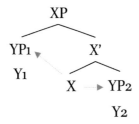
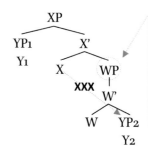

WP is a barrier between X and YP2 (see 1ii). Thus, X cannot govern YP2 and assign case to it.

Because there is a barrier in non-finite CP in (4), the head C *for* cannot check its accusative case against the accusative case feature of the DP *him*. To solve this problem, syntacticians propose that TP be a weak barrier because it is non-finite. Thus, Condition (1ii) above needs to be revised as follows: No barrier (WP) except TP[non-finite] intervenes between X and Y.

4.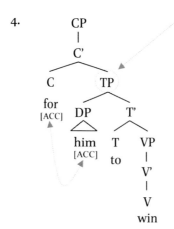

Based on (1), this TP can be a barrier that prevents head C (*for*) from checking the accusative case of the DP (*him*). However, this TP is non-finite. It is now an exception, and should not be considered a barrier any longer. Due to this exception in the principles of government, we call structures such as (*for him to win*) an EXCEPTIONAL CASE MARKING construction. Due to these new modifications, case checking in (4) can now proceed, and the accusative case of the head C (*for*) can be checked against the accusative case of the DP (*him*).

UNIT 164

Exceptional Case Marking IV

Exceptional Case Marking

According to the modifications made for **EXCEPTIONAL CASE MARKING** constructions, the government principles are revised as follows.

1. Principles of Government
   X governs Y iff
   iii. X *m-commands* Y, and
   iv. No barrier (WP) except TP[non-finite] intervenes between X and Y

Although TP[non-finite] is no longer a barrier, TP[finite] and all other XP are still barriers.

2. She believes that he wins.   3. She needs for him to win.

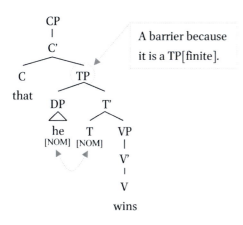
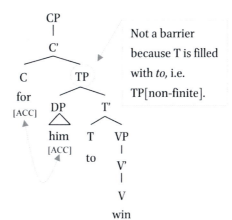

In (2), the head T checks its nominative case against that of the DP in spec,TP. Given that the TP[finite] is a barrier in (2), the head C *that* cannot check any case on the DP in spec,TP[finite]. In fact, the head C *that*, like the head T[non-finite] in (3), is not a case-checker in English. It is also obvious that the head C *that* is different from the head C *for*, which looks like the preposition *for*. Thus, like other prepositions, the head C *for* checks the accusative case. In light of these observations, we can conclude that case-checkers in English are the heads listed in (4). Heads in (4e) do not check any case in English.

4. Case-checkers in English
   a. The head T[finite] checks the nominative case of the DP in spec,TP.
   b. The head D checks the genitive case of the DP in the spec,DP.
   c. The heads V and P check the accusative case of the DP in their complements.
   d. The head C[for] checks the accusative case of the DP in spec,TP[non-fnite]
   e. The heads C[that/whether/∅], T[non-finite], N & A do not check cases in English.

UNIT 165

Exceptional Case Marking v

Exceptional Case Marking

Besides the exceptional case marking (ECM) construction in (1), let us introduce another instance of ECM in (2).

1. She needs for him to win. (ECM)
2. She expects him to win. (ECM)

There are two possible ways to derive example (2). Let us consider the two possible derivations for (2), as shown in (3) and (4), and determine which derivation is superior.

3. Derivation (I) for (2)   4. Derivation (II) for (2)

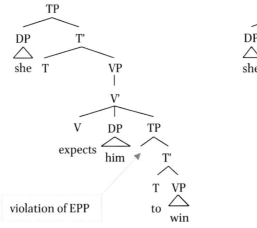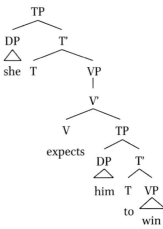

The difference between the two derivations—(I) and (II) in (3) and (4) respectively—follows from the treatment of the DP *him*. In derivation (I), the DP *him* is treated as an object of the verb *expects*, followed by TP[non-finite] *to win*. In contrast, derivation (II) treats the DP *him* as a subject in spec,TP[non-finite]. Thus, according to each derivation, the verb *expects* takes two different subcategorization frames.

5. *expects*, V [__ DP TP$_{[non-finite]}$] for derivation (I)
              θ   θ   θ

6. *expects*, V [__ TP$_{[non-finite]}$]   for derivation (II)
              θ   θ

The problem with derivation (I) in (3) is that spec,TP[non-finite] is empty, and this is a violation of the EPP. In contrast, derivation (II) in (4) respects EPP because the DP *him* functions as a subject and occupies spec,TP[non-finite]. In evaluation of the two proposals, derivation (II) seems superior to derivation (I) as far as the EPP is concerned. In the next unit, we will present more challenges to derivation (I) in favor of derivation (II).

UNIT 166

Exceptional Case Marking VI

Exceptional Case Marking

Theta Role Assignment also shows that derivation (II) is superior to derivation (I). Consider the subcategorization frames of the verbs *expects* and *win* for each derivation below.

1. She expects him to win. (ECM)

2. Derivation (I) for (1)   3. Derivation (II) for (1)

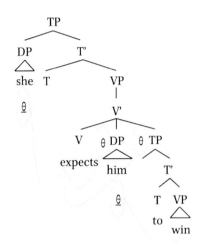 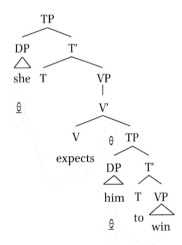

4. *expects*, V [__ DP TP$_{[\text{non-finite}]}$]   5. *expects*, V [__ TP$_{[\text{non-finite}]}$]
                    θ θ θ   θ θ

6. *win*, V [__]   7. *win*, V [__]
            θ   θ

The θ-role distribution in (2) violates the Principles of Theta Role Assignment in (8).

8. Principles of Theta Role Assignment
   i. Assign one θ-role to every complement (i.e. internal arguments)
   ii. Assign one θ-role to the subject (i.e. the external argument), unless it is an expletive.

In (2), the DP *him* is assigned two θ-roles: an internal θ-role from the verb *expects*, and an external θ-role from the verb *win*. This is a violation of the principles in (8) which require that every argument must receive one θ-role. As for derivation (II) in (3), each argument receives one θ-role, and the DP *him* receives an external θ-role from the verb *win*. As a third advantage, the verb *win* is very close to its agent *him* in (3) (both are inside one TP) and can assign its theta role to it. However, the verb *win* in (3) is far removed from the DP *him*.

UNIT 167

Exceptional Case Marking VII

Exceptional Case Marking

Due to violations of the EPP and the Principles of Theta Role Assignment, we concluded that derivation (11) is superior to derivation (1). Thus, the proper structure for (1) is given in (3).

1. She expects him to win. (ECM)

2. *expects*, V [___ TP[non-finite]]
       θ   θ

3. Tree for (1).

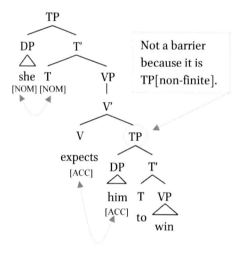

Recall that the TP[non-finite] in (3) should not function as a barrier. This is according to the Principles of Government in (4), particularly condition (4ii).

4. Principles of Government
   X governs Y iff
   i. X *m-commands* Y, and
   ii. No barrier (WP) except TP[non-finite] intervenes between X and Y

Given that TP[non-finite] in (3) is not a barrier, the verb *expects* can check its accusative case against that of the DP *him*. Therefore, the structure is called ECM.

In conclusion, there are two types of ECM in English: (i) the first is when the complementizer *for* checks the accusative case of the DP *him* as in (5) and (ii) the second is when the verb (like *expects*) checks the accusative case of the DP *him* as in (6).

5. She needs [CP **for** [TP[non-finite] him to win]]. (ECM)
6. She **expects** [TP[non-finite] him to win]. (ECM)

UNIT 168

Unaccusative I

Unaccusative Advancement

UNACCUSATIVE ADVANCEMENT occurs in passive constructions where the object of the verb is not marked in the accusative case, so it moves to spec,TP for the nominative case.

1.   The ball was kicked by *the player*.   (passive)

In Units 132 through 134, we discussed the passive structure, and reached the conclusion that a passive form is not syntactically derived from its active form. The passive verb *kicked* in (1) has the following subcategorization frame.

2.   *kicked*[passive], V [___ DP (PP[by])]   (for passive)

To derive (1), it is assumed that the passive verb *kicked* selects the object *the ball* as the first complement and the optional PP *by the player* as a second complement. The derivation of the passive structure in (1) is represented in (3) and (4) below.

3.   DS for (1)   4.   SS for (1)

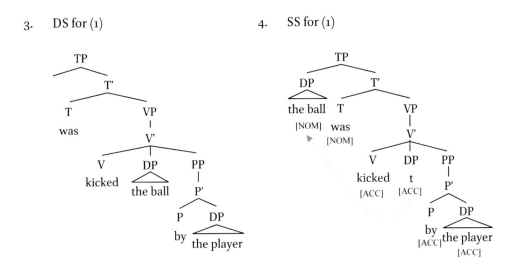

To satisfy the EPP, it has been suggested that the DP *the ball* in the passive structure in (3) moves to spec,TP as in (4). However, there is a problem with this proposal. In (4), the DP *the ball* appears in two case-checking configurations: (i) in the complement position of the verb *kicked*, which checks the accusative case, and (ii) in spec,TP whose head T checks the nominative case. We know that the DP *the ball* must be marked in the nominative case because it eventually becomes the subject as in (1). However, how can we prevent the DP *the ball* from being checked by the accusative case from the verb *kicked*? The DP *the ball* is the complement of the verb *kicked* before it moves to spec,TP. Thus, it may have two cases: the accusative case (before the movement) and the nominative case (after the movement). This is a problem for case theory as one argument might end up with two case features.

UNIT 169

Unaccusative 11

Unaccusative Advancement

As discussed earlier, unaccusative advancement in passive structures raises a problem for Case Theory. The case of the DP in the complement position of the verb can be checked against the accusative case. Then, after the DP moves to spec,TP, it can be re-checked against the nominative case. The DP will end up with two unneeded cases. The assumption that the accusative case is checked on the DP in the complement position, and is then overwritten by the nominative case in spec,TP does not solve the problem. The Italian Linguist Luigi Burzio offers a solution. He provided evidence that verbs do not check the accusative case if they do not assign an external θ-role. This is known as **BURIZIO'S GENERALIZATION** (Burzio, 1986).

1. **Burizio's Generalization:** A verb can check the accusative case iff it assigns an external theta role. If the verb does not assign an external theta role, its ability to check the accusative case is eliminated.

That means that all verb heads that check the accusative case are expected to assign an external θ-role. An external θ-role is the semantic role assigned by the verb to the subject.

2. *The player* **kicked** the ball.   (active)
3. The ball **was kicked** by *the player*.   (passive)

In (2), the active verb *kicked* assigns an external θ-role to the subject of the sentence *the player*, which is the agent, i.e. the initiator of the action *kicking*. It also assigns an internal θ-role to the object *the ball*, which is the theme, i.e. the one that undergoes the action *kicking*. This is demonstrated in the subcategorization frame of the verb *kicked* in (4). Since the active verb *kicked* assigns an external θ-role, this verb checks the accusative case against any DP in its complement position, e.g. *the ball* as in (2).

4. *kicked*, V [__ DP]   (for active)
              θ   θ

In (3), however, the passive verb *kicked* does not have an agent in its subject position. Although the DP *the ball* appears in a subject position, it is not the initiator of the action *kicking*. As in subcategorization frame (5), the passive verb *kicked* selects two complements, thus assigning two internal θ-roles to them. There is no external θ-role assigned by the passive verb *kicked*. As a result, we can conclude that the passive verb *kicked* in (2) does not check the accusative case at all.

5. *kicked*[passive], V [__ DP (PP[by])]   (for passive)
                    θ   θ

UNIT 170

Unaccusative III

Unaccusative Advancement

For the sake of simplicity, let us state the following: if the subcategorization frames of any verb assigns an external θ-role, it means that there must be DP in its spec,TP at the d-structure. However, if the verb does not assign an external θ-role, spec,TP may appear empty at the d-structure as in passive structures or in raising constructions (see Unit 177).

1. *kicked*, V [___ DP]   (for active)
            θ   θ

2. *kicked*[passive], V [___ DP (PP[by])]   (for passive)
                    θ   θ

In light of these facts, Burzio's generalization states that the active verb *kicked* in (1) can check the accusative case of its DP-complement because it assigns an external θ-role. In contrast, the verb *kicked*[passive] in (2) cannot check the accusative case because there is no external θ-role in its subcategorization frame. There are only two internal θ-roles assigned to its two complements. Consider the syntactic tree structures for (3) and (4).

3.   The player kicked the ball   4.   The ball is kicked by the player

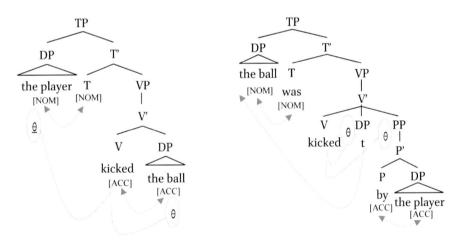

The earlier problem—that the DP *the ball* in passive constructions might have two cases (the accusative and nominative) before and after its movement—is now resolved. In (3), the active verb *kicked* assigns an external θ-role to the subject *the player*; thus, it checks the accusative of the object *the ball*. However, the passive verb *kicked* in (4) does not assign an external θ-role. Therefore, it has no [ACC] feature, and cannot check any accusative on the DP *the ball*. The nominative case of the DP *the ball* is checked only after the DP moves to spec,TP.

UNIT 171

Binding Theory I

Binding Theory

BINDING THEORY is a theory that regulates the syntactic relations between noun phrases, pronouns and anaphors in a sentence. There are three principles in binding theory.

1. Principle A: Anaphors must be bound in their binding domain.
2. Principle B: Pronouns must be free in their binding domain.
3. Principle C: Referring expressions must be free.

We will discuss these principles in the above order in the following units.

Anaphors

An **ANAPHOR** is an expression that receives its interpretation from another preceding word in the sentence. Consider the following examples:

4. Ahmed$_i$ respects himself$_i$.   Meaning: *himself = Ahmed*.
5. Fatima$_j$ respect herself$_j$.   Meaning: *herself = Fatima*

In (4) and (5), the words *himself* and *herself* are called anaphors. Other anaphors are *myself, yourself, ourselves, themselves* and *itself*. Anaphors receive their meaning from preceding words in the sentence. In (4), the anaphor *himself* refers to *Ahmed*, whereas *herself* in (5) refers to *Fatima*. These preceding expressions that provide meaning to the anaphors are called **ANTECEDENTS**. As shown in (4), the anaphor *himself$_i$* is **CO-INDEXED** with the antecedent *Ahmed$_i$* with the subscript (i), while the anaphor *herself$_j$* in (5) is co-indexed with the antecedent *Fatima$_j$* with the subscript (j). **CO-INDEXATION** is a reference operation where two words are linked together by an index such as (i) or (j). Consider the following ungrammatical sentences.

6. *Himself$_i$ respects Ahmed$_i$
7. *Herself$_j$ respect Fatima$_j$.

In (6) and (7), the anaphors *himself* and *herself* precede the antecedents *Ahmed* and *Fatima* respectively. Although they are properly co-indexed with subscripts, these sentences are ungrammatical. The ungrammaticality of (6) and (7) follows from the violation of the requirement that anaphors must always follow antecedents as shown in (4) and (5). These facts explain the first part of Principle A in binding theory in (8): An anaphor must be bound. In simple terms, 'bound' in (8) means 'preceded by an antecedent'. In the next units, we will address the concept *binding* and *binding domain* using more technical terms.

8. Principle A
   An anaphor must be bound in its binding domain.

UNIT 172

Binding Theory II

Anaphors

We showed that anaphors must follow the antecedents from which they receive their meanings as in (1). If anaphors precede antecedents, the sentence becomes ungrammatical as in (2). This condition of word order refers to the first part of Principle A in (3).

1. Ahmed$_i$ respects himself$_i$.
2. *Himself$_i$ respects Ahmed$_i$

3. Principle A
   An anaphor must be bound in its binding domain.

Technically speaking, the word *bound* in (3) means *c-commanded*. Binding is accomplished by a c-command relationship between elements in the tree structure. If A is bound by B, A is c-commanded by B. C-command is defined as follows.

4. C-command relationship
   A c-commands B iff:
   i. A does not dominate B, and B does not dominate A
   ii. The first node that dominates A dominates B

Consider the tree structures below, where the anaphor *himself* is bound/c-commanded by the antecedent *Ahmed* in (5), but is not bound/c-commanded by *Ahmed* in (6).

5. Tree for (1) 6. Tree for (2)

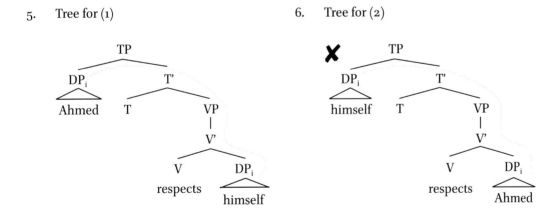

In (5) and (6), both the anaphor *himself* and the antecedent *Ahmed* are DPs co-indexed with the subscript (i), i.e DP$_i$. However, in (5), the DP$_i$ *Ahmed* c-commands and binds the DP$_i$ *himself*. In other words, the anaphor is bound/c-commanded by the antecedent; this relationship respects the first part of principle A in (3). However, in (6), the anaphor *himself* is above the antecedent *Ahmed* in the tree. Thus, the anaphor cannot be bound/c-commanded by the antecedent at all, and this relationship violates the first part of Principle (3) making the sentence (2) ungrammatical. In conclusion, antecedents must be structurally above anaphors.

UNIT 173

Binding Theory III

Anaphors

Consider the following examples.

1. $Ahmed_i$ thinks that Ali_j respects $himself_j$.   Meaning: *himself* = *Ali*
2. *$Ahmed_i$ thinks that Ali_j respects $himself_i$.   Meaning: *himself* = *Ahmed*

Sentence (1) is grammatical because the anaphor $himself_j$ is bound by the antecedent Ali_j, and both are co-indexed with the subscript (j). However, sentence (2) is ungrammatical because the anaphor $himself_i$ is bound by the antecedent $Ahmed_i$, not Ali_j. Although *Ahmed* and *himself* in (2) are both co-indexed by the subscript (i), and *himself* is bound and c-commanded by *Ahmed*, sentence (2) is still ungrammatical. The ungrammaticality of (2) results from a violation of the second part of Principle A in (5). The binding/c-commanding/co-indexation must be held within one binding domain. In English, TP is a binding domain. Thus, anaphors and antecedents must appear in one TP for binding to occur. In (1) and (2), there are two TPs: the first TP is *Ahmed thinks*, and the second TP is *Ali respects himself*. When *himself* refers to *Ali* as in (3), both the anaphor and the antecedent appear in the same (second) TP. However, in (4), the anaphor *himself* is in the second TP, whereas the antecedent *Ahmed* is in the first TP; in other words, they are not in the same binding domain (TP). This condition renders sentence (2) ungrammatical.

3. Tree for (1)   4. Tree for (2)

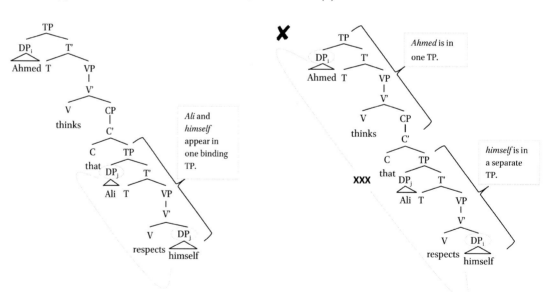

5. Principle A
   An anaphor must be bound in its binding domain (i.e. TP).

UNIT 174

Binding Theory IV

Pronouns

The distribution of pronouns differs from that of anaphors.

1. Ahmed$_i$ respects him$_j$.   Meaning: *him = Ali, Saeed etc., but not Ahmed.*
2. *Ahmed$_i$ respects him$_i$.   Meaning: *him = Ahmed.*

In (1), the antecedent *Ahmed$_i$* and the pronoun *him$_j$* are not co-indexed with the same subscript. That is, the pronoun *him$_j$* does not mean *Ahmed$_i$*; it may mean *Ali, Saeed* or other persons. However, in (2), the antecedent *Ahmed$_i$* and the pronoun *him$_i$* are co-indexed; therefore, the sentence becomes ungrammatical. It is obvious that the pronoun *him* should not take its interpretation from the antecedent *Ahmed*. It must not be bound; it must be free. In short, pronouns must be free in their binding domain (TP) as stated in Principle B in (3).

3. Principle B
   Pronouns must be free* in their binding domain (TP).
   (*Free means *not bound*.)

Now consider the following examples.

4. Ahmed$_i$ thinks that Ali$_j$ respects him$_i$.   Meaning: *him = Ahmed*
5. *Ahmed$_i$ thinks that Ali$_j$ respects him$_j$.   Meaning: *him = Ali.*
6. Ahmed$_i$ thinks that Ali$_j$ respects him$_k$ Meaning: *him = John, Saeed, etc.*

In (4) through (6), there are two TPs: the first TP is *Ahmed thinks*, and the second TP is *Ali respects him*. In (4), the co-indexation is possible between the antecedent *Ahmed$_i$* and the pronoun *him$_i$* because each appears in a different TP: *Ahmed$_i$* is in the first TP, while *him$_i$* is in the second TP. For this reason, the pronoun *him$_i$* can be bound and co-indexed with the antecedent *Ahmed$_i$*. However, because the antecedent *Ali$_j$* and the pronoun *him$_j$* appear in the same (second) TP in (5), binding is disallowed, and the sentence is ungrammatical. In (5), the pronoun *him$_j$* should not refer to *Ali$_j$* at all. In conclusion, pronouns can be bound by other antecedents if both appear in different TPs as in (4), but they must not be bound in the same TP as in (5); instead, they must be free in their binding domain as in (3). This is the opposite behavior of anaphors, which need to appear with their antecedents in the same TP.

In contrast to anaphors, the interpretation of pronouns is not necessarily captured via binding. Put differently, pronouns do not need antecedents to be interpreted. As shown in (6), the pronoun *him$_k$* does not need to receive its meaning from the antecedent *Ahmed$_i$* or *Ali$_j$*. In (6), the pronoun *him$_k$* refers to other persons in the world such as *John* and *Saeed*. This indicates that pronouns, unlike anaphors, may or may not be bound by an antecedent in a different TP. In contrast, anaphors must always be bound, and must receive their interpretation from an antecedent in the same TP.

UNIT 175

Binding Theory v

Pronouns

We have concluded that the distribution of pronouns differs from that of anaphors as shown below.

1. Ahmed$_i$ respects him$_j$.   Meaning: *him = Ali, Saeed, John etc.*
2. *Ahmed$_i$ respects him$_i$.   Meaning: *him = Ahmed.*
3. *Ahmed$_i$ thinks that Ali$_j$ respects him$_j$. Meaning: *him = Ali.*
4. Ahmed$_i$ thinks that Ali$_j$ respects him$_i$/$_k$. Meaning: *him = Ahmed or John/Saeed.*

Unlike anaphors that must be bound/co-indexed by an antecedent in their binding domain (TP), pronouns must be free in their binding TP as in (1), (2) and (3). Outside the binding domain, pronouns may, or may not, be bound/co-indexed as in (4).

5. Tree for (4)   6. Tree for (3)

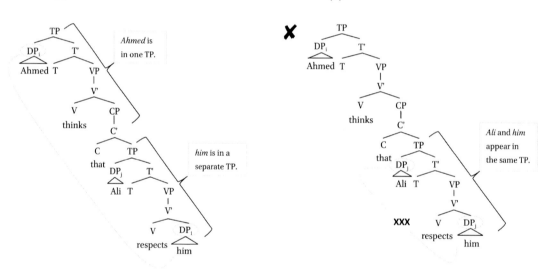

In (5), since the antecedent *Ahmed$_i$* and the pronoun *him$_i$* appear in two different binding domains (TPs), the pronoun *him$_i$* can be bound/co-indexed by the antecedent *Ahmed$_i$*. However, in (6), because the antecedent *Ali$_j$* and the pronoun *him$_j$* appear in the same binding domain (TP), the sentence is ungrammatical. In conclusion, the distribution of pronouns must respect Principle B in (7).

7. Principle B
   Pronouns must be free in their binding domain (TP).

UNIT 176

Binding Theory VI

R-Expressions

We have covered the distribution of anaphors (Principle A in Binding Theory) and pronouns (Principle B in Binding Theory). The third principle in binding theory relates to **REFERRING EXPRESSIONS**, abbreviated as **R-EXPRESSIONS**. Referring expressions are words (i.e. proper or common nouns) that refer to persons or entities in the world. Unlike anaphors that **must** receive their interpretation from an antecedent, and pronouns that **may** receive their meaning from an antecedent, R-expressions do not receive their interpretations from any antecedent.

1. Ahmed$_i$ respects Ali$_j$.
2. *Ahmed$_i$ respects Ali$_i$.   Meaning: *Ali = Ahmed*
3. Ahmed$_i$ thinks that Ali$_j$ respects Saeed$_k$.
4. *Ahmed$_i$ thinks that Ali$_j$ respects Saeed$_i$.   Meaning: *Ahmed = Saeed*

In (1) through (4), all these proper nouns are R-expressions. Their meanings are not elicited from other words in the sentence. In (1), the R-expression *Ali* does not mean *Ahmed*, thus they are not co-indexed with the same subscript. If the latter does happen, the sentence becomes ungrammatical as in (2). Whether R-expressions are in the same binding domain (TP) as in (1), or in two separate domains (TPs) as in (3) and (4), they must not be co-indexed with antecedents. Sentence (4) is ungrammatical if *Saeed* is taken to refer to *Ahmed*. Thus, Principle C states that R-expressions must be free regardless of their domains.

5. Principle C
   R-expressions must be free.

The same applies to common noun phrases such as *the man, the ball* etc. because they are among the R-expressions.

Summary

In English, words can receive their interpretation in two ways: (i) from words within the same sentence, or (ii) from the outside world.
 Anaphors must take their interpretation from their antecedents, and they both must appear in the same binding domain. Pronouns do not necessarily take their interpretation from their antecedents but, if they do, their antecedents must be in a different binding domain. R-expressions always take their meaning from the outside world. The three principles in binding theory are summarized below.

6. **Principle A:** An anaphor must be bound in its binding domain (TP).
7. **Principle B:** Pronouns must be free in their binding domain (TP).
8. **Principle C:** R-expressions must be free.

SECTION 10

Advanced Topics

∴

UNIT 177

Raising I

Raising

Consider the following examples.

1. It seems that **Ahmed** enjoys volleyball.   (Expletive Insertion)
2. It is likely that **Ahmed** enjoys volleyball.   (Expletive Insertion)

3. **Ahmed** seems to enjoy volleyball.   (Raising Construction)
4. **Ahmed** is likely to enjoy volleyball.   (Raising Construction)

In Units 126 through 131, we discussed constructions like (1) and (2). However, we did not come across constructions like (3) and (4). Note that (1) is semantically similar to (3), and (2) is similar in meaning to (4). Let us recap what we said about (1) and (2), and move from there to an analysis of (3) and (4). It has been proposed that both the verb *seems* and the adjective *likely* in (1) and (2) select CP [*that Ahmed enjoys volleyball*], and assign an internal θ-role to it. However, they do not assign an external θ-role as shown in their subcategorization frames in (5) and (6).

5. *seems*, V [___ CP]
               θ

6. *likely*, A [___ CP]
               θ

Because the verb *seems* and the adjective *likely* do not assign an external θ-role, their d-structures do not have thematic subjects. To satisfy the EPP, the expletive *it* is inserted in spec,TP in tree structures (7) and (8).

7. DS for (1)   8. DS for (2)

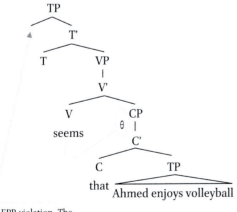
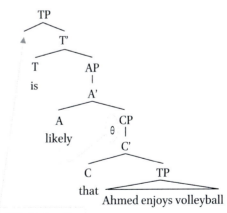

EPP violation. The expletive DP *it* is inserted here.

EPP violation. The expletive DP *it* is inserted here.

UNIT 178

Raising 11

Raising

We discussed constructions in (1) and (2), and claimed that they do not have thematic subjects; rather, the expletive *it* is inserted in their spec,TP for the EPP.

1. It seems that Ahmed enjoys volleyball.   (Expletive Insertion)
2. It is likely that Ahmed enjoys volleyball.   (Expletive Insertion)

3. Ahmed seems to enjoy volleyball.
4. Ahmed is likely to enjoy volleyball.

Let us now consider (3) and (4). Although the verb *seems* and the adjective *likely* select CP [*that Ahmed enjoys volleyball*] in (1) and (2), they select TP[non-finite] [*to enjoy volleyball*] in (3) and (4). Thus, we assume that the subcategorization frames of the verb *seems* and the adjective *likely* in (3) and (4) are different from (1) and (2) in that they select TP[non-finite].

5. *seems*, V [___ TP$_{[non-finite]}$]
       θ

6. *likely*, A [___ TP$_{[non-finite]}$]
       θ

It is obvious from (5) and (6) that the verb *seems* and the adjective *likely* do not assign external θ-roles as is the case in (5) and (6) in the previous unit. Proceeding from these assumptions, we will encounter problems. Consider the tree structures for (3) and (4) below.

7. DS for (3)   8. DS for (4)

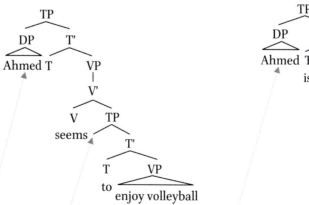
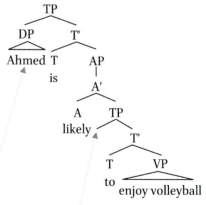

In (7) and (8), two problems appear. First, the lower spec,TP[non-finite] is not filled. This is a violation of the EPP. Expletive insertion cannot fix this problem. If an expletive *it* is added, it will yield an ungrammatical sentence such as *Ahmed seems it to enjoy volleyball* or *Ahmed is likely it to enjoy volleyball*. Second, the higher spec,TP[finite] is filled with the thematic DP *Ahmed* at the d-structure, although the subcategorization frames in (5) and (6) do not assign an external θ-role.

UNIT 179

Raising III

Raising

In the last unit, we discussed a problematic analysis for the constructions in (1) and (2).

1. **Ahmed** seems to enjoy volleyball.
2. **Ahmed** is likely to enjoy volleyball.

As an alternative, we will not change the subcategorization frames in (3) and (4).

3. *seems*, V [__ TP[non-finite]]
                θ

4. *likely*, A [__ TP[non-finite]]
                θ

However, we will assume that the DP *Ahmed* originates in spec,TP[non-finite], and that the spec,TP[finite] is empty as suggested by the subcategorization frames in (3) and (4). Thus, the tree structures for (1) and (2) will be as follows.

5. DS for (1)   6. DS for (2)

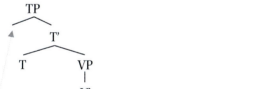
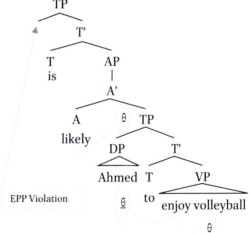

The assumption that the DP *Ahmed* starts in spec,TP[non-finite] is useful. Given that the embedded verb *enjoy* needs to assign an external θ-role to the DP *Ahmed*, which is the experiencer that feels the enjoyment, the DP *Ahmed* is sufficiently close to the verb *enjoy* to receive a θ-role. The only problem under the current assumption relates to the empty spec,TP[finite]. An expletive cannot satisfy the EPP requirement as shown in (7) and (8).

7. *It seems Ahmed to enjoy volleyball.
8. *It is likely Ahmed to enjoy volleyball.

UNIT 180

Raising IV

Raising

Thus far, we have assumed that the d-structures for (1) and (2) are as in (3) and (4).

1. **Ahmed** seems to enjoy volleyball.
2. **Ahmed** is likely to enjoy volleyball.

3. ___ seems **Ahmed** to enjoy volleyball.
4. ___ is likely **Ahmed** to enjoy volleyball.

To derive (1) and (2), syntacticians argue that the DP *Ahmed* originates in spec,TP[non-finite], and rises to spec,TP[finite] for the EPP. Consider the derivations of (1) and (2) below.

5. DS for (1)

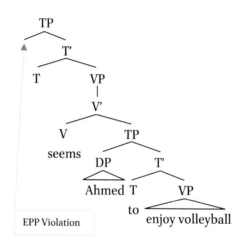

6. SS for (1)

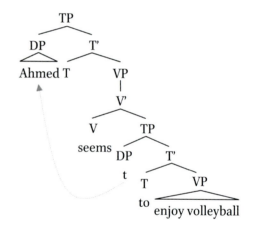

7. DS for (2)

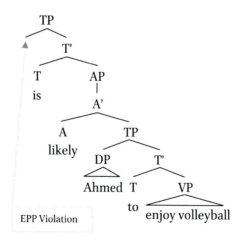

8. SS for (2)

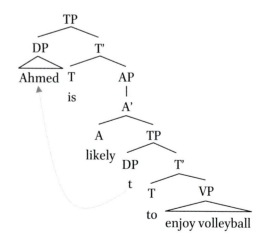

UNIT 181

Raising V

Raising

The constructions discussed in the earlier units are known as **RAISING** constructions. Raising constructions appear when the subject of a non-finite TP moves from its specifier to the specifier of a finite TP.

1. [TP[finite] __ seems [TP[non-finite] **Ahmed** to enjoy volleyball]]. (the d-structure)
2. [TP[finite] __ is likely [TP[non-finite] **Ahmed** to enjoy volleyball]]. (the d-structure)

3. [TP[finite] **Ahmed** seems [TP[non-finite] __ to enjoy volleyball]]. (raising)

4. [TP[finite] **Ahmed** is likely [TP[non-finite] __ to enjoy volleyball]]. (raising)

Because the subject *Ahmed* is raised from spec,TP[non-finite] to spec,TP[finite] in (3) and (4), such constructions are known as raising constructions. This type of construction is also called **SUBJECT-TO-SUBJECT RAISING**. The EPP has motivated these movements in the last unit. Now, we present Case as another motivation. Consider the d-structure for (3) and (4).

5. DS for (3)   6. DS for (4)

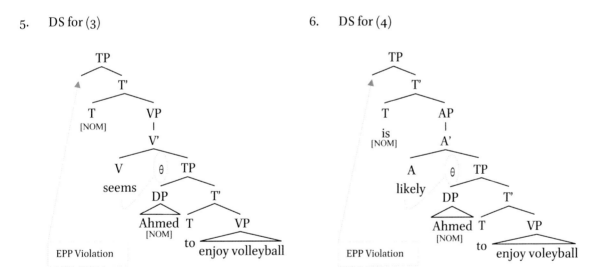

As required by the Case Filter, the DP *Ahmed* must be case-checked. Yet, the DP *Ahmed* is in a position where case checking does not hold. Since the DP *Ahmed* originates in spec,TP[non-finite], the head T[non-finite] cannot check the nominative case because it is not a case-checker. Also, the verb *seems* and the adjective *likely* cannot check the accusative case because of Burzio's Generalization, which stipulates that heads do not check the accusative case if they do not assign external θ-roles (see Unit 169). The verb *seems* and the adjective *likely* do not assign external θ-roles in (5) and (6). Thus, the DP *Ahmed* must move to spec,TP[finite], where its case can be checked by the nominative case of the head T[finite].

UNIT 182

Raising VI

Raising

We have argued that Subject-to-Subject Raising constructions occur when the subject rises from spec,TP[non-finite] to spec,TP[finite] as in the representations in (1) and (2).

1. [TP[finite] **Ahmed** seems [TP[non-finite] ___ to enjoy volleyball]]. (raising)

2. [TP[finite] **Ahmed** is likely [TP[non-finite] ___ to enjoy volleyball]]. (raising)

There are two reasons behind the movement of the subject to the empty spec,TP[finite]: (i) to satisfy the EPP, and (ii) to check its nominative case against the nominative case on the head T[finite]. Case checking will be accomplished as in the structures below given for (1) and (2).

3. DS for (1)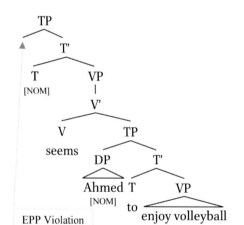

4. SS for (1)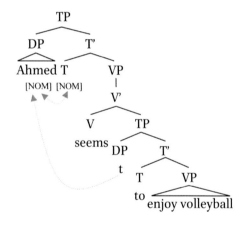

5. DS for (2)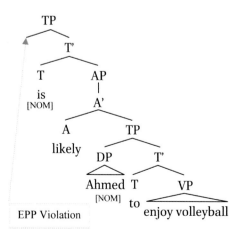

6. SS for (2)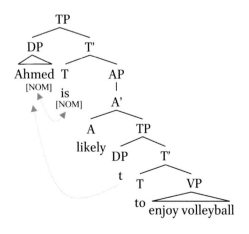

UNIT 183

Control Theory 1

Control Theory

CONTROL CONSTRUCTIONS are different from raising constructions. Consider the following examples.

1. Ahmed **seems** to enjoy volleyball.   (Raising Construction)
2. Saeed does not **seem** to come.   (Raising Construction)

3. Ahmed **plans** to play volleyball.   (Control Construction)
4. Saeed cannot **decide** whether to come.   (Control Construction)

Examples (1) and (2) are clearly raising constructions. At first glance, examples (3) and (4) seem to involve a raising structure. However, this is not the case, as there are two major differences between the two sets of examples. First, raising constructions involve verbs that do not assign any external θ-roles. The verb *seem* in (1) and (2) does not assign an external θ-role as shown in its subcategorization frame in (5); thus, it can take the expletive *it* as a subject in other relevant constructions as in (6) and (7).

5. *seems*, V [__ TP$_{[non-finite]}$]
    θ

6. *It* seems that Ahmed enjoys volleyball.
7. *It* seems that Saeed cannot come.

In contrast, the subcategorization frames of the verbs *plans* and *decide* in (3) and (4) assign external θ-roles to their subjects (see (10) and (11)). The subjects *Ahmed* and *Saeed* are agents, i.e. initiators of the actions *planning* and *deciding* respectively. Thus, these verbs do not allow the expletive *it* as a subject in other relevant constructions as in (8) and (9).

8. **It* plans that Ahmed plays volleyball.
9. **It* cannot decide that Saeed will come.

The second major difference is that the verb *seems* in (1) and (2) selects TP[non-finite] as a complement, whereas the verbs *plans* and *decide* in (3) and (4) select CP. The complementizer *whether* sometimes appears as in (4), and sometimes disappears (or appears as a null complementizer) as in (3). Thus, the subcategorization frames of the verbs *plans* and *decides* differ from that of the verb *seem* in (5) in that they select CP as in (10) and (11).

10. *plans*, V [__ CP$_{[\varnothing]}$]
    θ θ

11. *decide*, V [__ CP$_{[whether]}$]
    θ θ

UNIT 184

Control Theory 11

Control Theory

We concluded that the control constructions in (1) and (2) are different from the raising ones in (3) and (4) in that the verbs in the former assign external θ-roles and select CP[∅/whether], whereas the verbs in the latter select TP[non-finite] and do not assign external θ-roles.

1. Ahmed **plans** to play volleyball.   (Control Construction)
2. Saeed cannot **decide** whether to come.   (Control Construction)
3. Ahmed **seems** to enjoy volleyball.   (Raising Construction)
4. Saeed does not **seem** to come.   (Raising Construction)

We might nonetheless try to extend our analysis of raising constructions to control constructions. Let us consider the problems that this may cause.

5. DS for (2)

6. SS for (2)

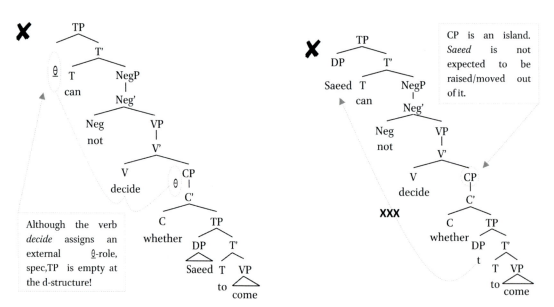

As shown in (5) and (6), a control construction cannot adopt the same analysis given to a raising one. First, in raising structures, spec,TP[finite] is empty at the d-structure because the verb *seem* does not assign an external θ-role. However, the verb *decide* requires a thematic subject to which it assigns an external θ-role. The d-structure in (5) is generated without any subjects, i.e. it is a violation of the theta criterion. Second, in raising structures, subjects can be raised from spec,TP[non-finite] to spec,TP[finite] because TP[non-finite] is not an island. However, in (6), CP is an undisputed island out of which subjects cannot be moved (see Unit 159). Consider (7), where a wh-subject is not allowed to move across CP.

7. **Who* does he think [$_{CP}$ that ___ will come].   (CP as an island)

UNIT 185

Control Theory III

Control Theory

In light of the discussions in the previous units, it is obvious that the control constructions in (1) and (2) need a separate analysis.

1. Ahmed **plans** to play volleyball. (Control Construction)
2. Saeed cannot **decide** whether to come. (Control Construction)

Because the verbs *plans* and *decide* assign external θ-roles to their subjects as in (3) and (4), spec,TP must be filled at the d-structure as shown in (5) and (6) for sentences (1) and (2).

3. *plans*, V [__ CP$_{[\emptyset]}$]
   $\underline{\theta}$ θ

4. *decide*, V [__ CP$_{[whether]}$]
   $\underline{\theta}$ θ

5. DS for (1)

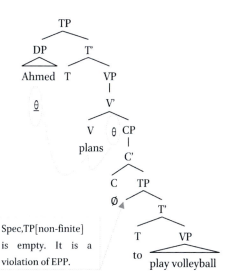

6. DS for (2)

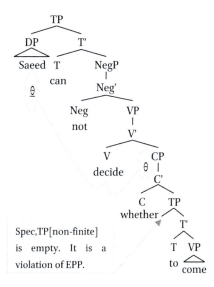

In (5) and (6), spec,TP[finite] is filled with a thematic subject. These thematic subjects respect the subcategorization frames in (3) and (4) that require external arguments at the d-structure. However, there is still a problem in structures (5) and (6). Spec,TP[non-finite] is empty, violating the EPP. The expletive insertion cannot fix this problem because it yields ungrammatical sentences as in (7) and (8).

7. *Ahmed plans **it** to play volleyball.
8. *Saeed cannot decide whether **it** to come.

UNIT 186

Control Theory IV

Control Theory

In the control constructions in (1) and (2), we have shown that spec,TP[finite] is filled by a thematic subject, but spec,TP[non-finite] is empty in violation of the EPP.

1. [TP[finite] Ahmed **plans** [CP ∅ [TP[non-finite] ___ to play volleyball]. (Control)
2. [TP[finite] Saeed cannot **decide** [CP whether [TP[non-finite] ___ to come]. (Control)

To overcome this problem, it is important to note that *Ahmed* in (1) is the agent of both the actions *planning* and *playing*. Also, *Saeed* is the agent of the actions *deciding* and *coming*. Thus, we may want spec,TP[non-finite] to be filled with something related to the subjects *Ahmed* and *Saeed* respectively. For this reason, syntacticians propose that spec,TP[non-finite] be filled with a covert subject. This covert subject is a pronominal determiner phrase (DP) but without phonological content. In other words, it is a null unpronounced pronoun. In theory, it is called **PRO** (read as "big PRO", because there is also a "small **pro**", which falls outside the scope of this textbook). Therefore, spec,TP[non-finite] is filled with DP as in (3) and (4).

3. Tree for CP in (1) 4. Tree for CP in (2)

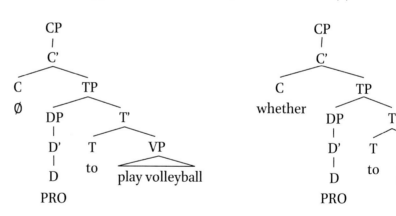

The PROs in spec,TP[non-finite] in (3) and (4) are DPs but they are not pronounced. Because *Ahmed* is the agent of both the actions *planning* and *playing* in (1), and *Saeed* is the agent of the actions *deciding* and *coming* in (2), PRO in (3) and (4) must refer to *Ahmed* and *Saeed* respectively. The subjects *Ahmed* and *Saeed* are called **CONTROLLERS** because they control PRO, and PRO receives its interpretation from them. Thus, for interpretation, PRO must be bound and co-indexed by a controller. Recall that *bound* means *c-commanded* as in (5).

5. C-command relationship:
   A *c-commands* B iff
   i. A does not dominate B, and B does not dominate A
   ii. The first node that dominates A dominates B

UNIT 187

Control Theory v

Control Theory

In control constructions, spec,TP[non-finite] is now filled by an unpronounced DP known as big PRO. This PRO receives its interpretation from a controller, in this case another DP in spec,TP[finite]. PRO must be bound and co-indexed with controllers as shown in (1) and (2).

1. [TP[finite] Ahmed$_i$ **plans** [CP ∅ [TP[non-finite] PRO$_i$ to play volleyball].   (Control)
2. [TP[finite] Saeed$_j$ cannot **decide** [CP whether [TP[non-finite] PRO$_j$ to come]. (Control)

In (1), the unpronounced pronoun PRO$_i$ is co-indexed with the controller *Ahmed$_i$* with the subscript (i), whereas PRO$_j$ in (2) is co-indexed with the subject *Saeed$_j$* with the subscript (j). Given that PRO receives its interpretation from its controller, PRO means *Ahmed* in (1), and *Saeed* in (2). The full tree structures for (1) and (2) are as follows.

3. Tree for (1)   4. Tree for (2)

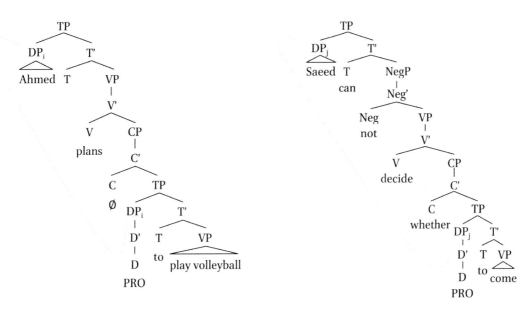

The PRO in spec,TP[non-finite] in (3) and (4) is part of **EMPTY CATEGORIES**. An empty category is a term proposed by Noam Chomsky (1981), and it refers to a covert unpronounced element governed by a higher element from which it receives interpretation. Therefore, traces in the original positions of moved elements are also instances of empty categories. For this reason, one may wrongly assume that PRO functions like a trace for the subjects *Ahmed* and *Saeed*. However, PRO is not a trace; *Ahmed* and *Saeed* are only co-indexed with PRO. They are not raised from spec,TP[non-finite] leaving PRO behind. A raising-construction-based analysis of control constructions is problematic (see Unit 184).

UNIT 188

Control Theory VI

Control Theory

We have now reached our final analysis of control constructions. Spec,TP[non-finite] is filled with PRO, and PRO is bound and co-indexed with the subject in spec,TP[finite] as shown in (1) and (2).

1. [TP[finite] Ahmed$_i$ **plans** [CP ∅ [TP[non-finite] PRO$_i$ to play volleyball]. (Control)
2. [TP[finite] Saeed$_j$ cannot **decide** [CP whether [TP[non-finite] PRO$_j$ to come]. (Control)

The position of PRO in spec,TP[non-finite] within CP has advantages. First, it satisfies the EPP. Second, PRO occurs in a position that does not violate the principles of Case theory. The position of PRO does not violate the Case Filter requirement in (3).

3. **Case Filter:** Every *pronounced* DP must have a case that is checked by another case feature in the same domain.

In (3), every pronounced DP must be case-marked. Because PRO is an unpronounced DP, we expect it not to be case-marked. Consider the position of PRO below.

4. Tree for CP in (1)   5. Tree for CP in (2)

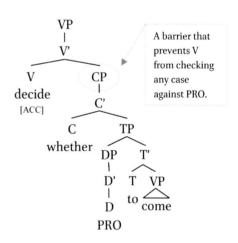

In (4) and (5), the complementizers *whether* and ∅ are not case-checkers, unlike the complementizer *for*. Thus, they cannot check any case on PRO. The head T[non-finite] is not a case-checker either. The only possible case-checkers are the head verbs *plan* and *decide*. However, they cannot check any case on PRO because CP is a barrier according to (6ii).

6. Principles of Government (for *Case Checking*)
    X governs Y iff
    i. X *m-commands* Y, and
    ii. No barrier (WP) except TP[non-finite] intervenes between X and Y

UNIT 189

Control Theory VII

Control Theory

We concluded that PRO is not in a case position because CP functions as a barrier that prevents any head from checking case on PRO.

1. [$_{TP[finite]}$ Ahmed$_i$ **plans** [$_{CP}$ ∅ [$_{TP[non-finite]}$ PRO$_i$ to play volleyball]. (Control)
2. [$_{TP[finite]}$ Saeed$_j$ cannot **decide** [$_{CP}$ whether [$_{TP[non-finite]}$ PRO$_j$ to come]. (Control)

Since PRO is an unpronounced pronoun/DP, we expect it never to appear in a case-checking position. In fact, PRO cannot appear in any position where it will possibly be case-marked.

Sentence		**Position of PRO**	**Case**
3. a.	*Ahmed$_i$ thinks that PRO$_i$ will come.	Subject	Nominative
b.	*Ahmed$_i$ praises PRO$_i$.	Object	Accusative
c.	*Ahmed$_i$ is angry at PRO$_i$.	Prepositional Object	Accusative
d.	*They$_i$ need for PRO$_i$ to win.	Spec,TP[non-finite]	Accusative
e.	*We know Ahmed$_i$. We read PRO$_i$ book	Possessor	Genitive

Theta Assignment in Control Constructions

Another advantage of the position of PRO in spec,TP[non-finite] follows from the fact that it does not violate locality constraints when it receives an external θ-role from the verbs inside the TP[non-finite]. We know that PRO functions as an agent of the embedded verbs. Consider the subcategorization frames of the verbs *play* and *come* in (4) and (5).

4. *play*, V [___ DP]   5. *come*, V [___]
       θ   θ   θ

As an agent, PRO in spec,TP[non-finite] is suitably close to theta-assigning verbs, so it can easily receive its θ-role from the embedded verbs as shown in (6) and (7).

6. Tree for CP in (1)   7. Tree for CP in (2)

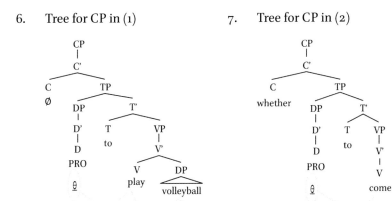

UNIT 190

Control Theory VIII

Object Control Constructions

Let us now introduce a new type of control construction. In control constructions, PRO does not always receive its interpretation from the subject in spec,TP[finite] as in (1). Sometimes, PRO is bound and co-indexed with the object of the verb as in (2).

1. [$_{TP[finite]}$ Ahmed$_i$ plans [$_{CP}$ [$_{TP[non-finite]}$ PRO$_i$ to play volleyball.]
2. [$_{TP[finite]}$ Ahmed$_i$ persuaded Ali$_j$ [$_{CP}$ [$_{TP[non-finite]}$ PRO$_j$ to play volleyball.]
3. *[$_{TP[finite]}$ Ahmed$_i$ persuaded Ali$_j$ [$_{CP}$ [$_{TP[non-finite]}$ PRO$_i$ to play volleyball.]

Given that the controller of PRO in (1) is the subject of TP[finite], i.e. *Ahmed*, this construction is known as **SUBJECT CONTROL**. In (2), PRO takes its interpretation from the object of the verb *persuaded*, namely *Ali*. Therefore, this construction is called **OBJECT CONTROL**. The agent that *plays volleyball* in (2) is *Ali* now; thus, both PRO$_j$ and *Ali$_j$* are co-indexed with the subscript (j). PRO cannot be co-indexed with *Ahmed* as in (3). Sentence (3) is ungrammatical because *Ahmed$_i$* is mistakenly assumed to be the one who plays volleyball, based on its co-indexation with PRO$_i$. Consider the tree structures for (2) and (3) below.

4. Tree for (2)   5. Tree for (3)

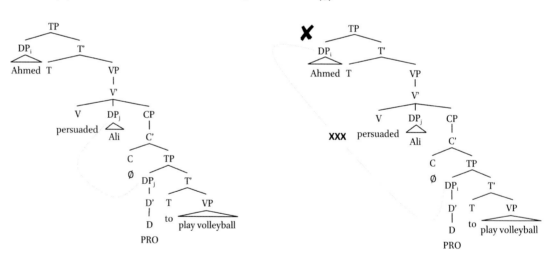

In (4), PRO$_j$ is bound and co-indexed with *Ali$_j$* and receives its interpretation from it. In (5), PRO$_i$ cannot be co-indexed with *Ahmed$_i$*. Note that the co-indexation between *Ahmed$_i$* and PRO$_i$ in (5) is not allowed because they do not appear in the same binding domain (namely TP). In the preceding units, we saw examples where PRO was co-indexed with *Ahmed* in different domains (see (3) in Unit 187, for example). The co-indexation in (5) seems to be disallowed because *Ali* blocks PRO from receiving its interpretation from *Ahmed*.

UNIT 191

Control Theory IX

Control Theory

There are two types of control constructions: (i) Subject Control Constructions, where the subject of the TP[finite] is the controller as in (1), and (ii) Object Control Constructions, where the object of the verb is the controller as in (2).

1. [$_{TP[finite]}$ Ahmed$_i$ plans [$_{CP}$ [$_{TP[non-finite]}$ PRO$_i$ to play volleyball.]
2. [$_{TP[finite]}$ Ahmed$_i$ persuaded Ali$_j$ [$_{CP}$ [$_{TP[non-finite]}$ PRO$_j$ to play volleyball.]

If a DP intervenes as an object, PRO cannot be co-indexed with the subject as in (3). In (3), *Ahmed* is supposed to be the player, not *Ali*, which would be an incorrect interpretation.

3. *[$_{TP[finite]}$ Ahmed$_i$ persuaded Ali$_j$ [$_{CP}$ [$_{TP[non-finite]}$ PRO$_i$ to play volleyball.]

To account for the ungrammaticality in (3), it is obvious that PRO can only be co-indexed with the closest c-commanding DP. In (3), PRO cannot be co-indexed with *Ahmed* because the closest c-commanding DP to PRO is *Ali*. In syntactic theory, this constraint is known as the **MINIMAL DISTANCE PRINCIPLE (MDP)**.

4. **Minimal Distance Principle (MDP):** PRO must be co-indexed with the closest c-commanding DP.

The MDP in (4) accounts for the grammaticality in (2) and the ungrammaticality in (3).

5. Tree for (2)

6. Tree for (3)

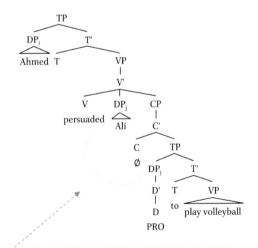

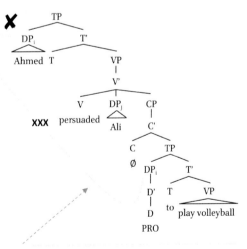

This is in accordance with the **Minimal Distance Principle**, because PRO is co-indexed with the closest c-commanding DP *Ali*.

This is in violation of the **Minimal Distance Principle**, because PRO is co-indexed with the furthest c-commanding DP *Ahmed*.

UNIT 192

Control Theory x

Control Theory

Let us summarize and move on. Control constructions are of two types: (i) Subject Control Constructions, where the subject of the TP[finite] is the controller as in (1), and (ii) Object Control Constructions, where the object of the verb is the controller as in (2).

1. [$_{TP[finite]}$ Ahmed$_i$ *plans* [$_{CP}$ [$_{TP[non-finite]}$ PRO$_i$ to play volleyball.]
2. [$_{TP[finite]}$ Ahmed$_i$ *persuaded* Ali$_j$ [$_{CP}$ [$_{TP[non-finite]}$ PRO$_j$ to play volleyball.]

Note that the control constructions in (1) and (2) appear with the verbs *plans* and *persuaded* that take CP as a complement. Let us call these structures **VERBAL CONTROL CONSTRUCTIONS**. Control constructions may also involve adjectives such as *eager, reluctant, happy* etc. These adjectives are followed by CP. We will call these constructions **ADJECTIVAL CONTROL CONSTRUCTIONS**. Consider the following examples.

3. [$_{TP[finite]}$ Ahmed$_i$ is *happy* [$_{CP}$ [$_{TP[non-finite]}$ PRO$_i$ to play volleyball.]
4. [$_{TP[finite]}$ Ahmed$_i$ is *eager* [$_{CP}$ [$_{TP[non-finite]}$ PRO$_i$ to play volleyball.]
5. [$_{TP[finite]}$ Ahmed$_i$ is *reluctant* [$_{CP}$ [$_{TP[non-finite]}$ PRO$_i$ to play volleyball.]

In (3) through (5), PRO$_i$ is co-indexed with the subject *Ahmed$_i$*, who is *happy/eager/reluctant* regarding *playing volleyball*. Consider syntactic tree structure (6) given to (3). This same basic structure can be used as representative and assigned to (4) and (5), simply replacing *happy* with *eager* and *reluctant* respectively. In English, adjectives are not case-checkers. Even if they were assumed to be case-checkers, they would not check any case against PRO because of the CP-barrier.

6. Tree for (4)

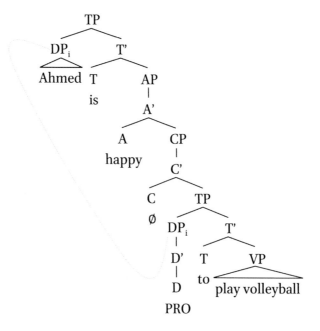

UNIT 193

Control Theory XI

Control Theory

Before we complicate matters with more terms, let us recap. There are two types of control: (A) Verbal Control Constructions that include (i) Subject Control Constructions, where the subject of the TP[finite] is the controller as in (1), and (ii) Object Control Constructions, where the object of the verb is the controller as in (2); and (B) Adjectival Control Constructions that involve adjectival phrases with a subject controller as in (3).

1. [$_{TP[finite]}$ Ahmed$_i$ *plans* [$_{CP}$ [$_{TP[non-finite]}$ PRO$_i$ to play volleyball.]
2. [$_{TP[finite]}$ Ahmed$_i$ *persuaded* Ali$_j$ [$_{CP}$ [$_{TP[non-finite]}$ PRO$_j$ to play volleyball.]
3. [$_{TP[finite]}$ Ahmed$_i$ is *happy* [$_{CP}$ [$_{TP[non-finite]}$ PRO$_i$ to play volleyball.]

In all the examples above, PRO receives its interpretation either from the subject as in (1) and (3), or from the object as in (2). We call these constructions **OBLIGATORY CONTROL CONSTRUCTIONS** (OCC). OCC means that PRO is obligatorily controlled by a controller from which it receives its interpretation.

In certain cases, however, PRO does not receive its interpretation from any word in the sentence, but instead refers to people and things in the outside world. Let us recall how such a PRO reference occurs in pronouns before we examine how it occurs in unpronounced pronouns.

4. Ahmed$_i$ thinks that Ali$_j$ respects **him**$_i$.   Meaning: *him= Ahmed*
5. Ahmed$_i$ thinks that Ali$_j$ respects **him**$_k$ Meaning: *him = John, Saeed, etc.*

In (4), the pronoun *him*$_i$ is obligatorily co-indexed with the antecedent *Ahmed*$_i$. However, it is possible that the pronoun *him*$_k$ does not refer to anything in the sentence; it may refer to other people (*John, Saeed* etc.) as in (5). This means that the pronoun *him*$_k$ is not obligatorily co-indexed with any word in the sentence. The same applies to PRO. Consider the following examples.

6. It stinks [$_{CP}$ PRO$_{arb}$ to play volleyball.]   (Verbal Control)
7. [$_{CP}$ PRO$_{arb}$ To play volleyball] stinks.   (Verbal Control)
8. It is possible [$_{CP}$ PRO$_{arb}$ to play volleyball.] (Adjectival Control)
9. [$_{CP}$ PRO$_{arb}$ To play volleyball] is possible.   (Adjectival Control)

In (6) through (9), PRO does not receive its interpretation from any word in the sentence. Rather, it refers to all people in the world, thus being co-indexed by *arb* (= arbitrary). These constructions are known as **NON-OBLIGATORY CONTROL CONSTRUCTIONS** (NCC), because PRO is not obligatorily controlled by any word in the sentence. NCC can be found in verbal or adjectival constructions as in (6) through (9). The subject in NCC can be either the expletive *it* or CP.

UNIT 194

Control Theory XII

Control Theory

We have seen that there are two types of control constructions: (i) Obligatory Control Constructions (OCC), where PRO must receive its interpretation from a word in the sentence (Verbs: *plan, persuade* etc., or Adjectives: *happy, eager, reluctant* etc.) as in (1) through (3), and (ii) Non-Obligatory Control Constructions (NCC), where PRO does not obligatorily receive its interpretation from any word in the sentence (Verbs: *stink, scare* etc., or Adjectives: *possible, likely* etc.) as in (4) through (7). The difference between the two types depends on whether the verbs/adjectives assign external θ-roles or not. If they assign external θ-roles, they are OCC as in (1) through (3); if not, they are NCC as in (4) through (7).

Obligatory Control Constructions (OCC)

1. Ahmed$_i$ ***plans*** [$_{CP}$ PRO$_i$ to play volleyball.]   (Verbal Control: Subject)
2. Ahmed$_i$ ***persuaded*** Ali$_j$ [$_{CP}$ PRO$_j$ to play volleyball.]   (Verbal Control: Object)
3. Ahmed$_i$ is ***happy*** [$_{CP}$ PRO$_i$ to play volleyball.]   (Adjectival Control: Subj)

Non-Obligatory Control Constructions (NCC)

4. It ***stinks*** [$_{CP}$ PRO$_{arb}$ to play volleyball.]   (Verbal Control)
5. [$_{CP}$ PRO$_{arb}$ To play volleyball] ***stinks***.   (Verbal Control)
6. It is ***possible*** [$_{CP}$ PRO$_{arb}$ to play volleyball.]   (Adjectival Control)
7. [$_{CP}$ PRO$_{arb}$ To play volleyball] is ***possible***.   (Adjectival Control)

The subcategorization frames of these verbs/adjectives are shown in (8) and (9).

8. **Obligatory Control Constructions**   9. **Non-obligatory Control Constructions**
   plans, V [__ CP[∅]]   *stinks*, V [__ CP[∅]]
              θ θ   θ
   persuaded, A [__ DP (CP[∅])]   *possible*, A [__ CP[∅]]
                   θ θ θ   θ
   happy, A [__ CP[∅]]
              θ θ

A simple way to decide whether or not these verbs/adjectives assign external θ-roles is to test whether or not they allow the expletive *it* in other relevant constructions. If the expletive *it* is not allowed, they assign external θ-roles; thus, they are OCC as in (10). If the expletive *it* is allowed, they do not assign external θ-roles; thus, they are NCC as in (11).

10. Obligatory Control Constructions
    *It ***plans*** that Ahmed plays volleyball.
    *It ***persuaded*** Ali to play volleyball.
    *It is ***happy*** that Ahmed plays volleyball.

11. Non-obligatory Control Constructions
    ✓It ***stinks*** that Ahmed plays volleyball.
    ✓It ***stinks*** that Ali plays volleyball.
    ✓It is ***possible*** that Ahmed plays volleyball.

UNIT 195

Control Theory XIII

Control Theory

Let us end our discussion of control constructions with Non-obligatory Control Constructions (NCC), where PRO is not obligatorily controlled by any controller as in (1) through (4).

1. It **stinks** [$_{CP}$ PRO$_{arb}$ to play volleyball.]   (Verbal Control)
2. [$_{CP}$ PRO$_{arb}$ To play volleyball] **stinks**.   (Verbal Control)
3. It is **possible** [$_{CP}$ PRO$_{arb}$ to play volleyball.]   (Adjectival Control)
4. [$_{CP}$ PRO$_{arb}$ To play volleyball] is **possible**.   (Adjectival Control)

NCC only occurs with verbs/adjectives that do not assign external θ-roles as can be seen from the d-structure for (1) and (2) given in (5), and the d-structure for (3) and (4) given in (6). Because these verbs/adjectives do not assign external θ-roles, the subject position (spec,TP[finite]) will be empty at the d-structure.

5. *___ **stinks** [$_{CP}$ PRO$_{arb}$ to play volleyball.]   (Verbal Control)
6. *___ is **possible** [$_{CP}$ PRO$_{arb}$ to play volleyball.]   (Adjectival Control)

Because the empty spec,TP[finite] is a violation for the EPP, it is filled either by the insertion of the expletive *it* as in (7), or by the movement of CP as in (8). Consider the syntactic structures for (3) and (4) as representative.

7. Tree for (3)

8. Tree for (4)

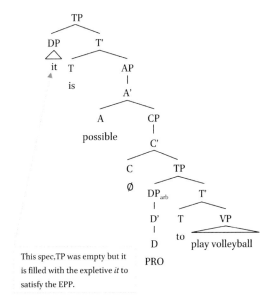

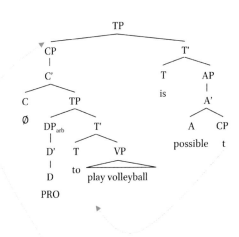

UNIT 196

Raising vs. Control 1

Raising Constructions vs. Control Constructions

For some students, it may still be difficult to differentiate between (i) Raising Constructions as in (1), and (ii) Control Constructions as in (2). Consider the following examples.

1. [$_{TP[finite]}$ Ahmed seems [$_{TP[non-finite]}$ ~~Ahmed~~ to play volleyball]   (Raising)
2. [$_{TP[finite]}$ Ahmed$_i$ plans [$_{CP}$ ∅ [$_{TP[non-finite]}$ PRO$_i$ to play volleyball.]   (Control)

Both verbs in (1) and (2) are followed by the infinitival phrase [*to play volleyball*]. However, the verb *seems* in (1) is followed by TP[non-finite], while the verb *plans* in (2) is followed by CP[∅]. The agent that initiates the action *playing* in both (1) and (2) is *Ahmed*. However, *Ahmed* in (1) is simply raised from spec,TP[non-finite] to spec,TP[finite], whereas *Ahmed* in (2) is directly base-generated in spec,TP[finite] and co-indexed with a PRO occupying spec,TP[non-finite]. In (1) and (2), both ~~Ahmed~~ and PRO occupy spec,TP[non-finite] and satisfy the EPP requirement. Consider the tree structures of (1) and (2) below.

3. Tree for (1): raising   4. Tree for (2): control

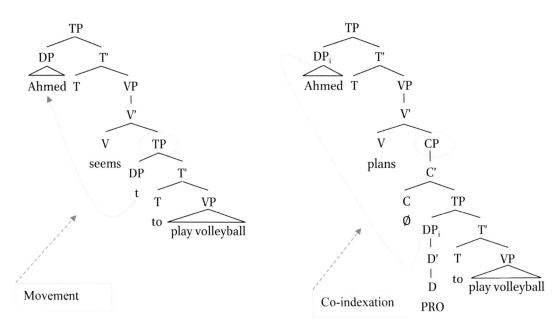

In (3), the DP *Ahmed* moves from spec,TP[non-finite] to spec,TP[finite]. In (4), there is no movement; co-indexation is held between PRO$_i$ in spec,TP[non-finite] and *Ahmed$_i$* in spec,TP[finite]. Although the structural representations of raising and control constructions split them apart, one might not be able to decide whether the predicate [*to play volleyball*] in (1) and (2) is TP[non-finite] or CP[∅], simply because they are identical in their surface representation. In the next unit, we will introduce diagnostic tests that determine whether the predicate [*to play volleyball*] is CP (i.e. control) or TP[non-finite] (i.e. raising).

UNIT 197

Raising vs. Control II

Raising Constructions vs. Control Constructions

External Theta Role Assignment is the best test to distinguish (i) Raising Constructions in (1) and (2) from (ii) Control Constructions in (3) and (4).

1. Ahmed seems [$_{TP}$ ~~Ahmed~~ to play volleyball]   (Raising Constructions)
2. Ahmed is likely [$_{TP}$ ~~Ahmed~~ to play volleyball]   (Raising Constructions)
3. Ahmed$_i$ plans [$_{CP}$ PRO$_i$ to play volleyball.]   (Control Constructions)
4. Ahmed$_i$ is eager [$_{CP}$ PRO$_i$ to play volleyball.]   (Control Constructions)

The primary difference lies in the fact that the verbs/adjectives in raising constructions do not assign external θ-roles as in (5), thus allowing the expletive *it* in other constructions as in (6).

5. a. *seems*, V [__ TP$_{[non\text{-}finite]}$]   b. *likely*, V [__ TP$_{[non\text{-}finite]}$]
              θ   θ

6. a. *It seems that Ahmed plays volleyball.*   b. *It is likely that Ahmed plays volleyball.*

In contrast, the verb/adjectives in control constructions assign external θ-roles as in (7), thus disallowing the insertion of the expletive *it* in other relevant constructions as in (8).

7. a. *plans*, V [__ CP[∅]]   b. *eager*, A [__ CP[∅]]
            θ   θ   θ   θ

8. a. **It **plans** that Ahmed plays volleyball.*   b. **It is eager that Ahmed plays volleyball.*

Note, however, that only in non-obligatory control constructions do the verbs/adjectives not assign external θ-roles as in (9), thus allowing the expletive to appear in constructions (10).

9. a. *stinks*, V [__ CP[∅]]   b. *possible*, A [__ CP[∅]]
                θ   θ

10. a. *It stinks to play volleyball.*   b. *It is possible to play volleyball.*

To determine whether a verb assigns an external θ-role, passive-active synonymy is another helpful test. If the active and passive forms are synonymous using a given verb, such a verb does not assign an external θ-role, e.g. *seem* in (11). If both forms, active and passive, are non-synonymous using a given verb, such a verb assigns an external θ-role, e.g. *plan* in (12).

11. *Ahmed **seems to play** volleyball.*   =   *Volleyball **seems to be played** by Ahmed.*

12. *Ahmed **plans to play** volleyball.*   ≠   *Volleyball **plans to be played** by Ahmed.*

UNIT 198

ECM vs. Control 1

ECM Constructions vs. Object Control Constructions

For some students, it may be difficult to differentiate between (i) ECM in (1), and (ii) Object Control Constructions (OCC) in (2).

1. [TP[finite] She expects [TP[non-finite] him to win]   (ECM)
2. [TP[finite] She persuaded him$_i$ [CP ∅ [TP[non-finite] PRO$_i$ to win.]   (OCC)

In Units 165–167, we discussed ECM construction (1), where the verb *expects* selects TP[non-finite] as shown in its subcategorization frame in (3). In Unit 190, we explored OCC (2), of which the subcategorization frame for the verb *persuaded* is proposed in (4).

3. *expects*, V [___ TP$_{[non-finite]}$]
               θ θ

4. *persuaded*, V [___ DP CP$_{[∅]}$]
               θ θ θ

The derivations for the two constructions are different. Consider the structure for ECM in (5), and that of OCC in (6).

5. Tree for (1)   6. Tree for (2)

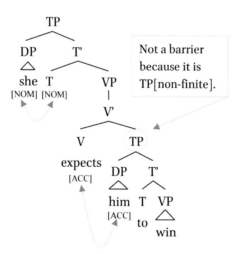

Not a barrier because it is TP[non-finite].

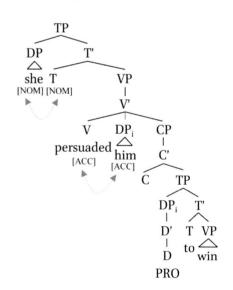

In ECM, spec,TP[non-finite] is filled with the DP *him*, whose accusative case is checked by the verb *expects*. However, in OCC, spec,TP[non-finite] is filled with PRO, which is co-indexed with the object of the verb *persuaded*, i.e the DP *him*. In the next unit, we will introduce two diagnostic tests to differentiate between ECM and OCC.

UNIT 199

ECM vs. Control 11

ECM Constructions vs. Control Constructions

To know whether a construction is ECM as in (1) or OCC as in (2), there are two diagnostic tests related to (i) the expletive *there*, and (ii) the idiomatic chunks.

1. [$_{TP[finite]}$ She expects [$_{TP[non-finite]}$ him to win]]   (ECM)
2. [$_{TP[finite]}$ She persuaded him$_i$ [$_{CP}$ ∅ [$_{TP[non-finite]}$ PRO$_i$ to win.]]   (Control)

As for the first diagnostic test, note first of all that the expletive *there* can appear in a subject position as in (3), but not in an object position as in (4).

3. **There** is a book on the table.   (Subject Position)
4. *A book is **there** on the table.   (Object Position)

In other related constructions, the expletive *there* is allowed in the object position of ECM constructions as in (5), but it cannot be allowed in an object position in OCC as in (6).

5. She **expects** there to be many people.   (ECM)
6. *She **persuaded** there to be many people.   (Control)

Thus, the allowability of the expletive *there* in an object position can indicate whether a given construction is ECM or OCC. If *there* is allowed, the construction is ECM. If not, it is OCC.

As for the second diagnostic test, let us learn first that an idiom as in (7) and (8) is a group of words that has an established meaning not deducible from those of the individual words.

7. Let the cat out of the bag
8. The shit hits the fan.

The idiom in (7) means 'reveal a secret', while that in (8) means 'things get chaotic and out of control'. Each of the above sentences may have a literal meaning, though it is unlikely; we may safely assume that they are idioms. Note that both idioms have external arguments, i.e. *the cat* and *the shit* respectively. These arguments can appear in an object position in ECM in (9) and (10) while keeping their idiomatic meanings, but they cannot appear in an object position in OCC in (11) and (12) unless they have non-idiomatic meanings.

9. She **expects** the cat to be out of the bag.   (it has an idiomatic meaning)
10. She **expects** the shit to hit the fan.   (it has an idiomatic meaning)
11. She **persuaded** the cat to be out of the bag. (only non-idiomatic meaning)
12. She **persuaded** the shit to hit the fan.   (only non-idiomatic meaning)

Thus, to differentiate between ECM and OCC constructions, it is important to test them using the idioms in (7) and (8). If the external argument of the idiom can appear in an object position and yield an idiomatic meaning, the construction is ECM. If it yields only a non-idiomatic meaning, the construction is OCC.

SECTION 11

Split Projections

∴

UNIT 200

Split DP Hypothesis 1

Split Projections

In the previous units, we discussed lexical and functional phrases. **LEXICAL PHRASES** include NP, VP, AP, PP and AdvP; they all have semantic lexical contents. **FUNCTIONAL PHRASES** are DP, TP and CP; they have grammatical functions. To account for data from languages other than English, syntacticians have introduced various new kinds of phrases. For instance, DP is split into phrases such as Quantifier Phrase (QP), Demonstrative Phrase (DemP), Number Phrase (NumP) and Classifier Phrase (ClassP), whereas CP is expanded into Force Phrase (ForcP), Topic Phrase (TopP), Focus Phrase (FocP), and Inflection Phrase (InfP). We will discuss these phrases in more detail in the next units using data from foreign languages; however, we will provide English examples as far as possible.

Split DP

Since the introduction of DP-hypothesis (Abney, 1987), many scholars have introduced new projections to account for advanced data. Consider the following examples.

1. [The new books] arrived.
2. [Ahmed's books] arrived.

The examples above can be structurally drawn as in (3) and (4) respectively.

3. Tree for (1)   4. Tree for (2)

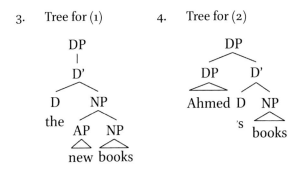

It is clear that the head D can be filled with a determiner such as *the/a/an* as in (3) or the possessive morpheme *-'s* as in (4). Spec,DP in (4) hosts the possessor. Consider the following data.

5. [**All** Ahmed's books] arrived.
6. [**Many** a man] has been destroyed by booze.
7. [**Both** my brothers] are immigrants.
8. I will come in [**half** an hour].

The current DP-hypothesis is inadequate and cannot account for the data in (5) through (8). Words like *all, many, both,* and *half* precede the determiner phrase; thus, they must project above the DP.

UNIT 201

Split DP Hypothesis II

Quantifier Phrase

QUANTIFIERS are words such as *all, many, half, both* etc. that appear before possessors as in (1), or before determiners such as *a, my, an* as in (2) through (4).

1. [**All** Ahmed's books] arrived.
2. [**Many** a man] has been destroyed by booze.
3. [**Both** my parents] are immigrants.
4. I will come in [**half** an hour].

To account for the above facts, a **QUANTIFIER PHRASE** (QP) is proposed above DP as in (5).

5. QP
    |
    Q'
    ╱╲
    Q DP

Thus, the phrases in (1) through (4) can be drawn as in (6) through (9) respectively.

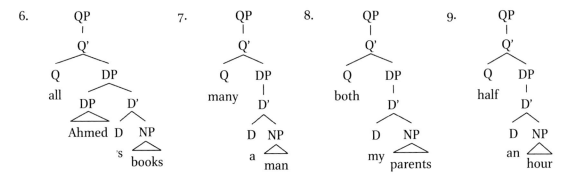

Demonstrative Phrase

DEMONSTRATIVES are words such as *this, that* etc. Arabic demonstratives cannot precede the quantifier *kull* 'all' in (10); they follow it and precede the definite article *ʕal-* 'the' in (11).

10. *[haðihi kull ʕal kutub] wasˤalat   (✗ Dem+Q+D+Noun)
    [these all the books] arrived
    'All these books arrived'.

11. [kull haðihi ʕal kutub] wasˤalat   (✓ Q+Dem+D+Noun)
    [all these the books] arrived
    'All these books arrived'.

UNIT 202

Split DP Hypothesis III

Demonstrative Phrase

As discussed in the previous unit, Arabic demonstratives must follow the quantifier *kull* 'all' but precede the definite article *ʕal-* 'the' as in (1).

1. [*kull haðihi ʕal kutub*] *wasˤalat* (✓Q+Dem+D+Noun)
    [all these the books] arrived
    'All these books arrived'.

Example (1) proposes a **DEMONSTRATIVE PHRASE** (DemP) between QP and DP as in (2). Thus, the derivation of (1) will be as shown in (3).

2. Tree for DemP   3. Tree for (1)

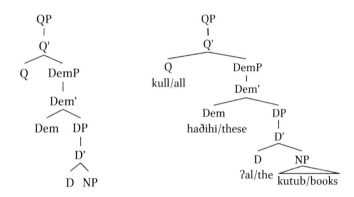

Number Phrase

Thus far, we have proposed QP and DemP above the DP. Let us introduce new phrases that appear below the DP. Consider the following examples.

4. [The **three** books] arrived.

NUMBERS like *three* appear between D and NP. Ritter (1991) argues that the number *three* in (4) projects a **NUMBER PHRASE** (NumP) as in (5) and occupies the head Num° as in (6).

5. Number Phrase (NumP)   6. Tree for (4)

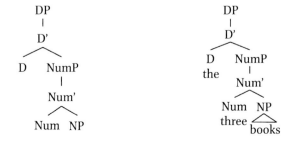

UNIT 203

Split DP Hypothesis IV

Classifier Phrase

CLASSIFIERS or **MEASURE WORDS** are words used in Chinese when the noun is quantified by a number. Phrases such as 'one person' or 'three books' are translated into Chinese by inserting a classifier (having a function but not a meaning) between the number and the noun. Consider the following example (cf. Xupin Li, 2013:17).

1. [san   tiao   he]
   [three CLASSIFIER   river]
   'Three rivers'

Since classifiers are placed between the number and the noun, it is assumed that **CLASSIFIER PHRASE** (ClP) projects between NumP and NP as in (2). The structure for (1) is given in (3).

2. Classifier Phrase (ClP)   3. Tree for (1)

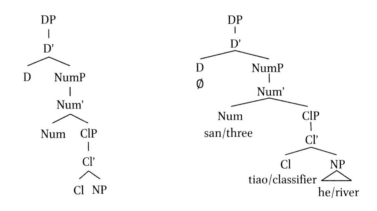

Summary

To graphically illustrate the foregoing facts, the DP is split into different layers as in (4).

4. Split DP analysis

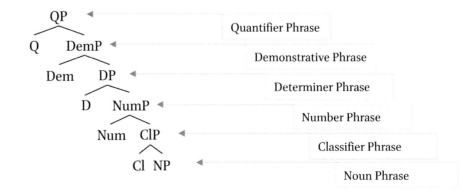

UNIT 204

Split VP Hypothesis 1

Split VP Hypothesis

The current analysis of verb phrases (VPs) has a few drawbacks. Consider the following examples.

1. Ahmed [$_{VP}$ damaged [$_{DP}$ his bike]].
2. Ahmed [$_{VP}$ smashed [$_{DP}$ his bike] [$_{PP}$ into a wall]].

The VPs in (1) and (2) are structurally drawn as in (3) and (4) respectively.

3. Tree for (1)

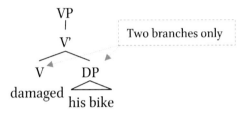

Two branches only

4. Tree for (2)

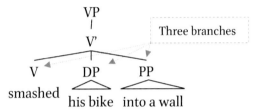

Three branches

Although all the X'-theory trees are represented in a binary branching as in (3), the branching becomes ternary when the verb takes two complements as in (4). This is an inconsistency in the X' structural representation, and it needs to be revised. The second problem follows from the fact that the two complements *his bike* and *into a wall* function as a single constituent. The two complements in (5), taken together, can be replaced by the proform *it* in (6).

5. Ahmed [$_{VP}$ smashed [$_{DP}$ his bike] [$_{PP}$ into a wall]].
6. Ahmed [$_{VP}$ smashed [it]].   *it = his bike into a wall*

7. Tree for (5)

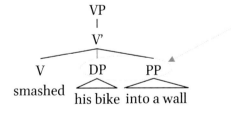

The problem follows from the fact that these two DPs are in separate nodes. If they were grouped under one node, we could substitute them both together with the proform *it*.

Another piece of evidence that these two DPs form one constituent comes from the fact that they can be coordinated with other similar constituents as in (8). Such a coordinated structure confirms that these two DPs need to be grouped under one node, not separate nodes.

8. Ahmed smashed [$_{constituent}$ his bike into a wall] and [$_{constituent}$ his kite into a tree].

All the facts above suggest that the structure of VP needs to be revised.

UNIT 205

Split VP Hypothesis II

Split VP Hypothesis

As discussed earlier, the current structure of VP with two complements, because of its ternary branching, presents problems to the X'-theory scheme. Moreover, it does not capture the constituency facts as the two complements are not combined under one node. A third piece of evidence for their constituenthood comes from binding conditions (see Carnie, 2013:413).

1. Ahmed showed Ali$_i$ himself$_i$.
2. *Ahmed showed himself$_i$ Ali$_i$

In (1), the anaphor *himself$_i$* must be bound/c-commanded by the antecedent *Ali$_i$*, but not vice versa as in (2). However, based on the binary branching structure in (3), *Ali* c-commands *himself*, and *himself* c-commands *Ali* (asymmetric c-commanding). Thus, both the sentences in (1) and (2) should be grammatical based on structure (3), yet (2) is ungrammatical.

3. Tree for (1)

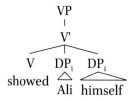

Binding conditions suggest that *Ali* must be above the anaphor *himself* in the tree for c-commanding. This high position of *Ali* will rule out (2) because *himself* will be too low in the structure to c-command *Ali*. The structure should be roughly like the one in (4).

4. Tree for (1)

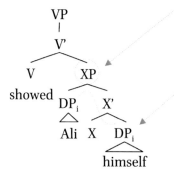

Under this new structure, all the branching is binary. Also, both the DPs *Ahmed* and *himself* are under one node (i.e. XP), thus they form one constituent.

The anaphor *himself* is also bound/c-commanded by the DP *Ali*, yielding sentence (1). *Himself* is very low in the structure and it cannot bind *Ali*, thus eliminating sentence (2).

Structure (4) is better than the one in (3) because it (i) features binary branching, (ii) respects constituenthood (both DPs under XP) and (iii) explains binding facts. But what is the XP?

UNIT 206

Split VP Hypothesis III

Split VP Hypothesis

Based on earlier findings, VP in (1) is revised and split into two layers in (2) (Larson, 1988).

1. Ternary Branch (Old Structure)   2. Binary Branch (New Structure)

Larson (1988) argues that the VP in (2) is in fact a light verb phrase (vP), whereas the XP is the big V, i.e. the VP. Thus, the tree in (2) should be revised as in (3).

3. Split VP hypothesis

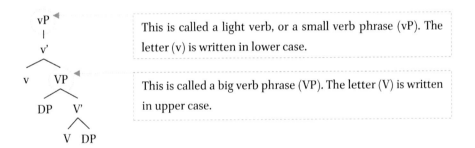

This is called a light verb, or a small verb phrase (vP). The letter (v) is written in lower case.

This is called a big verb phrase (VP). The letter (V) is written in upper case.

Thus, the structural representation of sentence (4) will be as shown in (5) and (6).

4. Ahmed [showed [$_{DP}$ Ali$_i$] [$_{DP}$ himself$_i$]]

5. DS for (4)   6. SS for (4)

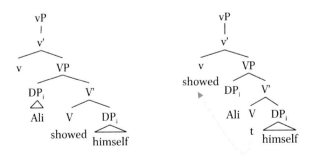

Since the verb is generated in V in (5), this yields an undesirable word order, namely *Ali showed himself*. Thus, it is proposed that the verb move from V to v. The resulting structure in (6) respects precedence, binary branching, constituenthood and binding conditions.

UNIT 207

Split VP Hypothesis IV

Split VP Hypothesis

From now on, all the verbs that take two complements, be they DP-DP, DP-PP or DP-AP as in (1) through (3) respectively, must receive the new structural representations in (4) through (6). The main verb always moves from big V to small v.

1. Ahmed [_VP_ gave [_DP_ Ali] [_DP_ a prize]]. (DP-DP complements)
2. Ahmed [_VP_ smashed [_DP_ his bike] [_PP_ into a wall]]. (DP-PP complements)
3. Ahmed [_VP_ deemed [_DP_ the story] [_AP_ very controversial]]. (DP-PP complements)

4. Tree for (1)
5. Tree for (2)
6. Tree for (3)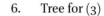

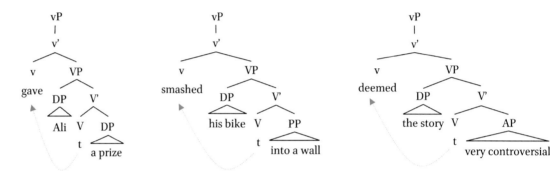

vP-Internal Subject Hypothesis

In light of the new analysis given to the VP, note that spec,vP is empty, whereas spec,VP is filled with the first complement. In the syntax literature, it has been argued that the subject (DP) starts '(or is base-generated)' in spec,vP, as in (7). It then moves from spec,vP to spec,TP to satisfy the EPP. This hypothesis is known as **vP-INTERNAL SUBJECT HYPOTHESIS**, originally proposed by Speas and Fukui (1986).

7. vP-Internal Subject Hypothesis

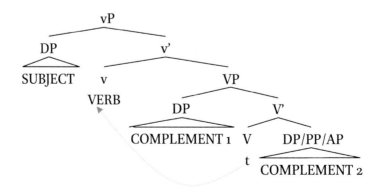

UNIT 208

Split VP Hypothesis V

vP-Internal Subject Hypothesis

One piece of evidence that the subject originates in spec,vP before it moves to spec,TP comes from **QUANTIFIER FLOAT** (Sportiche, 1988; Koopman and Sportiche, 1991). Quantifier Float is a construction where the DP moves as a pronoun out of the QP. After DP-movement, the quantifier is left behind, i.e. floating. Consider the following examples.

1. **All** the students must drink water.
2. They **all** must drink water.
3. They must **all** drink water.
4. *They must drink **all** water
5. *They must drink water **all**.

According to the examples above, it is obvious that the quantifier *all* (meaning 'all of them', i.e. the students) cannot follow the verb *drink* in (4) or the noun *water* in (5). However, it can come before the verb *drink* as in (3). This position of the quantifier *all* in (3) supports the idea that the subject appears right before the VP. The subject *they* originates in spec,vP and moves from there to spec,TP, leaving *all* behind. Consider the tree structures given to (3).

6. DS for (3) 7. SS for (3)

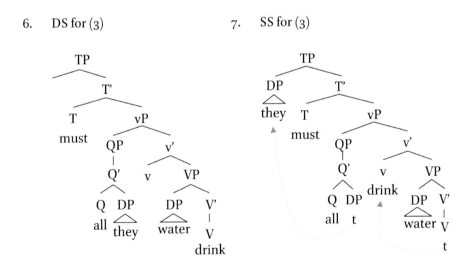

As shown in (6), the subject *all they* starts in spec,vP as a quantifier phrase. The DP then moves out of the QP to spec,TP for the EPP as in (7) (Sportiche, 1988). The quantifier *all* is left stranded before the verb *drink*. This accounts for (3), where *all* occurs before the verb, but not after the verb as in (4) or after the object as in (5). The verb *drink* must also move from V to v to generate the correct word order, namely *drink water*. Without movement, the phrase will be *water drink*. This V-to-v movement is necessary for precedence and constituency. It ensures that when verbs have two complements, they still move from V to v.

UNIT 209

Split VP Hypothesis VI

vP-Internal Subject Hypothesis

The vP-internal Subject Hypothesis states that the subject starts in spec,vP before it moves to spec,TP. The verb must move from V to v as well. Consider the two transformations below.

1. Move DP from spec,vP to spec,TP   Phrasal Movement   EPP
2. Move V to v   Head-to-Head Movement   Word Order

The two rules in (1) and (2) are theoretically motivated. Since theta role assignment must occur in a local configuration, the verb assigns an external θ-role to the subject and internal θ-roles to its complements, and both the subject and the complements must be close enough to the theta-assigning verb, i.e. in its configuration. Thus, the verb with two complements first assigns its internal θ-roles to the two objects that occur in its spec,VP and in its complement position. Since the subject is now positioned in spec,vP, the verb moves from V to v, and assigns an external θ-role to the subject. Consider sentence (3) and the subcategorization frame of the verb *smashed* in (4).

3. Ahmed has smashed his bike into the wall.

4. *smashed*, V [___ DP PP]

The derivation of (3) will be as follows.

5. DS for (3)

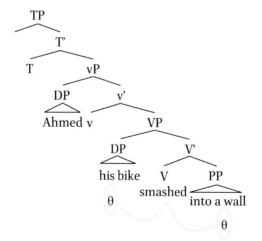

6. SS for (3)

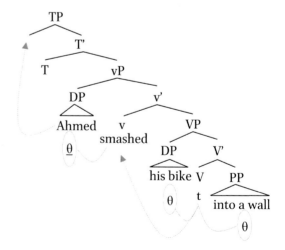

In (5), the verb *smashed* assigns two internal θ-roles to its complements (DP and PP). Then, it moves from V to v to assign an external θ-role to the subject *Ahmed*. After the theta assignment is accomplished as in (6), the subject *Ahmed* moves to spec,TP for the EPP.

UNIT 210

Split TP Hypothesis 1

Split TP Hypothesis

In the previous units, split analyses were proposed for DP and VP. To avoid unnecessary movement illustrations, we will not adopt the vP-analysis of verbs unless the verbs under investigation have two complements. As for the vP-internal subject hypothesis, we will adopt it only for theoretical motivations, and retain our view that the subject is directly positioned in spec,TP. Let us consider how TP and CP are expanded into different layers.

Split TP Hypothesis

It is well-established that the TP projects between the VP and the CP as shown in (1).

1.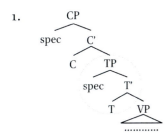

The literature of generative syntax has split TP into different layers, one of which is specified for **AGREEMENT**. In theories that precede the case-checking proposal, TP was assumed to include **AGREEMENT PHRASE** (AgrP), where the verb agrees with the subject in **PHI-FEATURES** (person, number, gender) and assigns case to it. Consider (2) through (5).

2. He runs.
   [**He:** 3rd person, singular] *agrees* with [**runs:** 3rd person, singular]

3. *He run.
   *[**He:** 3rd person, singular] *does not agree* with [**run:** 3rd person, plural]

4. They run.
   [**They:** 3rd person, plural] *agrees* with [**run:** 3rd person, plural]

5. *They runs.
   *[**They:** 3rd person, plural] *does not agree* with [**runs:** 3rd person, singular]

In English, the subjects *he* and *they* agree with the verbs *runs* and *run* as in (2) and (4) respectively. This process is known as **SUBJECT-VERB AGREEMENT**. Sentences (3) and (5) are ungrammatical because the subject-verb agreement is not established. Certain languages, such as Swahili and Fulfulde, have **OBJECT-VERB AGREEMENT** (Pawlak, 2012). Although English does not show morphological agreement between the verb and the object, it is assumed that it has an abstract object-verb agreement that we cannot see morphologically.

UNIT 211

Split TP Hypothesis 11

Split TP Hypothesis

For agreement and case, two types of agreement phrase (AgrP) have been proposed around the TP: (i) **AGREEMENT SUBJECT PHRASE** (**AgrSP**) and (ii) **AGREEMENT OBJECT PHRASE** (**AgrOP**). AgrSP is put above the TP, while AgrOP is put below the TP as shown in (1). Bear in mind that AgrPs were eventually eliminated from syntactic theory and are no longer in use.

1. Agreement Subject/Object Phrases

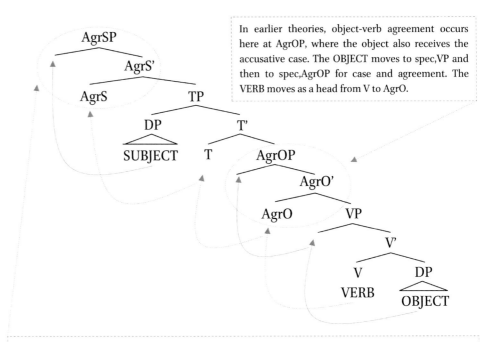

In earlier theories, object-verb agreement occurs here at AgrOP, where the object also receives the accusative case. The OBJECT moves to spec,VP and then to spec,AgrOP for case and agreement. The VERB moves as a head from V to AgrO.

Subject-verb agreement occurs here at AgrSP, where the subject also receives the nominative case. The SUBJECT moves from spec,TP to spec,AgrSP for case and agreement. The VERB keeps moving as a head from V to AgrO to T, and finally to AgrS.

Subject-verb or object-verb agreements must occur in a spec-head configuration as in (2) and (3) below. The subject and the object land in spec,AgrSP and spec,AgrOP respectively, while the head verb keeps moving from V to AgrO to T to AgrS to check the cases of the subject and the object at each destination. Despite these consecutive movements, the word order will always be preserved, i.e. Subject-Verb-Object.

2. Subject-Verb Agreement/Case 3. Object-Verb Agreement

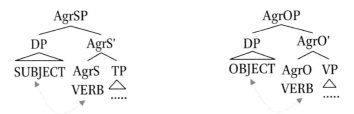

UNIT 212

Split TP Hypothesis III

Split TP Hypothesis

TP has further been expanded to include other functions like **TENSE**, **ASPECT**, and **MOOD**. **TENSE–ASPECT–MOOD**, abbreviated as TAM, is a linguistic grammatical system that regulates the expression of **TENSE** (a point in time: past, present, future), **ASPECT** (nature of time—continuous, perfect, repetitive, etc.), and **MOOD** or **MODALITY** (degree of necessity, obligation, probability, ability etc.) (Bybee et al., 1994). Cinque (1999) argues that there are 30 possible TAMs in English, thus adding two functional projections to TP: **MOOD PHRASE** (ModP) and **ASPECT PHRASE** (AspP). These phrases serve all of the 30 TAMs. From a structural perspective, TP projects over ModP, which in turn projects over AspP as in (1). The words listed in boxes below can occupy the heads T, Mod or Asp (Cinque, 1999).

1. Tense-Aspect-Mood Projections

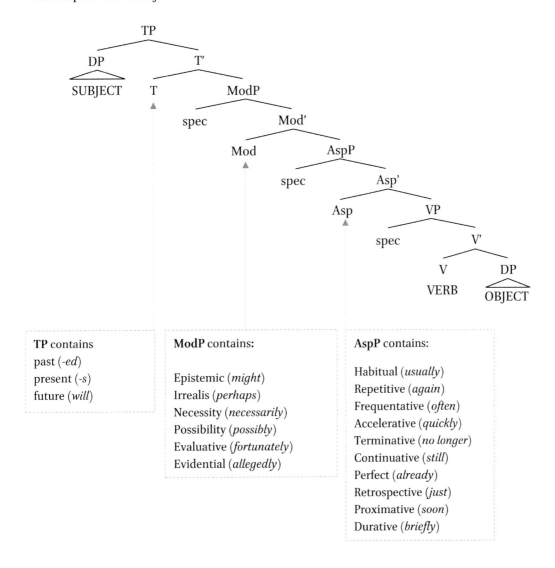

TP contains
past (*-ed*)
present (*-s*)
future (*will*)

ModP contains:

Epistemic (*might*)
Irrealis (*perhaps*)
Necessity (*necessarily*)
Possibility (*possibly*)
Evaluative (*fortunately*)
Evidential (*allegedly*)

AspP contains:

Habitual (*usually*)
Repetitive (*again*)
Frequentative (*often*)
Accelerative (*quickly*)
Terminative (*no longer*)
Continuative (*still*)
Perfect (*already*)
Retrospective (*just*)
Proximative (*soon*)
Durative (*briefly*)

UNIT 213

Split CP Hypothesis 1

Split CP Hypothesis

CP is among the functional phrases that undergo splitting analyses as well. Rizzi (1997) was the first syntactician to provide a split CP analysis. He proposed that CP be expanded into the phrases in (1).

1. **Force-Finiteness System:** Force Phrase (ForcP) > Topic Phrase* (TopP*) > Focus Phrase (FocP) > Topic Phrase* (TopP*) > Finite Phrase (FinP)   (Rizzi, 1997)

The phrases with an asterisk—such as (TopP*)—are iterative. Note the differences between Focus and Force, which are abbreviated to Foc and Forc respectively. The structural representation for (1) is given in (2).

2. Split CP hypothesis (Rizzi, 1997)

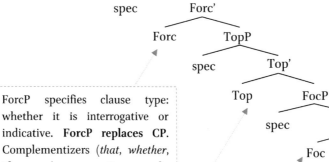

ForcP specifies clause type: whether it is interrogative or indicative. **ForcP replaces CP.** Complementizers (*that, whether, if*), yes/no questions, wh-questions appear in this projection (ForcP).

TopP hosts **topic phrases**, i.e. any old-information phrases that have already been mentioned in the context, and are moved to the front of the sentence.

FocP hosts **focused phrases**, i.e. any new-information phrases that are not known from the context, and are moved to the front of the sentence.

TopP hosts **topic phrases**, i.e. any old-information phrases that have already been mentioned in the context, and are moved to the front of the sentence.

FinP marks finiteness and hosts tense information. **FinP replaces TP** according to Rizzi's structure.

UNIT 214

Split CP Hypothesis II

Split CP Hypothesis

According to the force-finiteness system by Rizzi (1997) in (1), CP is replaced by ForcP (the highest projection), and TP is replaced by FinP (the lowest projection). Let us discuss focus and topic phrases, which are sandwiched between ForcP and FinP.

1. **Force-Finiteness System:** Force Phrase (ForcP) > Topic Phrase* (TopP*) > Focus Phrase (FocP) > Topic Phrase* (TopP*) > Finite Phrase (FinP)   (Rizzi, 1997)

To differentiate between topic and focus phrases, Rizzi indicates that both are moved to the front of the sentence for emphasis. However, **topic** brings **old information** to the front, whereas **focus** brings **new information**. Consider (2) and (3) elicited from Rizzi (1997).

2. **Your book**, you should give ___ to Paul (not to Bill).   Topic
3. **Your book** (not mine), you should give ___ to Paul.   Focus

In (2), the phrase *your book* is known to the addressee; what is not known is to whom it should be given: Paul or Bill. Thus, the phrase *your book* is considered to be a topic phrase. However, in (3), the phrase *your book* is not known to the addressee; they know that it should be given to Paul, but not that the book in question is their own book. It is new information to them; thus, the phrase *your book* in (3) is a focus phrase. According to Rizzi (1997), (2) and (3) should receive different structures as in (4) and (5).

4. Tree for (2)   5. Tree for (3)

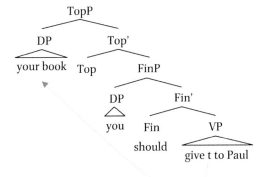
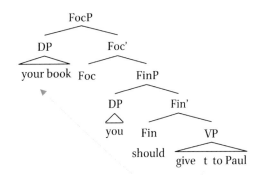

In (4), the phrase *your book*, as old information, is moved from the complement of the verb *give* to spec,TopP. The same applies to the phrase *your book* as new information; however, it moves to spec,FocP, not spec,TopP. In other words, based on whether the information is old or new, it moves to either spec,TopP or spec,FocP. It is important to note that Rizzi (1997) uses FinP rather than TP. In the coming units, we will keep using TP rather than FinP. The FinP in structures (4) and (5) is presented only to illustrate Rizzi's ideas.

UNIT 215

Split CP Hypothesis III

Split CP Hypothesis

In certain cases, all the three phrases (i.e. ForcP, TopP, FocP) in (1) appear in one example.

1. **Force-Finiteness System:** Force Phrase (ForcP) > Topic Phrase* (TopP*) > Focus Phrase (FocP) > Topic Phrase* (TopP*) > Finite Phrase (FinP)   (Rizzi, 1997)

Consider example (2) (cf. Radford, 2009:326).

2. He had seen something truly evil: prisoners being ritually raped, tortured and mutilated. He prayed *that atrocities like those*, *never again* would he witness.

According to Ratford's analysis, and as shown in the simplified structure in (3), the complementizer *that* takes the head position in ForcP. The phrase *atrocities like those* is a topic phrase because it is old information, referring to rape, torture and mutilation mentioned earlier in the sentence. As illustrated in (3), this topic phrase moves from the object position of the verb *witness* and lands in spec,TopP. As for the focus phrase *never again*, it is an adverb phrase bearing new information, thus it is moved to spec,FocP. The auxiliary *would* finally moves from head Fin to head Foc so the sentence obtains the correct word order.

3. Tree for (2)

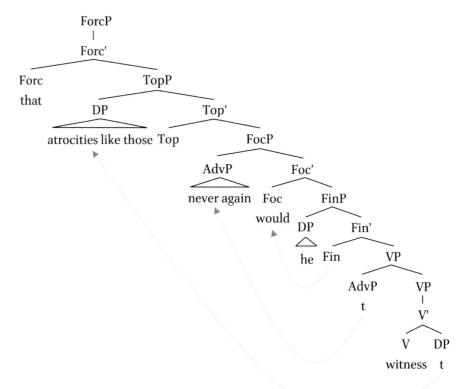

SECTION 12

Minimalist Program

∴

UNIT 216

Introduction

Minimalist Program

MINIMALIST PROGRAM (MP) is a recent framework developed by Noam Chomsky (1995) to pursue the inquiry of language. MP claims that all the variations in the world languages are only lexical (i.e. words are different), yet the syntactic structures of these languages are the same and follow Universal Grammar. Unlike earlier approaches, MP promotes economy in derivation and representation, hence the term 'minimalist'. MP minimizes principles and machinery in syntactic computation.

Chomsky (1995) modifies and eliminates many concepts and principles that were discussed earlier. As he puts it, '[T]hough the general framework remains, the modifications at each point are substantial. Concepts and principles regarded as fundamental ... are challenged and eliminated. These include the basic ideas of the Extended Standard Theory that were adopted in the [Principles and Parameters] approaches: D-Structure; S-Structure; government; the Projection Principle and the θ-Criterion; other conditions held to apply at D- and S-Structure; the Empty Category Principle; X-bar theory generally; the operation Move α; the split-I[nfl] hypothesis; and others. (...). Whether these steps are on the right track or not, of course, only time will tell' (Chomsky, 2015:9). Some of these modifications and developments will be discussed in more detail in the following units.

Minimalist Program Grammar Architecture

The MP grammar architecture is illustrated in (1).

1.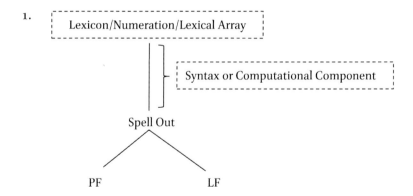

According to MP, a given sentence is built out of a number of lexical items (i.e. words) taken from the **LEXICON**. This portion of the lexicon is called the **NUMERATION** or the **LEXICAL ARRAY**. Then, the syntax applies rules and principles to construct the structure/sentence out of these lexical items, and sends it to **SPELL OUT**. At **SPELL OUT**, the structure diverges into two interfaces: **PHONETIC FORM** (= PF, for phonology) where the structure is pronounced, and **LOGICAL FORM** (= LF, for semantics) where the structure is interpreted.

UNIT 217

Feature Checking 1

Features

Unlike earlier approaches, MP is a feature-based framework stipulating that lexical items are endowed with certain features. These features play a major role in constructing structures and organizing words into well-formed phrases. They also play an important role in moving a head X or a phrase XP from one position to another.

FEATURES are 'properties of lexical elements' (den Dikken, 2000:5) or 'properties of syntactic atoms' (Adger & Svenonius, 2011:2). In MP, every word is endowed with information from three sources: phonology (how the word is pronounced), semantics (how the word is interpreted) and morpho-syntax (the property/category of the word and how it is distributed). Thus, a word can be a composition of several features as in (1) below.

1. *A word may include*
   PHONOLOGICAL FEATURES: voicing, manner, place features etc.
   Examples: [voice], [labial], [sonorant], [consonantal], [back], [high], [low], etc.

   SEMANTIC FEATURES: the semantic properties of an entity in the world.
   Examples: [human], [adult], [animate], [male], etc.

   MORPHOSYNTACTIC FEATURES: categories, gender, person, number, tense, case etc.
   Examples: [N], [V], [masculine], [3rd person], [plural], [past], [nominative] etc.

Since we are concerned with morphology (how a word is inflected) and syntax (how the word is distributed), we will focus only on **MORPHOSYNTACTIC FEATURES** such as [N], [plural], [past], [nominative], etc. According to MP, features can be of two types: **INTERPRETABLE** and **UNINTERPRETABLE**. Interpretable features are features that have meaning at the semantic interface LF. This feature is put between two square brackets as [F], where [F] means 'feature'. Uninterpretable features have no meaning, and they are abbreviated as [uF], where [u] means 'uninterpretable'. Both interpretable and uninterpretable features occur in the syntax.

However, after the structure is sent to LF, every element must receive interpretation/meaning. This is based on a principle known as **FULL INTERPRETATION** given in (2).

2. **FULL INTERPRETATION:** every element at the semantic interface LF must receive interpretation/meaning.

Because interpretable features already have meaning, they cause no problem at LF. However, uninterpretable features have no meaning, so they will violate the principle in (2). These uninterpretable features must be removed during syntactic derivation before they reach LF, but how?

UNIT 218

Feature Checking II

Feature Checking

We have argued that lexical items enter syntax bearing multiple morphosyntactic features. These features can either be interpretable [F], or uninterpretable [uF]. These [F] vs [uF] are only representative, and they might be [Past] vs. [uPast], [Plural] vs. [uPlural], etc. Because of the Full Interpretation in (1), all uninterpretable features must be removed during the syntactic derivation before they reach LF and cause a problem, i.e. make the sentence ungrammatical.

1. **FULL INTERPRETATION**: every element at LF must receive interpretation.

The removal of uninterpretable features is achieved via a mechanism called **FEATURE CHECKING**, where 'checking' means 'deleting'. Feature checking establishes a relationship between two matching features: the uninterpretable feature [uF] is checked against another matching interpretable feature [F]. If an uninterpretable feature [uF] is checked, it is deleted, indicated by a strikethrough [~~uF~~]. The deletion of an uninterpretable feature [~~uF~~] will cause no problem at LF, because it does not violate the Full Interpretation in (1), and it now receives meaning from another interpretable feature [F] via feature checking.

Feature checking can be done via the approach **AGREE** given in (2). Agree can be induced between two matching features: one is called **PROBE** (it is the feature that searches and requests to agree) and **GOAL** (the feature that accepts to agree with the requesting feature).

2. Agree approach
    A feature [uF] (probe) agrees with another matching feature [F] (goal) iff
    i. [uF] c-commands [F] (remember that [uF] and [F] are features of the same type)
    ii. There is no matching feature $[F_x]$ checking against [uF] that is closer to [uF] than [F] is.

The closeness condition in (2ii) is defined in (3).

3. Closeness
    $[F_x]$ is closer to [uF] iff
    i. [uF] c-commands both [F] and $[F_x]$ (see tree 5)
    ii. $[F_x]$ c-commands [F] but [F] does not c-command $[F_x]$. (see tree 5)

Thus, Agree between [uF] and [F] can be established as illustrated in (4), but not as in (5).

4. This is a possible Agree 5. This is not a possible Agree

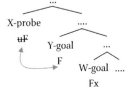
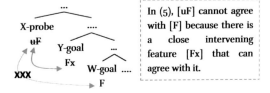

In (5), [uF] cannot agree with [F] because there is a close intervening feature [Fx] that can agree with it.

UNIT 219

Feature Checking III

Feature Checking

We have concluded that feature checking is accomplished via Agree (i.e. a c-commanding relationship between two matching features). We can therefore expect feature checking to be accomplished under **SISTERHOOD** as well, because sisters c-command each other. If two constituents are sisters, one of which has [uF] and the other has [F], feature checking can occur between these two features because one sister must c-command the other. This local configuration is known as **FEATURE CHECKING CONFIGURATION**. There are three possible feature checking configurations where two constituents become sisters:

1. Head-Head Configuration
2. Head-Complement Configuration
3. Specifier-Head Configuration

Let us examine the first configuration in (4) below.

4. **HEAD-HEAD CONFIGURATION**

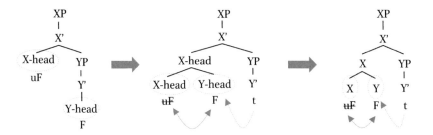

In (4), the head Y moves and adjoins the head X. Thus, Y and X become sisters. This head-to-head movement constitutes what is known as a head-head configuration, where feature checking can be accomplished. The feature [uF] on X can c-command the [F] on Y and agree with it. Thus, [uF] is checked and deleted under sisterhood.

Also, feature checking can still be accomplished if [uF] is on Y while [F] is on X, i.e. the reverse situation. There will be no problem because adjoined heads always c-command each other. The [uF] on Y can c-command the [F] on X and agree with it. Thus, [uF] is checked and deleted as shown in (5) below.

5. **HEAD-HEAD CONFIGURATION**

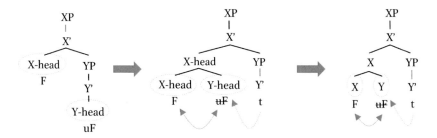

UNIT 220

Feature Checking IV

Feature Checking

The second configuration where feature checking occurs is the head-complement configuration as in (1).

1. **HEAD-COMPLEMENT CONFIGURATION**

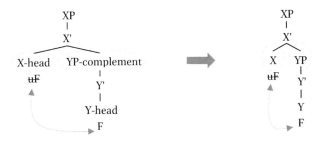

In (1), X is a head and YP is its complement (= they are sisters). The head X has [uF], and its complement YP has [F], on its head Y. In this head-complement configuration, feature checking occurs. The [uF] on the head X c-commands the [F] inside the complement YP and agrees with it. Thus, [uF] is checked and deleted under sisterhood.

If the uninterpretable feature [uF] is inside the complement YP, and the interpretable feature [F] is on the head X as in (2), there will be a problem in the c-commanding relationship. The [uF] is embedded in the complement YP, and cannot c-command the [F] on the head X. Agree cannot be accomplished, i.e. the [uF] cannot be checked and deleted. The solution comes from **FEATURE PERCOLATION**, proposed by Lieber (1980). Feature percolation simply assumes that the feature(s) on the head Y can percolate and rise to the phrase level YP. Thus, we assume that the [uF] percolates/rises from the head Y to the phrase YP. Then, the [uF] can be checked because it c-commands the [F] on X and agrees with it.

2. **HEAD-COMPLEMENT CONFIGURATION**

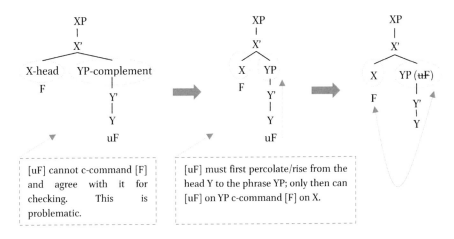

UNIT 221

Feature Checking v

Feature Checking

The third configuration where features can be checked under sisterhood is the specifier-head configuration as in (1).

1. **SPEC-HEAD CONFIGURATION**

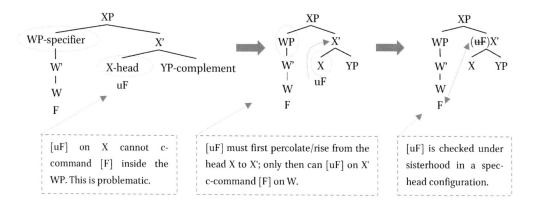

Feature checking can occur under sisterhood in a spec-head configuration. Although the specifier WP is clearly not a sister to the head X, Boblajik (1996) claims that WP is a sister to X', which is a projection of X. In (1), if the head X has the [uF] and the specifier WP has [F], there will be a problem in the c-commanding relationship. The [uF] cannot c-command the [F] inside the WP. For that reason we propose that the [uF] percolate from the head X to the X' level. After percolation, the [uF] on the X' can c-command the [F] inside the WP and agree with it. Thus, [uF] is checked and deleted.

What is the situation when the reverse occurs, i.e. when the [uF] appears inside the specifier WP, and the [F] is on the head X as shown in (2)? Under such circumstances, the [uF] must percolate from the head W and rise to the phrase level WP. Therefore, [uF] on the WP can c-command the [F] on the head X and agree with it. The [uF] is then checked and deleted.

2. **SPEC-HEAD CONFIGURATION**

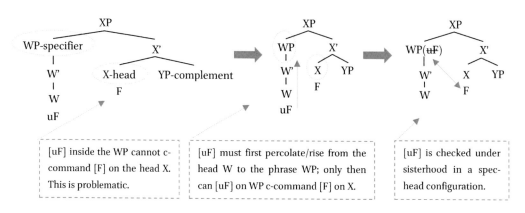

UNIT 222

Feature Checking VI

Feature Checking

To summarize, lexical items enter the syntax endowed with features. These features can be interpretable [F] (e.g. [plural], [past], [nominative] etc.) or uninterpretable [uF] (e.g. [uplural], [upast], [unominative] etc.). When the structure is sent to LF (for semantics), the full interpretation principle requires that every item (words or features) must have meaning. Thus, because the uninterpretable features [uF] have no meaning, they need to be removed during the syntax before they reach LF; otherwise, the structure will crash. The removal of these uninterpretable features [uF] can be done via Agree as in (1).

1. Agree approach
    A feature [uF] (probe) agrees with another matching feature [F] (goal) iff
    i.   [uF] c-commands [F]
    ii. There is no matching feature [F_x] checking against [uF] that is closer to [uF] than [F] is.

Thus, any [uF] can be checked and deleted if it c-commands a matching interpretable feature [F] below it. This can be done even if [uF] is far away from [F] in the structure as in (2).

2.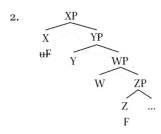

Another direct way to check [uF] is via sisterhood as in (3). In the coming units, however, we will not show how features percolate for every case. We will always assume that feature percolation occurs when necessary; thus, we will keep it simple as in (4), (5) and (6).

3. **Checking under Sisterhood**
    An uninterpretable feature [uF] on a syntactic element, Y, is checked when Y is sister to another syntactic element, Z, which bears a matching interpretable feature [F] (Adger, 2003:67). There are three configurations for checking under sisterhood: (i) head-head as in (4), (ii) head-complement as in (5) or (iii) spec-head as in (6).

4. Head-Head   5. Head-Complement   6. Spec-Head

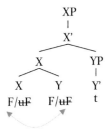 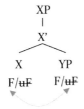 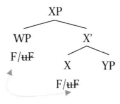

UNIT 223

Category Features

Category Features

To demonstrate the ideas discussed earlier, MP proposes that words bear features that represent their categories, i.e. their parts of speech. If a word is a noun, it bears a **CATEGORY FEATURE** [N]. If a given word is a verb, an adjective, a preposition or a determiner etc., we assume that it has a **CATEGORY FEATURE** such as [V], [A], [P] or [D]. In short, category features are the features attached to lexical items that tell us what category those lexical items belong to. Category features are interpretable because they add meaning to the lexical items they are associated with. Being interpretable, they must be written as [N], [V], [A], [P], [D] etc. Consider the following examples.

1. A journalist wrote these wonderful reports.
2. A journalist reports on the issue.

Sentence (1) consists of six lexical items: *A* (D), *journalist* (N), *wrote* (V), *these* (D), *wonderful* (A), and *reports* (N). There are six lexical items in sentence (2) as well: *A* (D), *journalist* (N), *reports* (V), *on* (P), *the* (D), and *issue* (N). Note that the lexical item *reports* is a noun in (1) but a verb in (2), although they are written alike. The syntactic position of such a lexical item determines its category. In the syntactic structure of sentences (1) and (2), it is assumed that each lexical item bears an interpretable category feature that it belongs to, i.e. [N], [V], [A], [P], or [D]. The structures (3) and (4) are given to (1) and (2) respectively.

3. Tree for (1)

4. Tree for (2)

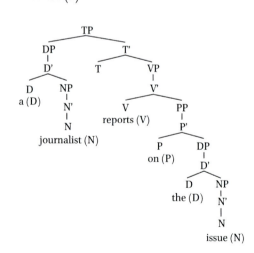

Notice that each word is endowed with a category feature. Although the features should technically be written between square brackets [D], [N], [V], [A], [P], the software used to draw these structures does not allow the use of the square brackets [ ]; thus, they are written between round brackets, e.g. (D), (N), (V), (A) and (P).

UNIT 224

Subcategorization Features 1

Categorization Selectional Features

We learned in Unit 19 and 20 that a lexical item may select one or more complements. The complement selection is known as subcategorization. Such information is written in subcategorization frames as shown in (1) for the verb *destroy*.

1. *destroy*, V [___ DP]

2. He destroyed the city.
3. *He destroyed.

As in (2), the verb *destroy* must select a DP, i.e. *the city*. If not, the sentence becomes ungrammatical as in (3). Thus, in (1), the verb *destroy* requires DP as a complement.

Complement selection, or subcategorization, can also be reduced to features. Since a lexical item has an interpretable category feature such as [N], [V], [A] or [P], we can assume that they also bear **CATEGORIZATION SELECTIONAL FEATURES** (shortened to **C-SELECTIONAL FEATURES**). These features are also known as **SUBCATEGORIZATION FEATURES** (shortened to **SUBCAT FEATURES**). Subcat features such as [uN], [uV], [uA], [uP], [uD] etc. are always uninterpretable. We can put these subcategorization features within the subcategorization frames. For example, subcategorization frames can be revised following the format in (4). (1) should be revised as in (5).

4. Word   category feature   subcategorization feature
5. *destroy*   [V]   [uD]

The subcategorization information in (5) means that the lexical item *destroy* is a verb because it has an interpretable category feature [V]. It also means that this verb *destroy* must select a determiner phrase because it has an uninterpretable subcat feature [uD]. Being uninterpretable, the feature [uD] needs to be checked against a matching interpretable feature [D], either by Agree or sisterhood. Otherwise, it will cause the derivation to crash at LF.

The uninterpretable feature [uD] stipulates that the verb *destroy* must select a DP because only determiners have interpretable category features [D]. If the verb *destroy* (that has an uninterpretable subcat feature [uD]) selected a DP (that has an interpretable category feature [D]), we would expect the [uD] on the verb to be checked against the feature [D] of the determiner. This would remove the [uD] from the verb, making the sentence grammatical.

If the verb *destroy* did not select a DP, this would definitely make the sentence ungrammatical as in (3). The sentence would become ungrammatical because the feature [uD] on the verb is not checked by any means; there is no determiner phrase (with [D]) close to the verb that can check its subcat feature [uD] and remove it.

UNIT 225

Subcategorization Features 11

Categorization Selectional Features

To reiterate the foregoing, a lexical item might have two features. The first one is an interpretable category feature such as [N], [V], [A], [P], [D] etc., which decides its category as a noun, a verb, an adjective, a preposition or a determiner. The second feature is an uninterpretable subcat feature such as [uN], [uV], [uA], [uP], [uD] etc., which decides the category of the complement it selects. Suppose we have the subcategorization frames in (2) and (3).

1. Lexical Item   Interpretable Category Feature   Uninterpretable Subcat Feature
2. *Destroy*   [V]   [uD]
3. *the*   [D]   to be discussed later

As for category features, the lexical item *destroy* is a verb bearing [V]; *the* is a determiner bearing [D]. We know that the verb *destroy* selects DP as a complement. Thus, we represent this complement selection with an uninterpretable subcat feature, [uD], on the verb. The syntactic tree for the following verb phrase *destroy the city* will be as shown in (4).

4. Tree for the VP *destroy the city*   5. Tree for the VP *destroy the city*

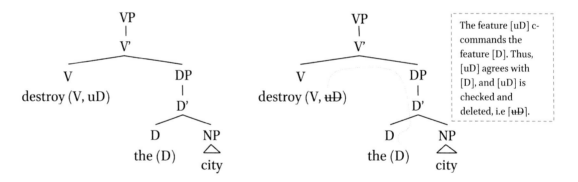

As shown in (4), the verb *destroy* has two features: [V] and [uD]. However, the determiner *the* has [D]. The feature [uD] is problematic for LF because it violates the Full Interpretation. It needs to be checked and removed. The [uD] on the verb *destroy* can be checked against the [D] on the determiner *the* and removed. This can be done either under sisterhood (in a head-complement configuration) or via Agree, where the probe (feature [uD]) c-commands a goal (an interpretable feature [D]) and agrees with it according to the conditions in (6). The [uD] is then checked and deleted as in (5) above.

6. **Agree approach**
   A feature [uF] (probe) agrees with another matching feature [F] (goal) iff
   i. [uF] c-commands [F]
   ii. There is no matching feature [F$_x$] checking against [uF] that is closer to [uF] than [F] is.

UNIT 226

Subcategorization Features III

Categorization Selectional Features

We have learned that MP executes complement selection via feature checking. A lexical item can have an uninterpretable subcat feature [uF] that must be checked by selecting a complement that has an interpretable category feature [F]. Consider the following phrases.

1. [N destruction [PP [P of [DP [D the [NP city]
2. [A afraid] [PP of [DP [D the [NP city]

The lexical items in (1) and (2) are *destruction* (N), *afraid* (A), *of* (P), *the* (D) and *city* (N). We assume that they have interpretable category features: [N] for *destruction*, [A] for *afraid*, [P] for *of*, [D] for *the* and [N] for *city*. Each lexical item in (1) and (2) selects a complement. Both the noun *destruction* and the adjective *afraid* select PP. We assume that each of them has an uninterpretable subcat feature [uP]. As for the preposition *of*, it selects a DP, thus we assume that it has an uninterpretable subcat feature [uD]. The determiner *the* selects NP, thus it has [uN]. The subcategorization frames for these lexical items can be summarized in (3).

3. | Lexical Item | Interp. Category Feature | Uninterp. Subcat Feature |
   |---|---|---|
   | destruction | [N] | [uP] |
   | afraid | [A] | [uP] |
   | of | [P] | [uD] |
   | the | [D] | [uN] |
   | city | [N] | nothing (no complement) |

All the uninterpretable subcat features ([uP], [uD], [uN]) will be problematic at LF and need to be checked and removed during the syntactic derivation. They can be checked against the interpretable category features of their complements ([P], [D] and [N]) either under sisterhood (in a head-complement configuration) or via Agree as shown below.

4. Tree for (1) 5. Tree for (2) and (3)

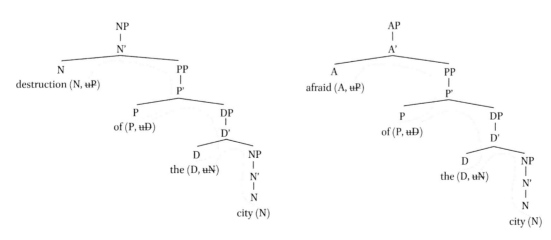

UNIT 227

Subcategorization Features IV

Categorization Selectional Features

Let us derive a full sentence and show how complement selection is represented in MP via a feature checking approach.

1. The professor will deliver a lecture quickly.

Each word in (1) has an interpretable category feature: [D] for *the*, [N] for *professor*, [T] for *will*, [V] for *deliver*, [D] for *a*, [N] for *lecture*, [Adv] for *quickly*. As for complement selection, the determiners *the* and *a* select NP, thus having an uninterpretable subcat feature [uN]. The tense word *will* selects VP, so it has [uV]. The verb *delivered* selects DP; therefore, it has [uD]. The word *quickly* is an adjunct, thus it does not select any complement. The subcategorization frames of the lexical items in (1) are summarized as follows.

2. | Lexical Item | Interp. Category Feature | Uninterp. Subcategorization Feature |
   |---|---|---|
   | *the/a* | [D] | [uN] |
   | *professor/lecture* | [N] | nothing (no complement) |
   | *will* | [T] | [uV] |
   | *deliver* | [V] | [uD] |
   | *quickly* | [Adv] | nothing (no complement) |

In MP, sentence (1) is represented as in (3).

3. Tree for (1)

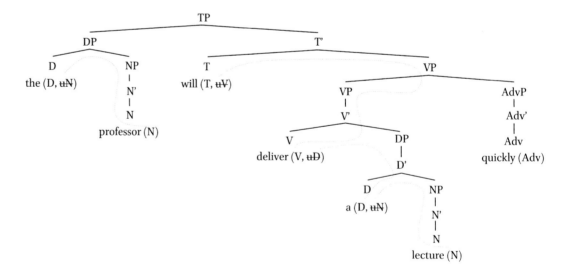

Although this is how complement selection is represented by features in MP, we will not show these technicalities in the future units, where the focus will be on other features instead.

UNIT 228

Feature-Driven Movements I

Minimalist Program

In the 1980s, many transformational rules were proposed. Consider the **head-to-head movements** or **phrasal movements** we discussed earlier.

1. Move V to T   Head-to-Head Movement   Verb-Movement
2. Move T to C   Head-to-Head Movement   Yes/No Question
3. Move DP to Spec,CP   Phrasal Movement   Wh-Question
4. Move XP to adjoin TP Phrasal Movement   Adjunction Rule
5. Move DP to Spec,TP   Phrasal Movement   Passive
6. Move CP to Spec,TP   Phrasal Movement   EPP

The earlier approaches proposed that an element move from a given position to a landing site simply because it can move. Thus, movements are free and do not need independent motivation. As long as the structure requires a specific word order, we move elements from one position to another.

However, in the 1990s, MP challenged this stance and proposed that every movement must be theoretically motivated. An element in the structure cannot move unless there is a valid reason that drives it to move. That is, we need to understand why auxiliaries, modals, and *do*-forms move from T to C in yes/no questions, or why the *wh*-words move from their positions to spec,CP in wh-questions. There must be something that prompts those elements to move to these specific landing sites. MP attempts to provide a motivation for such movements.

For this reason, MP proposes that every movement must be driven by features. If an element moves from a given position to a certain landing site, this is because the landing site has a feature that attracts a head X or a phrase XP bearing a matching feature to its configuration. Either the moved element or the landing site must have an uninterpretable feature that needs to be checked by an interpretable matching feature found on the other one. All feature checking that motivates movements can be done under **SISTERHOOD** in a special feature checking configuration as discussed earlier. There are three configurations as shown in (7) through (9).

7. Head-Head   8. Head-Complement   9. Spec-Head

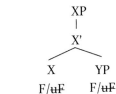
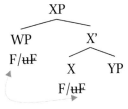

UNIT 229

Feature-Driven Movements II

Minimalist Program

Suppose we have the following structure in (1).

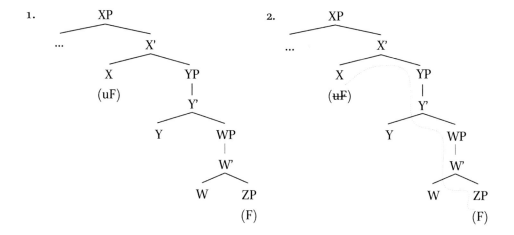

According to the **AGREE** approach, feature [uF] on X can simply agree with feature [F] on ZP because X c-commands ZP as shown in (2). Thus, feature [uF] is checked and deleted. For this reason, one might assume that there will be no need for the movement of ZP to spec,XP for feature checking as long as Agree can reach across a long distance. However, MP proposes that **AGREE** should not be enough if an uninterpretable feature is strong. Uninterpretable features can differ in terms of **STRENGTH**. They can be either (i) **WEAK** uninterpretable features written as [uF], or (ii) **STRONG** uninterpretable features written as [*uF] (with an asterisk). Weak uninterpretable features can be checked by **AGREE** as in (2) above. However, strong uninterpretable feature [*uF] must be checked in a special configuration: (i) head-head, (ii) head-complement or (ii) spec-head. Thus, if X has a strong uninterpretable feature [*uF] as in (3) below, the element ZP that has the interpretable feature [F] must move to spec,XP to check this strong feature in a spec-head configuration as in (4).

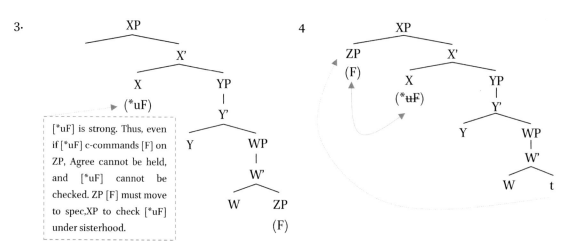

UNIT 230

Feature-Driven Movements III

Feature-Driven Movements

To sum up, features can be (i) interpretable [F] or (ii) uninterpretable [uF]. Uninterpretable features can be (i) weak [uF], needing to be checked by Agree or under sisterhood, or (ii) strong [*uF], needing to be checked under sisterhood in a special configuration head-head, head-complement or spec-head. This summary can be illustrated in (1) below.

1. Feature Checking

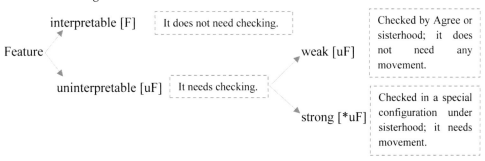

Feature-Driven Movement

To illustrate how strong uninterpretable features [*uF] cause movement, consider (2).

2. Is Ahmed ___ coming?

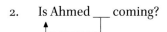

3. Move T to C   Head-to-Head Movement   Yes/No Question

To generate (2), it is argued that, as shown in (4), the head C is endowed with an interpretable question feature, namely [Q]. C does not have this feature when the CP is indicative, for example a statement such as a *that*-clause. C has [Q] only if the structure is a question, because [Q] adds an interrogative meaning to the whole CP. The auxiliary *is* in (4) is endowed with a strong uninterpretable feature [*uQ]. This strong uninterpretable feature [*uQ] needs to be checked; thus, it has to move to an appropriate checking configuration, in this case a T-C configuration, where it is checked against the interpretable feature on C as shown in (5).

4. Tree for (2) before checking   5. Tree for (2) after checking

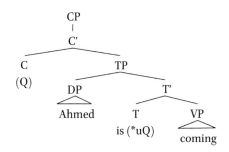
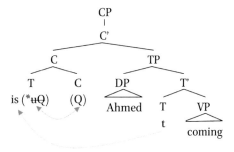

UNIT 231

Feature-Driven Movements IV

Feature-Driven Movements

As discussed earlier, yes/no questions are formed because the head C has an interpretable feature [Q], and the auxiliary T has a strong uninterpretable feature *[uQ]. This strong feature [*uQ] moves from the head T to the head C [Q], yielding the appropriate configuration for checking: a head-head configuration. As a result, the feature [*uQ] is checked. Wh-questions follow the same ideas as in (2).

1. Ahmed *is* buying what?
2. What *is* Ahmed ___ buying ___ ?

3. Move T to C   Head-to-Head Movement   Yes/No Question
4. Move DP to spec,CP   Phrasal Movement   Wh-Question

In (2), it is assumed that the head C has two interpretable features, [Q] and [WH], which add interrogative meaning to the CP. The auxiliary *is* will move with its feature [*uQ] from T to C to check it against the [Q] on C in a **head-head configuration**. The wh-word *what* will have a strong uninterpretable feature [*uWH]. Thus, it will also move from its position to spec,CP to check its feature against [WH] on C in another checking configuration: a **spec-head configuration**. This is shown in (5) and (6).

5. Tree for (2) before checking

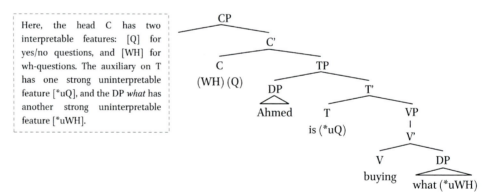

6. Tree for (2) after checking

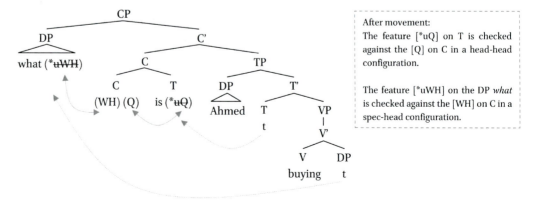

UNIT 232

Feature-Driven Movements V

Feature-Driven Movements

Strong features can also be used to motivate the EPP expressed in (1).

1. **Extended Projection Principle (EPP):** All sentences/clauses must have a subject. Technically speaking, spec,TP must be filled.

According to the EPP, a sentence must have a subject as in (2); otherwise it will be ungrammatical as in (3).

2. **Ahmed** plays football.
3. *plays football.

We have discussed many ways to satisfy the EPP. The EPP can simply be satisfied by an apparent subject as in (2). However, the subject position is sometimes filled with the expletive *it* or *there* as in (4) and (5) respectively; with CP as in (6); with the object of an unaccusative verb as in the passive structure in (7); with an embedded DP as in the raising structure in (8); or with PRO as in the control construction in (9).

4. [$_{DP}$ It] is likely that he left. (Expletive *it*)
5. [$_{DP}$ There] exist many solutions. (Expletive *there*)

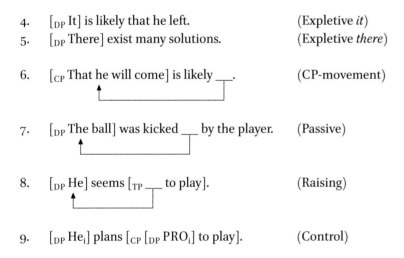

6. [$_{CP}$ That he will come] is likely ___. (CP-movement)

7. [$_{DP}$ The ball] was kicked ___ by the player. (Passive)

8. [$_{DP}$ He] seems [$_{TP}$ ___ to play]. (Raising)

9. [$_{DP}$ He$_i$] plans [$_{CP}$ [$_{DP}$ PRO$_i$] to play]. (Control)

All the different mechanisms of expletive-insertion, DP/CP-movement or PRO base-generation in (4) through (9) are proposed to fill spec,TP and satisfy the EPP. Thus, one might propose a strong uninterpretable EPP feature [*uEPP] on the head T. This feature [*uEPP] attracts DP or CP to spec,TP, and in certain cases requires the insertion of a DP-expletive or PRO. However, we know that DP/CP does not have an interpretable [EPP] feature, and there is no justification for having such a feature on them to check the [*uEPP]. Since most of the elements filling spec,TP are DPs, DPs already have [D] as an interpretable category feature. It is therefore proposed that the strong uninterpretable feature on T be [*uD], not [*uEPP]. During the syntactic derivation, this [*uD] on T can be checked under sisterhood in a spec-head configuration by any element that has the interpretable feature [D].

UNIT 233

Feature-Driven Movements VI

Feature-Driven Movements

To illustrate the satisfaction of the EPP under the feature approach, consider the sentence in (1) and its tree structures in (2) and (3).

1. The kids are sleeping.

2. Tree for (1) before checking   3. Tree for (1) after checking

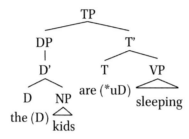 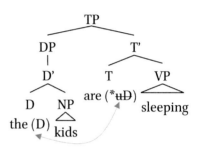

In (1), the DP *the kids* is the subject of the sentence, satisfying the EPP. In its structural representation in (2), the head T has a strong uninterpretable feature [*uD] that represents the EPP, which requires spec,TP to be filled with an element having an interpretable feature [D]. The DP is known to have an interpretable feature [D], which is the category feature of the determiner *the*. This feature [D] checks the strong feature [*uD] under sisterhood in a spec-head configuration as in (3). The EPP is now satisfied, and its feature [*uD] is successfully removed from the syntax. The same applies to expletive-insertion in (4) below.

4. It is likely that he left.

5. Tree for (4) before checking   6. Tree for (4) after checking

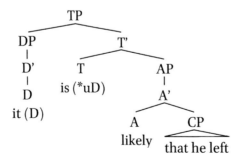 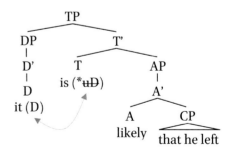

Although the expletive *it* has no semantic content, its category feature [D] is interpretable. [D] is a category feature and has nothing to do with the meaning of the word *it*. Under sisterhood, and in a spec-head configuration, [D] checks [*uD] and deletes it. The same analysis applies to the DP-expletive *there* (e.g. 5 in Unit 232).

UNIT 234

Feature-Driven Movements VII

Feature-Driven Movements

A potential problem follows from the CP-satisfaction of the EPP as in (1) represented in (3).

1. [$_{CP}$ That he will come] is likely ___.

2. Move CP to Spec,TP   Phrasal Movement   EPP

3. Tree for (1)

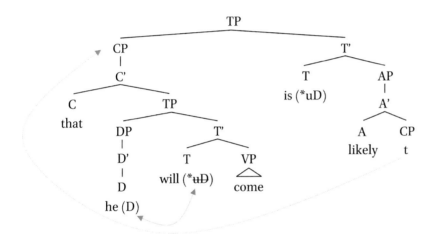

In (3), there are two spec,TPs, so two instances of the EPP must be satisfied. Thus, we have two instances of strong [*uD]: on the head T *is* of the matrix clause, and on the head T *will* of the embedded clause CP. The feature [*uD] in the embedded clause can be easily checked by the [D] of the subject *he* in spec,TP as shown in (3). However, it is not clear what checks the [*uD] on the head T *is*. The solution to this problem is to assume that the feature [*uD] on T percolates to T' and gets checked by the same feature [D] under sisterhood as in (4).

4.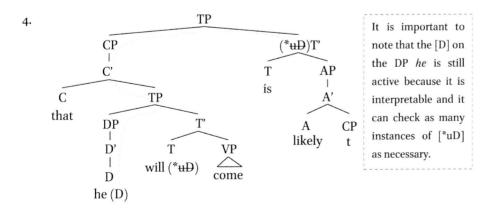

It is important to note that the [D] on the DP *he* is still active because it is interpretable and it can check as many instances of [*uD] as necessary.

UNIT 235

Feature-Driven Movements VIII

Feature-Driven Movements

Consider the passive constructions in (1), where the DP *the ball* having the [D] moves from the complement position to spec,TP to check [*uD] on T as shown in (2) below.

1. [DP The ball] was kicked ___ by the player.   (passive)

2. Tree for (1) after checking

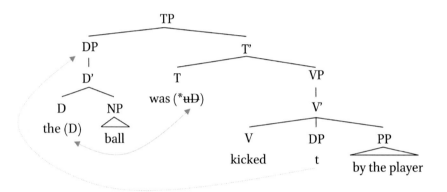

As for the raising constructions in (3), it is assumed that there are two strong features [*uD] as in (4): one is on the non-finite T (where the infinitival *to* occurs) and the other is on the finite T. The DP *he* having the category feature [D] can check both the lower and higher [*uD] at the same time as in (5).

3. [DP he] seems [TP ___ to play].   (Raising)

4. Tree for (3) after checking lower [*uD]

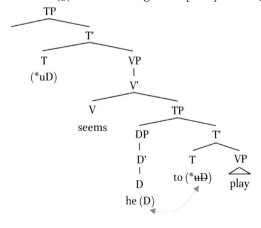

5. Tree for (3) after checking higher [*uD]

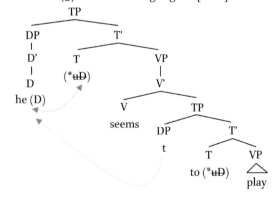

UNIT 236

Feature-Driven Movements IX

Feature-Driven Movements

Consider the control constructions in (1), and notice how the DP (PRO) satisfies EPP.

1. [$_{DP}$ He$_i$] plans [$_{CP}$ [$_{DP}$ PRO$_i$] to play football].   (Control)

In control constructions, there will be two strong features of [*uD] as in (2). One is on the non-finite T *to* and is checked by the unpronounced pronoun PRO, which is DP and has an interpretable feature [D]. The other is on the finite T and it is checked by the pronounced pronoun DP *he*. These feature checking operations are shown in (2).

2. Tree for (1)

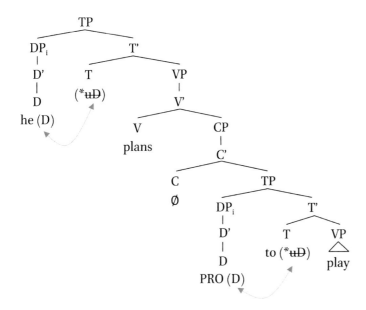

Summary of EPP Checking

In MP, the EPP is reduced to a strong uninterpretable feature [*uD] that is found either on the finite or the non-finite head T, or both. In both positions, this feature [*uD] is checked under sisterhood in a spec-head configuration by the interpretable category feature [D], which is only found on DPs. Sometimes the same DP checks two instances of [*uD] as in raising constructions or constructions beginning with CP. In other cases, and regardless of their semantic contents, the expletives *it/there* and the unpronounced PRO in control constructions also check [*uD] because they are simply DPs with an interpretable category feature [D].

UNIT 237

Agreement and Case I

Feature-Driven Movements

We have covered different types of morphosyntactic features, including interpretable category features, uninterpretable subcategorization features and the EPP feature [*uD]. Phi-features, technically written as φ-features, are a set of features that includes NUMBER, GENDER and PERSON. In English, any noun is either singular (SG) or plural (PL) in number, e.g. *man* vs. *men*. As for gender, a noun is either masculine (MASC) or feminine (FEM), e.g. *man* vs. *woman*. The person feature is specific to pronouns, and it distinguishes between the speaker (1st person such as *I* and *we*), the addressee (2nd person such as *you*) and others (3rd person such as *he, she, it* and *they*). In addition to phi-features, there are **CASE** features. English only has three cases: nominative (NOM) for subjects (e.g. [*he*] came), accusative (ACC) for objects of the verb or the preposition (e.g. met [*him*] or to [*him*]) or genitive (GEN) for the possessor (e.g. [*his*] book). Consider the summary given below.

1. φ-Features plus Case Features
   Number: [SG] = *man*   [PL] = *men*
   Gender: [MASC] = *man*   [FEM] = *woman*
   Person: [1st] = *I, we* [2nd] = *you*   [3rd] = *he/she/it/they*
   Case: [NOM] = *he*   [ACC] = *him*   [GEN] = *his*

The φ-features manifest themselves in **SUBJECT-VERB AGREEMENT**, where the verb agrees with the subject in number, gender and person. These agreement markers can be MORPHOLOGICAL (i.e. we see them on the verb as affixes or morphological changes) or ABSTRACT (we do not see their morphology). In all the examples below, only sentences that show subject-verb agreement are grammatical as in (2) and (3), but those that fail to induce agreement between the subject and the verb are ungrammatical as in (4) and (5).

2. He runs.
3. They run-∅.
4. *They runs.
5. *He run-∅.

In (2), the verb *runs* agrees with the singular 3rd person pronoun *he* and takes the singular 3rd person suffix -s. In (3), the verb *run-∅* agrees with the plural 3rd person plural pronoun *they* and takes the plural suffix -∅. In (4) and (5), the verbs *runs* and *run* do not agree with the subjects *they* and *he* respectively. Although the agreement in (2) and (3) is based on number and person (in this case singular and 3rd person), it is assumed that the agreement is also held for gender; however, gender in English does not manifest itself morphologically on the verb. Thus, in every subject-verb agreement, we assume that the verb fully agrees with the subject in all the phi-features (number, gender and person). If a feature does not manifest itself morphologically on the verb, we assume it to be abstract.

UNIT 238

Agreement and Case II

Feature-Driven Movements

Subject-verb agreement is established under sisterhood in a spec-head configuration. The φ-features are interpretable on the subject because DPs (functioning as subjects) add meanings related to number, gender and person to the whole structure. Thus, we can represent the interpretable φ-features on the subject DP as [φ]. However, the φ-features on the verb do not add any meaning; they are thus uninterpretable, and are represented as [uφ]. The uninterpretable φ–features [uφ] on the verb are checked by the interpretable features [φ] on the subject in a spec-head configuration as represented in (2) and (3) for sentence (1).

1. He runs

2. Tree for (1): after checking   3. Tree for (1): affix hopping

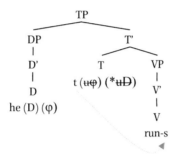

In (2), the uninterpretable EPP feature [*uD] and the uninterpretable φ-features [uφ] are on T. They are checked by the interpretable category feature [D] and the interpretable φ-features [φ] on the pronoun *he* in a spec-head configuration. This agreement yields the morpheme -s, which is then lowered from T to V as in (3). Under the vP-internal subject hypothesis, where the subject is located in spec,vP, subject-verb agreement is also possible, as represented below. The [uφ] on T can simply c-command and agree with the internal subject DP having [φ] as shown in (4). Because T still has [*uD], the DP moves from spec,vP to spec,TP to check [*uD] in a spec-head configuration as in (5). As for merging the suffix -s with the verb, the verb is assumed to move from V to v, and the suffix -s is lowered form T to v.

4. Tree for (1): checking of φ-features   5. Tree for (2): checking of EPP

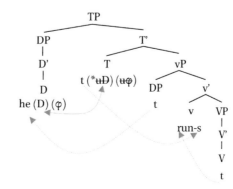

UNIT 239

Agreement and Case III

Feature-Driven Movements

With respect to case in MP, it is proposed that case be an uninterpretable feature [uCase] on the DP, either [uNOM], [uACC] or [uGEN]. This feature cannot be checked by any matching interpretable features, because Case has no meaning and its feature is always uninterpretable. If we assume that there is an uninterpretable case feature on T, and an uninterpretable case feature on the subject DP, two uninterpretable features cannot be checked against each other because one of them must be interpretable. Chomsky (2001) proposes an idea that can be termed **REFLEX FEATURE CHECKING**, where Case feature is checked as a reflex of the checking of other features. That is, case feature [uNOM] on the subject DP is checked as a product of the agreement between the interpretable φ-feature of the subject and the uninterpretable features [uφ] on T. Consider the checking of [uNOM] below.

1. He runs.

2. Tree for (1) checking of φ-feature   3. Tree for (1) after Case checking

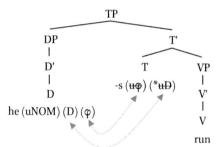
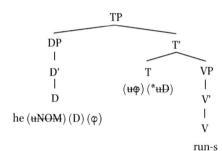

In (2), the DP first agrees with T in the φ-feature, i.e. the [uφ] on T is checked by [φ] on the DP in a spec-head configuration. As a result of this agreement, the Case feature [uNOM] on D is automatically checked in (3), simply as a reflex of φ-feature checking. Under the vP-internal subject hypothesis, the scenario is no different. The [uNOM] feature is assumed to be checked while the subject is in spec,vP, as a result of φ-feature checking shown in (4). The DP then moves from spec,vP to spec,TP to check the strong [*uD] as in (5).

4. Tree for (1) checking of φ-features and case   5. Tree for (1) checking [*uD]

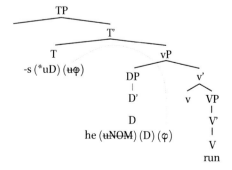
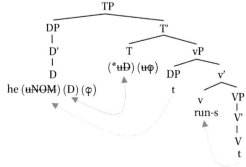

UNIT 240

Agreement and Case IV

Feature-Driven Movements

If [uNOM] on the subject DP is checked as a result of φ-feature checking, what about the accusative case, i.e. [uACC], that appears on the object of the verb? There is no object-verb agreement in English. In fact, Chomsky (1995) assumes that there is agreement between the verb and the object in English as well but this agreement is abstract, i.e. we do not see any morphological markers on the verb showing its agreement with the object. In other languages, object-verb agreement is obvious as in (1) from Hindi.

1. *Anil-ne   kitaabẽ   becũ*
   Anil-ERG book.F.PL sell.PERF-F.PL
   'Anil sold the books' (cf. Mohanan 1995:83)

In (1), the verb *becũ* 'sold' agrees with the object *kitaabẽ* 'the books' in gender and number. Both the verb and the object take feminine and plural as shown in the glosses in (1). Such an example suggests a universal tendency. Verbs in English also agree with their objects as in (2), but we do not see any markers on the verb.

2. John read   the books.
   ↑_____|
     verb-object Agreement
         in φ-features

Example (2) is represented in (3) and (4).

3. Tree for (2) before checking   4. Tree for (2) after checking

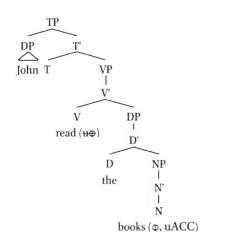
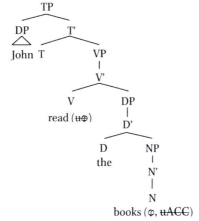

After [uφ] on the verb agrees with [φ] on the object DP, [uφ] is checked as in (3). As a reflex of this checking, the accusative case [uACC] is automatically checked as in (4).

UNIT 241

Agreement and Case v

Feature-Driven Movements

The same applies to [uGEN] that is checked as a reflex of φ-feature checking. Although there is no clear agreement between the possessor and the possessum (i.e. the thing which is possessed) in English, some languages show this agreement as shown in the examples from Finnish (cf. Johns, 2007:61) in (1) and (2).

1. *tei-dan   auto-nne*
   you.2.PL-GEN car-2.PL
   'your car'

2. *minu-n   vaimo-ni*
   1.1.SG-GEN   wife-1.SG
   'my wife'

As shown in (1), the possessor *tei* 'you', which is plural and 2nd person, agrees with the possessum *auto* 'car' in the same features: plural and 2nd person. The same occurs in (2), where the singular and 1st person possessor *minu* 'I' agrees with the possessum *vaimo* 'wife' in both number and person: singular and 1st person. Based on these facts, it is assumed that English possessive constructions also show an abstract agreement between the possessor and the possessum as in (3).

3.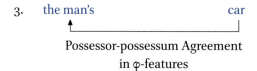

   Possessor-possessum Agreement
   in φ-features

Under this assumption, it is assumed that the head D has uninterpretable φ-features [uφ] and agrees with the possessor's interpretable φ-features. As a reflex of this agreement, the uninterpretable case feature [uGEN] on *the man* is automatically checked as in (5) below.

4. Tree for (3): checking of φ-features   5. Tree for (3): checking of [uGEN]

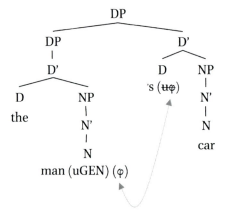   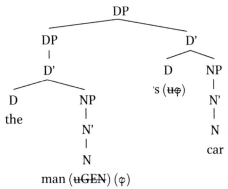

UNIT 242

Phases I

Phases

Phases (i.e. distinct stages in a series of events) constitute a central concept in MP. In 1998, Chomsky proposed that a structure be built in phases. Once a phase is structurally completed, it is sent to the interfaces (PF and LF) via the Spell-Out. CP and vP are phases in English. Thus, the structure is built from the bottom up, and once vP is finalized, it is sent to the interfaces before the rest of the structure. Consider the following sentence that is composed of two phases: vP and CP.

1. I thought that Ahmed had won the prize.

2. Tree for (1)

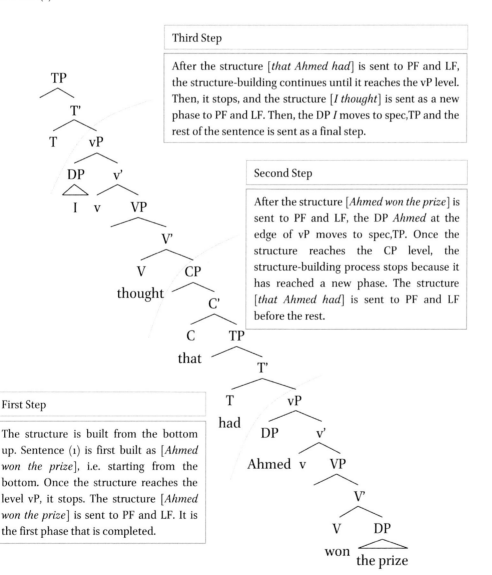

Third Step

After the structure [*that Ahmed had*] is sent to PF and LF, the structure-building continues until it reaches the vP level. Then, it stops, and the structure [*I thought*] is sent as a new phase to PF and LF. Then, the DP *I* moves to spec,TP and the rest of the sentence is sent as a final step.

Second Step

After the structure [*Ahmed won the prize*] is sent to PF and LF, the DP *Ahmed* at the edge of vP moves to spec,TP. Once the structure reaches the CP level, the structure-building process stops because it has reached a new phase. The structure [*that Ahmed had*] is sent to PF and LF before the rest.

First Step

The structure is built from the bottom up. Sentence (1) is first built as [*Ahmed won the prize*], i.e. starting from the bottom. Once the structure reaches the level vP, it stops. The structure [*Ahmed won the prize*] is sent to PF and LF. It is the first phase that is completed.

UNIT 243

Phases II

Phases

The idea of phases is that a syntactic structure is built in stages from the bottom up. A simple sentence is not fully structured all at once but built in phases: once the vP domain is completed, it is sent to PF and LF; once the CP that is above vP is completed, it is sent as a second phase, and so on. This cyclic structure-building suggests that once a phase is sent to PF and LF, all the elements inside this phase are inaccessible to any syntactic operations. Thus, no element is expected to move out of a phase except the element at the phase edge. This condition is known in syntactic theory as the **PHASE IMPENETRABILITY CONDITION (PIC)**, which is laid out in (1).

1. **Phase Impenetrability Condition (PIC):** If a phase (vP or CP) is completed and sent to the interfaces, only the head (v or C) and the specifiers of that phase (spec,vP or spec,CP) are accessible to any operations, which means they can move to the next higher phase. The other elements below the head are inaccessible to all operations, which means they cannot move out of the phase.

This condition stipulates that only elements in the head or the specifiers of a phase can move higher in the structure, but anything below the head is inaccessible and cannot move.

2. Representations of Phases vP/CP

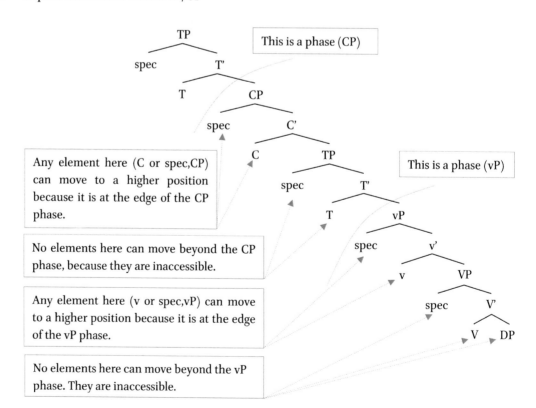

Phases III

Phases

Under phase theory, no elements can be moved out of the phase except those in its head or specifier. Thus, the derivation of sentence (1) will be as shown in (2).

1. I thought that Ahmed had won the prize.

2. Tree for (1)

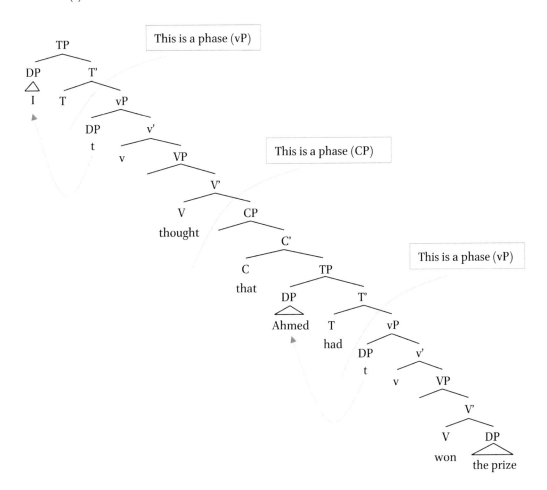

Given that any constituent in the head or the specifier of the phase are exceptions, and thus are allowed to move higher, the constituents *Ahmed* and *I* start in spec,vPs and move to spec,TPs without any violation of the Phase Impenetrability Condition (PIC). If these elements in spec,vPs are not exempted from the PIC and given the freedom to move, the sentence will be ungrammatical as in (3).

3. *I thought that had Ahmed won the prize.

UNIT 245

Copy Theory 1

Copy Theory

In pre-MP approaches, it was argued that a moved element leaves behind a null element called a **TRACE** (abbreviated as *t*). This trace forms a **CHAIN** with the moved element.

1. Will Ahmed come?

2. Tree for (1) before movement 3. Tree for (1) after movement

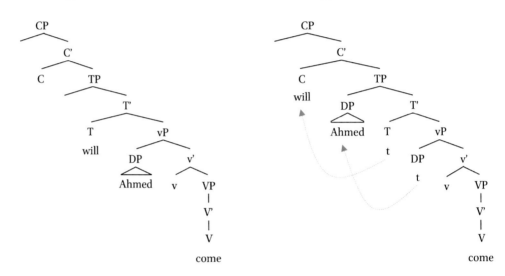

In MP, a **COPY THEORY OF MOVEMENT (CTM)** was proposed in place of trace theory (Chomsky, 1993). CTM assumes that the moved element leaves behind an exact copy of itself, not a null element as a trace. One might say that copy theory may cause a problem in that the structure will have two copies of the same element, and they may both be pronounced. The **REDUCTION CHAIN PRINCIPLE (RCP)** intervenes and decides which copy is pronounced. In English, only the highest copy is pronounced as in (4).

4. **Reduction Chain Principle (RCP):** Pronounce the highest copy in a movement chain.

For illustration, the moved element is a copy as in (6), not a trace as in (5).

5. Trace Theory of Movement   6. Copy Theory of Movement

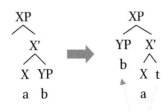
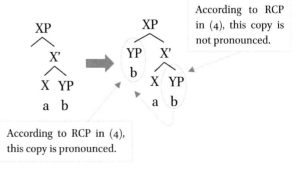

UNIT 246

Copy Theory II

Copy Theory

The motivation to adopt copy theory and reject trace theory comes from the fact that traces violate the inclusiveness principle stated in (1) as they add new information to the structure.

1. **Inclusiveness Principle**: No new information/words should be introduced by transformations during the derivation of a sentence.

The traces are new to the structure. However, copies of moved elements are not new; they are simply copies and duplicates of the same information. Thus, the derivation of question (2), "Ahmed will come", which was discussed in Unit 245, is revised in (3) and (4).

2. Will Ahmed come?

3. Tree for (1) before movement   4. Tree for (1) after movement

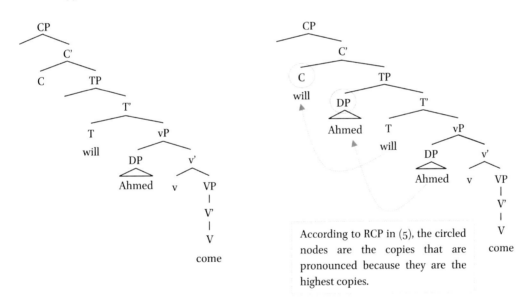

According to RCP in (5), the circled nodes are the copies that are pronounced because they are the highest copies.

According to the Chain Reduction Principle in (5), only the highest copies in (4) are pronounced at PF. The lower copies are not pronounced.

5. **Reduction Chain Principle**: Pronounce the highest copy in a movement chain.

Thus, at PF, the structure in (4) is pronounced as illustrated in (6). This is the same question as in (2).

6. Will Ahmed ~~will Ahmed~~ come?

UNIT 247

Bare Phrase Structure 1

Bare Phrase Structure

MP strives for the bare minimum by eliminating the deep and surface structures as they seem unnecessary. It also eliminates the X-bar level (X') and the phrase level (XP) in (1) because they violate the inclusiveness principle.

1. X'-Theory Scheme

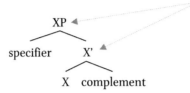

The X' level and the phrase level (XP) are new information and they are not part of the lexicon (i.e. the numeration or the lexical array). Thus, they violate the inclusiveness principle and need to be eliminated.

In place of these representations, MP proposes minimal machinery to derive a sentence. This yields the idea of **BARE PHRASE STRUCTURE**. All phrases, sentences and questions can be derived by only two operations: **MERGE** and **MOVE**. From the numeration or the lexical array (a limited number of lexical items needed for the derivation of a phrase), merge takes two lexical items and merge them together as in the computation process in (2).

2. Merge (α, β) → {α, {α, β}}

In (2), the items α, β are lexical items such as *man, in, food, eat*, etc. These items are taken from the numeration and merged together. This produces a new set. The head of the whole set projects and passes its label to the whole node as shown in (3).

3. Representation of (2)

```
    α
   ╱ ╲
  α   β
```

If the head of the whole set is β, β projects instead as in the computation in (4) represented in (5).

4. Merge (α, β) → {β, {α, β}}

5. Representation of (4)

UNIT 248

Bare Phrase Structure II

Bare Phrase Structure

Merge is a powerful and effective operation. It can apply iteratively until it builds the whole structure. Thus, the computation in (1) can be represented in (2).

1. Merge (δ, γ, α, β) → {δ, {δ, {γ, {γ, {α, {α, β}}}}}}

2. Representation of (1)

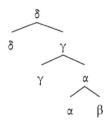

The Merge operation, discussed above, is sometimes called **EXTERNAL MERGE**. There is an **INTERNAL MERGE**, which is another term given to the second operation, **MOVE**. Move is assumed to **COPY** an already merged item and merge it again. Thus, if we want to move item α to the specifier of δ in (2), item α is simply copied and re-merged with δ as shown in (3).

3. Movement of α

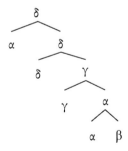

The re-merged item must be placed at the root of the structure (i.e. the top of the structure during the derivation). This condition ensures that the structure is extended only at the root, and guarantees that the derivation continues in cyclic steps and in one direction (i.e. bottom-up). This 'merging at the root' is in accordance with the principle known as **EXTENSION CONDITION** given in (4).

4. Extension Condition: all operations must extend the root (Chomsky, 1993:23).

In summary, there are two operations in minimalist syntax: (i) **Merge** (sometimes called **External Merge**) and (ii) **Move** (sometimes called **Internal Merge**; it includes **Copy**).

UNIT 249

Bare Phrase Structure III

Bare Phrase Structure

According to the discussion above, Bare Phrase Structure does not require X′ or XP level in their representations. All the nodes are X. When the head X projects, the label that passes to the whole projection is still X, not X′ or XP. This is the result of using two operations only: Merge and Move.

Thus, the X′-theory scheme in (1) is revised as in (2) for the Bare Phrase Structure.

1. X′-Theory Scheme   2. Bare Phrase Structure

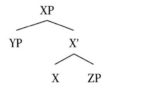

Notice that Bare Phrase Structure in (2) does not contain any X′ or XP. It is more basic and minimalist. The node X in (2) can be a head X, X′ or XP but these notations are not needed. Based on its structural position, we easily detect that the lower X in (2) is the head X, the intermediate X is the old X′, and the highest X is the old XP. In (1), YP is the specifier and ZP is the complement, but they are barely (i.e. in terms of Bare Phrase Structure) represented in (2) as Y and Z. We can readily observe that they are phrases, not heads, in these specific structural positions.

Consider the phrase *the man's car* in (3) that is represented according to X′-theory in (4) and the Bare Phrase Structure Rules in (5).

3. the man's car

4. X-Theory Representation   5. Bare Phrase Structure Derivation

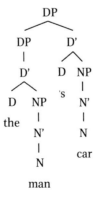
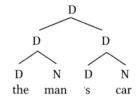

First, Merge applies to D [s] and N [car] and puts them together. Then, the head D projects, making a set ['s car]. Merge applies again to D [the] and N [man], and the head D [the] projects, making a new set [the man]. The new set [the man] is merged with the old set ['s car], making a bigger set [the man's car].

UNIT 250

Bare Phrase Structure IV

Bare Phrase Structure

Consider the structure of the question in (1) according to X'-Theory, shown in (2).

1. Have the boys played this game?

2. X'-Theory Representation for (1)

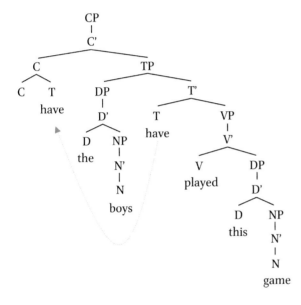

The structure can be revised according to the Bare Phrase Structure as in (3).

3. Bare Phrase Structure Derivation for (1)

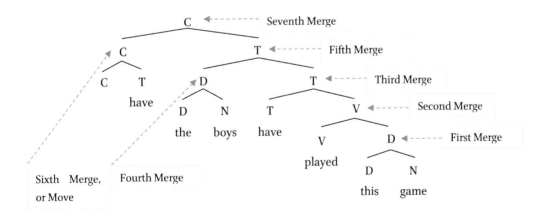

It is important to note as shown in (3), that after Merge applies to two items, it re-merges with other items, building the structure from the bottom up. The auxiliary *have* in head T undergoes Move, and is thus re-merged and adjoined to the head C. According to the Chain Reduction Principle, only the highest copy, i.e. *have*, is pronounced at PF.

Exercises

Units 1–2

Determine whether the following sentences are grammatical, ungrammatical, non-standard, disputable, anomalous or unambiguous. If ambiguous, provide their possible meanings.

1. Because he loves so much fun.
2. Colorless green ideas sleep furiously.
3. Flying planes can be very dangerous.
4. I ain't never done nothin' like that.
5. I can do that quicklier than you.
6. I will not buy nothing.
7. I'm reading a book about American history.
8. She seems to really like it.
9. The boy found in the house.
10. The chicken is ready to eat.
11. The oak tree is a beautiful animal.
12. Which journal was your article published in?
13. The dog has left me alone.
14. Thanks for that gift! It meaned a lot to me.

Units 8–15 (I)

Study the italicized words and determine their lexical category based on their inflection and syntactic distribution.

1. a. Sleep for a *while* before you travel.
   b. He *whiles* away his evenings playing games.
   c. *While* a good singer, she is a better dancer.

2. a. They live *near* the bus station.
   b. A lot of my *near* friends travelled overseas.
   c. The captain switched on the seat belt sign as we *neared* the airport.
   d. Come *nearer*, and I'll tell you the story.

3. a. The old man feels *down*.
   b. She ran *down* the street.
   c. The lady caught the *down* bus.
   d. The opposition *downed* the president.

4. a. Our chances are *even*.
   b. Let him *even* the ground.
   c. Do they *even* suspect danger?

5. a. Let us fly *above* the clouds.
   b. Have you understood the *above* sentence?
   c. See *above*.

Units 8–15 (II)

Determine the lexical category of the uncommon (blue) words below, and support your answer with three pieces of evidence, i.e. from semantics, morphology and syntax.

1. He absquatulated unexpectedly.
2. The muscles involved in deglutition were so tense that he couldn't swallow.
3. I woke up and stealthily crept downstairs
4. Past and present blurred together, flummoxing her still further.
5. These actors are much hunkier than the football players.
6. She goes to Arizona every January to lollygag in the sun.
7. We were struck by the sheer number of princely states in pre-independence India.
8. The lady gave me a withering look.
9. Being on a high mountaintop is ultimately an ineffable experience.
10. What's the matter? You look a little discombobulated!
11. The Scottish kids are guddling in the rivers.
12. We have ordered some delicious tiffins for dessert.
13. Eat fresh and think big.
14. Even the parsimonious Joe paid for drinks all round.
15. Two principles of good design are frangibility and non-penetration.
16. What's all the shouting for? Why are you making such a kerfuffle?
17. My sister has no job and is doing nothing to find one. She is so lackadaisical.
18. I don't like our English teacher ... he is a real curmudgeon.

Units 18–20 (I)

Provide subcategorization frames for the following heads. Indicate what complement(s) they select, and determine whether these are obligatory or optional. Also identify the head (if any) of each complement, e.g. PP$_{[of]}$, PP$_{[around]}$ etc.

1. *definitely*, Adv
2. *lock*, V
3. *protest*, V
4. *cover*, N
5. *submit*, V
6. *tired*, A
7. *inquire*, V
8. *over*, P
9. *fast*, Adv
10. *supply*, V
11. *debate*, N
12. *open*, V
13. *reliant*, A
14. *position*, N
15. *retreat*, V
16. *small*, A
17. *articulation*, N
18. *love*, V
19. *in*, P
20. *woman*, N

EXERCISES 285

Units 18–20 (II)

Consider the following sentences and determine the subcategorization frames for *surrender* and *abandon*.

1. The army *surrendered* the city to the enemy.
2. The army *abandoned* the city to the enemy.
3. The army *surrendered* the city.
4. The army *abandoned* the city.
5. The army *surrendered* to the enemy.
6. *The army *abandoned* to the enemy.
7. The army *surrendered*.
8. *The army *abandoned*.

Units 19–22

Determine whether the blue phrases are complements or adjuncts. Support your answer with evidence.

1. The use of computers in schools by students.
2. Ali plays the guitar professionally.
3. Fatima is fond of biscuits with her coffee.
4. The book on the table by Shakespeare with the blue cover that you gave me.
5. We gave John a smart watch.
6. He knew he would be reprimanded before he went in to see the boss.
7. They made him captain of the team this season.
8. She still talks about the moment when her life changed forever.
9. You should have your documents in the correct files during the meeting.
10. He wiped his forehead with a facial tissue before the interrogation.

Units 24–28

Determine whether the following blue phrases are constituents, and support your answer with at least three pieces of evidence, such as stand-alone, replacement, displacement, and coordination tests.

1. He fell in love with her.
2. She told him a joke.
3. I can't solve this problem.
4. I met you a couple months ago at the graduation party.
5. The company published several books on this topic.
6. I paid him the money.
7. She was already on the airplane when the flight was cancelled.
8. Ali was very happy.
9. I brought some food for the kittens.
10. We could not sign the contract.
11. The mailman brought two new magazines.

Units 47–53

Draw syntactic tree structures for the following phrases.

1. That relationship with the women
2. Good at mathematics
3. Satisfied with the results
4. Interested in the news
5. Good for you
6. Hit him on the head
7. Go!
8. Leave the house
9. Listen to the music
10. Invited him to the party
11. Drive so fast
12. The students and the teacher
13. Take it or leave it
14. Poor but clean
15. Proud of the community
16. The constraint on the rule
17. Some damage to the street
18. Your respect for the boss
19. Slept in the garden
20. An increase in the price
21. That he believes in God
22. Students from London

Units 50–56

Draw syntactic trees for the following sentences.

1. The fat mouse disappeared through a small hole.
2. The coach recommends that the players always eat healthy food
3. The mailman threw a colorful magazine on the doormat.
4. I doubt whether the first bus has already left.
5. They asked if the black bird had pecked at the bread on their table.
6. The villagers worked in the early morning for two hours.
7. In class, we will discuss many problems, and we will propose solutions to them.
8. Unfortunately he left to join the competition.
9. I think that that hamster will die from exhaustion.
10. We were watching this movie yesterday.

Unit 57 (1)

Read the following ambiguous sentences and provide possible meanings for them. Draw trees for FIVE structurally ambiguous sentences, linking the structures with their appropriate meanings.

EXERCISES

I   *Lexically Ambiguous Sentences*

1. Will Will will the will to Will?
2. She hit his nail with a hammer.
3. The businessman bought a club.
4. The glasses fell on the floor and broke.
5. She is looking for a match.
6. The Sheikh married my sister.
7. I have a really nice stepladder but I never knew my real ladder.
8. They passed the port at midnight.
9. He hit his son because he was drunk.
10. We decided to give it a fly.

II   *Structurally Ambiguous Sentences*

1. I saw a man on a hill with a telescope. (5 meanings)
2. We saw her duck. (3 meanings)
3. He fed her cat food. (3 meanings)
4. Look at the dog with one eye. (2 meanings)
5. Visiting relatives can be boring. (2 meanings)
6. Call me a taxi, please. (2 meanings)
7. I shot an elephant in my pajamas. (2 meanings)
8. Foreigners are hunting dogs. (2 meanings)
9. Passerby helped dog bite victim. (2 meanings)
10. A good life depends on a liver. (2 meanings)

Unit 57 (II)

Disambiguate the following humorous ambiguous headlines (cf. https://bit.ly/2WR7KuI).

I   Lexically Ambiguous Headlines

1. Antibusing Rider Killed By Senate
2. Astronaut Takes Blame For Gas In Spacecraft
3. Bar Trying To Help Alcoholic Lawyers
4. Bill Would Permit Ads On Eyeglasses
5. Blind Bishop Appointed To See
6. Blind Woman Gets New Kidney From Dad She Hasn't Seen In Years
7. Branch Avenue Bridge To Be Fixed Before Fall
8. Chef Throws His Heart Into Helping Feed Needy
9. Chinese Apeman Dated
10. Drunk Gets Nine Months In Violin Case
11. Ford Departs Peking; No Change In Ties
12. Include Your Children When Baking Cookies
13. Kids Make Nutritious Snacks
14. Man Struck By Lightning Faces Battery Charge
15. Red Tape Holds Up New Bridges
16. Rugby Team's Coach Set On Fire
17. Safety Experts Say School Bus Passengers Should Be Belted

18. Shouting Match Ends Teachers' Hearing
19. Stadium Air Conditioning Fails—Fans Protest
20. Women's Movement Called More Broad-Based

II *Structurally Ambiguous Headlines*

1. Aging Expert Joins University Faculty
1. Ban On Soliciting Dead In Trotwood
2. Beating Witness Provides Names
3. British Left Waffles On Falkland Islands
4. Carter Plans Swell Deficit
5. Chester Morrill, 92, Was FED Secretary
6. Child Teaching Expert To Speak
7. Chou Remains Cremated
8. Clinton Wins On Budget, More Lies Ahead
9. Complaints About NBA Referees Growing Ugly
10. Connie Tied, Nude Policeman Testifies
11. Hospitals are Sued by 7 Foot Doctors
12. Jumping bean prices affect poor
13. Killer Sentenced To Die For Second Time In 10 Years
14. Lawyers Give Poor Free Legal Advice
15. Lie Detector Tests Unreliable, Unconstitutional Hearing Told
16. Suspect Held in Killing of Reporter for Variety
17. Teacher Wants To Be Unveiled; Meeting Tonight
18. Teller Stuns Man With Stolen Check
19. Time For Football And Meatball Stew
20. Tuna Biting Off Washington Coast

Units 58–85

Draw trees for the blue phrases (some of them amounting to whole sentences) using the X′-theory scheme.

1. Their sister became a doctor in 1989.
2. Two scholars asked if we had invented that machine.
3. She was wondering whether her father will come.
4. Sarah and Khadija hope that everything is OK.
5. The old firm could be manufacturing many cars.
6. The company is experiencing growth.
7. Democrats are wondering whether they will be running in 2018.
8. Ali's restaurant provides delicious food to the customers.
9. Students would have been doing the homework.
10. This woman was cooking the broth on the stove.
11. No one can decide whether they should visit you.
12. The bus might have left by 5 p.m.
13. Some pupils had shown improvement.
14. Fatima will have finished her housework by today.
15. These boys might have won in the race.
16. The author has been publishing on politics.
17. All visitors shall meet our guide at the entrance.
18. I do not know if you will be able to understand his speech.

EXERCISES

Units 86–116

Draw trees for the sentences and questions below using X'-theory scheme.

1. Should our school have been preparing the tests?
2. Which ideas is the teacher referring to?
3. What will the jury be looking for in a month?
4. Is not it a right decision?
5. When should you see a physician about this symptom?
6. The three ladies would not have put scarfs round their necks.
7. These plants might have been changing colors in fall.
8. Who was walking across the road in front of his father?
9. Have not these tourists visited Jakarta?
10. What he will decide is anybody's guess.
11. Will the company maximize its profits?
12. Did you try on the shirt?
13. The police might not have been dispersing the rebels.
14. Will you take my brother to the station in your car?
15. How tall is this table?
16. Whose book is this?
17. The manager should have a new policy for his administration.
18. The popular book was sold all over the world.

Units 84–85

Discuss the differences between *did* in (1) and (2), and *have* in (3) and (4), and illustrate their differences via tree structures.

1. a. Ali did know
   b. Ali did not know.
   c. Ali didn't know.

2. a. Ali did him a favor.
   b. Ali didn't do him a favor.
   c. *Ali didn't him a favor.

3. a. I have come too early.
   b. I've come too early.

4. a. I have cars fixed.
   b. I have cars.
   c. *I've cars fixed.
   d. *I've cars.

Units 86–91

Recall that auxiliary-subject inversion is not allowed in embedded questions. Now consider the following examples from Belfast English (cf. Henry, 1995). Explain why auxiliary-subject inversion is allowed in Belfast English but not in Standard English.

1. She asked if they were leaving. (Standard English)
2. She asked were they leaving. (Belfast English)

3. We couldn't establish if he met them. (Standard English)
4. We couldn't establish did he meet them. (Belfast English)

5. The police investigated whether he had stolen the goods. (Standard English)
6. The police investigated had he stolen the goods. (Belfast English)

Units 98–101

Read the following examples from Early Modern English (cf. Radford, 1998) and consider the relative positions of the negation word *not* and the main verbs. Provide a syntactic derivation for sentences (2) and (4), and motivate any transformational rules you may need.

1. He heard not that. (Julia, Two Gentlemen of Verona, IV, ii)
2. I care not for her. (Thurio, Two Gentlemen of Verona, V, iv)
3. My master seeks not me. (Speed, Two Gentlemen of Verona, I, i)
4. I know not where to hide. (Trinculo, The Tempest, II, ii)
5. Thou thinkest not of this now. (Launce, Two Gentlemen of Verona, IV, iv)

Units 100–101

Compare the positions of the main verbs in English and French in the examples below (cf. Emonds, 1978). Provide a syntactic analysis for (2), (4) and (6) using transformational rules.

1. a. John does not like Mary.
   b. *John likes not Mary. (English)

2. *Jean n'aime pas Marie*
   Jean loves   not Marie
   'Jean does not love Marie' (French)

3. a. John often kisses Mary.
   b. *John kisses often Mary. (English)

4. *Jean embrasse souvent Marie*
   Jean kisses   often   Marie
   'Jean often kisses Marie' (French)

5. a. My friends all love Mary.
   b. *My friends love all Mary. (English)

6. *Mes amis   aiment tous Marie*
   My friends love all   Marie
   'My friends all love Marie' (French)

EXERCISES

Units 117–124

Consider the following blue phrases (i.e. participants) and decide which thematic roles they play in the whole sentence. Also, provide full subcategorization frames with thematic roles for the verbs and the adjectives in italics.

1. The river *provided* the village with water.
2. Nobody *likes* to *travel* from Brazil to Russia.
3. It *seems* that nobody *cares*.
4. The reporters *sound* very *eager* to *meet* you
5. The kids *bought* these notebooks for school.
6. We *made* these houses from clay for our kids.
7. That he will come is *unlikely*.
8. She *wrote* him a long letter, but he didn't *read* it.
9. The lady *folded* her handkerchief neatly.
10. The patient *hopes* for a speedy recovery.

Units 125–134

Draw syntactic trees for the following sentences.

1. It seems that love is blind.
2. That love is blind is true.
3. A huge whale overturned the boat.
4. The boat was overturned by a huge whale.

Units 138–151

Explain why the sentences below are ungrammatical, and determine which island is responsible for their ungrammaticality. Draw a syntactic tree for each sentence.

1. *Who do you think that ___ comes?
2. *What are you holding a pencil and ___ ?
3. *Who did you cancel the party because Ali invited ___?

Units 81–82, 106–112, 183–195

Review the applicable units and determine where the wh-words should be located in the structural representation.

1. I wonder *whether* I should sleep.   (finite clause)
2. I wonder *when* I should sleep.   (finite clause)
3. I wonder *where* I should sleep.   (finite clause)

4. I wonder *whether* to sleep.   (infinitive clause)
5. I wonder *when* to sleep.   (infinitive clause)
6. I wonder *where* to sleep.   (infinitive clause)

Units 171–176

Draw syntactic trees for the following examples and explain why (1) and (3) are grammatical and (2) and (4) are ungrammatical.

1. The quarrel with Salma has upset her.
2. *The quarrel with Salma has upset herself.
3. The quarrel with her has upset Salma.
4. *The quarrel with herself has upset Salma.

Units 171–176

Study the following grammatical examples carefully and explain how they still respect the principles of Binding Theory. Draw a syntactic tree for each sentence.

1. When he$_i$ got to the venue, Khalid$_i$ discovered that the exam had been postponed.
2. Which book about himself$_i$ does John$_i$ like?

Units 82–83, 161–167

Compare the sentences in each sentence pair below and discuss their similarities and differences. Provide a syntactic tree for each sentence.

1. a. I believe that Ahmed came.
   b. I believe Ahmed came.

2. a. We expect him to win.
   b. We let him win.

Units 196–197

Consider whether sentences (1) and (2) below feature control or raising constructions. Provide evidence for your answer, and draw tree structures for both sentences.

1. John tried to leave.
2. John seemed to leave.

Units 230–231 (I)

Study the examples below from Buhairi Arabic, a dialect spoken in the southwestern part of Saudi Arabia (cf. Alqarni, 2020). In (1) through (3), the wh-words *maða* 'what', *ʔay ab-kutib* 'which books' and *fin* 'who' move to the front of the sentence. In (4) and (5), however, the adverbial wh-words *wayn* 'where' and *mata* 'when' remain in situ, i.e. they do not move.

   Task 1: Develop a feature-based analysis and explain why the wh-words in (1) through (3) move, whereas the other wh-words in (4) and (5) do not.

   Task 2: Draw two syntactic trees, for (1) and (4), and motivate the use of any transformational rule you may need for their derivation.

1. *maða xið* ʕali
   what take.3.M.PERF Ali
   'What did Ali take?'

2. *ʔay ab-kutib* xið ʕali
   Which the-books take.3.M.PERF Ali
   'Which books did Ali take?'

3. *ʃin* ʕazam ʕali
   who invite.3.M.PERF Ali
   'Who did Ali invite?'

4. ʔali ra:ħ *wayn*
   Ali go.3.M.PERF where
   'Where did Ali go?' (*In-situ strategy*)

5. *b-ysa:fir* saʕad *mata*
   will-travel.3.M.S.IMPERF Saad when
   'When will Saad travel?'

Units 230–231 (11)

Develop a feature-based analysis of the wh-exclamatives in contrast to the wh-interrogatives below.

1. How badly are you disappointed?   (Wh-intorrogative)
2. How badly you are disappointed!   (Wh-exclamative)
3. *How badly are you disappointed!   (*Wh-exclamative)

4. What song did John write?   (Wh-question)
5. What a beautiful song John wrote!   (Wh-exclamative)
6. *What a beautiful song did John write! (*Wh-exclamative)

Glossary

Adverbial Clause Island: A syntactic island that requires that no elements can be moved out of adverbial clauses.

Agree Approach: A feature [uF] (probe) agrees with another matching feature [F] (goal) iff
  i. [uF] c-commands [F]
  ii. There is no matching feature [F_x] checking against [uF] that is closer to [uF] than [F] is.

A′-movement: A movement that transposes an element from any position to a position that is not potentially assigned a θ-role such as spec,CP, head C, adjoined positions and many others.

A-movement: A movement that transposes an element from any position to a potential θ-position such as spec,TP or the complement(s) of a verb.

Burizio's Generalization: A verb can check the accusative case iff it assigns an external theta role. If the verb does not assign an external theta role, its ability to check the accusative case is eliminated.

Case Filter: Every pronounced DP must have a case that is checked by another case feature in an appropriate configuration.

Checking under Sisterhood: An uninterpretable feature [uF] on a syntactic element, Y, is checked when Y is sister to another syntactic element, Z, which bears a matching interpretable feature [F].

Complex Noun Phrase Island: A syntactic island that dictates that no element can be moved from complex noun phrases.

Coordinate Structure Island: A syntactic island that stipulates that no elements in the coordinated DP can be moved out of the complex DP and asked about.

Coordination Test: A constituency test that examines whether a sequence of words can be coordinated with another sequence of the same lexical category.

Displacement Test: A constituency test that examines whether a sequence of words can be displaced or moved to the front of the sentence while the resulting sentence remains grammatical. This test is also known as **Movement Test**.

Dominance: A structural relation between tree nodes, represented in terms of top-down order.

Do-Support/Insertion: An operation that occurs at the d-structure, where a dummy *do* (or its other forms *does* and *did*) inserts in T based on its tense status.

Expletive Insertion: An operation that inserts the expletive *it* as a subject in sentences including adjectives or verbs that do not assign external θ-roles.

Extended Projection Principle (EPP): All sentences/clauses must have a subject.

Extension Condition: All operations must extend the root.

Full Interpretation: Every element at the semantic interface LF must receive interpretation/meaning.

Head Movement Constraint (HMC): Head X moves to head Y but cannot skip an intervening head Z between X and Y.

Inclusiveness Principle: No new information/words should be introduced by transformations during the derivation of a sentence.

Left Branch Island: A syntactic island that states that the left-hand elements within the DP spine (such as possessors or adjectives) cannot be extracted from, or moved out of, the DP.

M-command relationship: X *m-commands* Y iff
  iii. X does not dominate Y, and Y does not dominate X
  iv. The maximal projection of X (i.e. XP) dominates Y

No Extraction Constraint: If X moves to Z, then X cannot be extracted, i.e. move alone to the higher head Y without Z. X^Z must move together to a higher head position.

Phase Impenetrability Condition (PIC): If a phase (vP or CP) is completed and sent to the interfaces, only the head (v or C) and the specifiers of that phase (spec,vP or spec,CP) are accessible to any operations, which means they can move to the next higher phase. The other elements below the head are inaccessible to all operations, which means they cannot move out of the phase.

Precedence: A structural relation between tree nodes, represented in terms of left-to-right order.

Principles of Binding Theory
– Principle A: An anaphor must be bound in its binding domain (TP).
– Principle B: Pronouns must be free in their binding domain (TP).
– Principle C: R-expressions must be free.

Principles of Government: X governs Y iff
iii. X *m-commands* Y, and
iv. No barrier (WP) except TP[non-finite] intervenes between X and Y

Principles of Theta Role Assignment
i. Assign one θ-role to every complement (i.e. internal arguments)
ii. Assign one θ-role to the subject (i.e. the external argument), unless it is an expletive.

Projection Principle: Lexical properties and complement selection must be respected at both the d-structure and s-structure.

Proper Binding Condition (PBC): Traces must be bound.

Recoverability Principle: No information should be lost from the d-structure during the derivation.

Reduction Chain Principle: Pronounce the highest copy in a movement chain.

Stand-Alone Test: A constituency test that examines whether or not a sequence of words stands alone as an answer to a question. This test is also known as **Answer Ellipsis** or **Answer Fragment**.

Structure Preservation Principle: All derived structures must be identical to the base/d-structure. No movements should alter the X-theory scheme. The X′-Theory scheme must always be preserved.

Subjacency: Elements cannot move beyond two bounding nodes like two DPs or TPs.

Subject Island Constraint: A syntactic island that states that no element that occurs in a subject position can be moved out of the complex DP.

Substitution Test: A constituency test that examines whether a sequence of words can be substituted with or replaced by a single word while their relevant sentences remain grammatical. This test is also known as **Replacement Test**.

Wh-Island: A syntactic island that stipulates that no elements can be moved out of an embedded question.

References

Alqarni, Muteb. 2020. "The syntax of wh-interrogatives in Buhairi Arabic: documentation and analysis". *King Khalid University Journal of Humanities*, 28(1): 34–68.

Abney, Steven. 1987. The English Noun Phrase in its Sentential Aspect. PhD Dissertation, MIT.

Adger, David. 2003. Core Syntax. Oxford: Oxford University Press.

Adger, David, & Peter Svenonius. 2011. "Features in minimalist syntax". In: Gillian Ramchand and Charles Reiss (Eds.), The Oxford Handbook of Linguistic Minimalism, pp. 27–51. Oxford: Oxford University Press.

Bobaljik, Jonathan. 1994. "What does adjacency do?" In: Heidi Harley & Colin Phillips, The Morphology-Syntax Connection, pp. 1–32. The MIT Working Papers in Linguistics, 22.

Bobaljik, Jonathan. 1995. Morphosyntax: The Syntax of Verbal Inflection. PhD Dissertation, MIT.

Bresnan, Joan. 1982. The Mental Representation of Grammatical Relations. Cambridge, Massachusetts: MIT Press.

Burzio, Luigi. 1986. Italian Syntax: A Government-Binding Approach. Dordrecht, Holland: D. Reidel publishing Company.

Bybee, Joan, Revere Perkins, & William Pagliuca. 1994. The Evolution of Grammar: Tense, Aspect, and Modality in the Languages of the World. Chicago and London: University of Chicago Press.

Carnie, Andrew. 2013. Syntax: A Generative Introduction. New Jersey, US: Willey-Blackwell.

Chomsky, Noam. 1965. Aspects of the Theory of Syntax. Cambridge, Massachusetts: MIT Press.

Chomsky, Noam. 1970. "Remarks on nominalization". In: Roderick Jacobs & Peter Rosenbaum (Eds.) Reading in English Transformational Grammar, pp. 184–221. Waltham: Ginn.

Chomsky, Noam. 1981. Lectures on Government and Binding: The Pisa Lectures. Berlin: De Gruyter Mouton.

Chomsky, Noam. 1982. Some Concepts and Consequences of the Theory of Government and Binding. Cambridge, Massachusetts: MIT Press.

Chomsky, Noam. 1986. Knowledge of Language: Its Nature, Origin, and Use. Connecticut, US: Greenwood Publishing Group.

Chomsky, Noam. 1993. "A minimalist program for linguistic theory". In: Kenneth Hale and Samuel J. Keyser, The View from Building 20, pp. 1–52. Cambridge, Massachusetts: MIT Press.

Chomsky, Noam. 1995. The Minimalist Program. Cambridge, Massachusetts: MIT Press.

Chomsky, Noam. 1998. "Minimalist inquiries: the framework". In: Roger martin, David Michaels, Juan Uriagereka, Occasional Papers in Linguistics 15. Republished in 2000, Step By Step: Essays In Syntax in Honor of Howard Lasnik, pp. 89–155. Cambridge, Massachusetts: MIT Press.

Chomsky, Noam. 2001. "Derivation by phase". In: Michael Kenstowicz (Ed.), Ken Hale: A Life in Language, pp. 1–52. Cambridge, Massachusetts: MIT Press.

Chomsky, Noam. 2015. The Minimalist Program. Cambridge, Massachusetts: MIT Press.

Chomsky, Noam & Howard Lasnik. 1995. The Theory of Principles and Parameters. In: Noam Chomsky, The Minimalist Program, pp. 13–127. Cambridge, Massachusetts: MIT Press.

Cinque, Guglielmo. 1999. Adverbs and Functional Heads: A Cross-linguistic Perspective. New York, Oxford: Oxford University Press.

den Dikken, Marcel. 2000. "The syntax of features". *Journal of psycholinguistic research*, 29(1), 5–23.

Emonds, Joseph. 1970. Root and Structure-Preserving Transformations. PhD Dissertation, MIT.

Emonds, Joseph. 1978. "The verbal complex V'-V in French". *Linguistic Inquiry*, 9(1), 151–175.

Fiengo, Robert. 1977. "On trace theory". *Linguistic Inquiry*, 8(1), 35–61.

Gazdar, Gerald. 1981. "Unbounded dependencies and coordinate structure". *Linguistic Inquiry*, 12(2), 155–183.

Henry, Alison. 1995. Belfast English and Standard English. New York, Oxford: Oxford University Press.

Johns, Christopher 2007. Interpreting Agreement. PhD Thesis, Durham University.

Koopman, Hilda & Dominique Sportiche. 1991. "The position of subjects". *Lingua*, 85(1), 211–258.

Larson, Richard. K. 1988. "On the double object construction". *Linguistic Inquiry*, 19(3), 335–391.

Lasnik, Howard. 1994. "Verbal morphology: Syntactic structures meets the minimalist program". In Hector Campos and Paula Kempchinsky (Eds.), Evolution and Revolution in Linguistic Theory: Essays in Honor of Carlos Otero, pp. 251–275. Washington, D.C.: Georgetown University Press.

Lieber, Rochelle. 1980. On the Organization of the Lexicon. PhD Dissertation, University of New Hampshire.

Marantz, Alec. 1984. On the Nature of Grammatical Relations. Cambridge, Massachusetts: MIT Press.

Mohanan, Tara. 1995. "Wordhood and lexicality: noun incorporation in Hindi". *Natural Language and Linguistic Theory*, 13(1), 75–134.

Pawlak, Nina. 2012. "Morphological coding of verb-object agreement in African languages". In: Rocznik orientalistyczny, The Yearbook of Oriental Studies, pp. 158–170. Polish Academy of Sciences.

Radford, Andrew. 1998. Syntactic Theory and the Structure of English. Cambridge, UK: Cambridge University Press.

Radford, Andrew. 2009. Analysing English Sentences: A Minimalist Approach. Cambridge University Press.

Ritter, Elizabeth. 1991. "Evidence for number as a nominal head". *GLOW Newsletter 26*. Paper presented at GLOW-14.

Rizzi, Luigi. 1997. "The fine structure of the left periphery". In: Liliane Haegeman (Ed.), Elements of Grammar, pp. 281–337. Dordrecht: Kluwer.

Ross, John. 1967. Constraints on Variables in Syntax. PhD Dissertation, MIT.

Saito, Mamoru. 1985. Some Asymmetries in Japanese and their Theoretical Implications. PhD Dissertation, MIT.

Schachter, Paul. 1977. "Constraints on Coördination". *Language*, 53(1), 86–103.

Speas, Margaret & Naoki Fukui. 1986. "Specifiers and projections". In: Naoki Fukui, Tova Rapoport and Elizabeth Sagey (Eds.), MIT Working Papers in Linguistics 8, pp. 128–172. Cambridge, Massachusetts: MIT Press.

Sportiche, Dominique. 1988. "A theory of floating quantifiers and its corollaries for constituent structure". *Linguistic Inquiry*, 19(3), 425–449.

Stroik, Thomas & Michael Putnam. 2013. The Structural Design of Language. Cambridge: Cambridge University Press.

Tomlin, Russel. 1986. Basic Word Order: Functional Principles. London: Croom Helm.

Travis, Lisa. 1984. Parameters and Effects of Word Order Variation. PhD Dissertation, MIT.

Williams, Edwin. 1978. "Across-the-Board rule application". *Linguistic Inquiry*, 9(1), 31–43.

Xupin, Li. 2013. Numeral Classifiers in Chinese: The Syntax-Semantics Interface. Berlin: De Gruyter Mouton.

Yule, George. 2010. The Study of Language. Cambridge: Cambridge University Press.

For Further Reading

Aarts, Bas. 2008. English Syntax and Argumentation. New York: Palgrave Macmillan.

Aoun, Joseph. 1985. A Grammar of Anaphora. Cambridge, Massachusetts: MIT Press.

Baker, Mark. 2003. Lexical Categories. Cambridge: Cambridge University Press.

Baker, Mark, Kyle Johnson, & Ian Roberts. 1989. "Passive arguments raised". *Linguistic Inquiry* 20(1), 219–251.

Barker, Chris & Geoffrey K. Pullum 1990. "A theory of command relations". *Linguistics and Philosophy*, 13(1), 1–34.

Barss, Andrew & Howard Lasnik. 1986. "A note on anaphora and double objects". *Linguistic Inquiry*, 17(1), 347– 54.

Boeckx, Cedric. 2008. Understanding Minimalist Syntax: Lessons from Locality in Long-Distance Dependencies. Oxford, UK: Blackwell.

Borsley, Robert. 1996. Modern Phrase Structure Grammar. Oxford, UK: Blackwell.

Bresnan, Joan. 1972. Theory of Complementation in English. PhD dissertation, MIT.

Büring, Daniel. 2005. Binding Theory. Cambridge: Cambridge University Press.

Carnie, Andrew. 2010. Constituent Structure. Oxford: Oxford University Press.

Chomsky, Noam. 1980. "On binding". *Linguistic Inquiry* 11(1), 1–46.

Cook, Vivian & Mark Newson. 2007. Chomsky's Universal Grammar: An Introduction. Oxford, UK: Blackwell.

Cowper, Elizabeth. 1992. A Concise Introduction to Syntactic Theory: The Government and Binding approach. Chicago: University of Chicago Press.

Culicover, Peter. 1997. Principles and Parameters: An Introduction to Syntactic Theory. Oxford: Oxford University Press.

Culicover, Peter. and Ray Jackendoff. 2005. Simpler Syntax. Oxford: Oxford University Press.

Culicover, Peter; Thomas, Wasow & Adrian Akmajian (Eds.). 1977. Formal Syntax. New York: Academic Press.

Grimshaw, Jane. 1990. Argument Structure. Cambridge, Massachusetts: MIT Press.

Haegeman, Liliane. 1994. Introduction to Government and Binding Theory. Oxford, UK: Blackwell.

Haegeman, Liliane & Jacqueline, Guéron. 1999. English Grammar: A Generative Perspective. Oxford, UK: Blackwell.

Hornstein, Norbert. 1999. "Movement and control". *Linguistic Inquiry*, 30(1), 69–96.

Hornstein, Nobert; Jairo Nunes & Kleanthes Grohmann. 2005. Understanding Minimalism. Cambridge: Cambridge University Press.

Jackendoff, Ray. 1977. X-bar Syntax: A Theory of Phrase Structure. Cambridge, Massachusetts: MIT Press.

Lasnik, Howard. 1989. Essays on Anaphora. Dordrecht: Kluwer.

Lasnik, Howard. 1999. Minimalist Analyses. Oxford, UK: Blackwell.

Lasnik, Howard & Mamoru Saito 1984. "On the nature of proper government". *Linguistic Inquiry* 15(1), 235– 89.

Lasnik, Howard, Juan Uriagereka, and Cedric Boeckx. 2005. A Course in Minimalist Syntax. Oxford, UK: Blackwell.

O'grady, William, Michael Dobrovolsky & Francis Katamba. 1987. Contemporary Linguistics: An Introduction. London, New York: Longman

Ouhalla, Jamal. 1999. Introducing Transformational Grammar: From Principles and Parameters to Minimalism. London, UK: Hodder Education.

Radford, Andrew. 1997. Syntactic Theory and the Structure of English: A Minimalist Approach. Cambridge: Cambridge University Press.

Radford, Andrew. 2004. Minimalist Syntax: Exploring the Structure of English. Cambridge: Cambridge University Press.

Roberts, Ian. 1997. Comparative Syntax. London, UK: Edward Arnold.

Sells, Peter. 1985. Lectures on Contemporary Syntactic Theories. Stanford: CSLI.

Tallerman, Maggie. 2011. Understanding Syntax. London, UK: Hodder Education.

Index

A-movement 153
A'-movement 153
Abstract case 183
Adjectival Control Constructions 219
Adjunction Rules 128
Adjuncts 26
Adverbial Clause Island 171, 294
Affix Hopping 119
Agreement 239
Ambiguous sentences 6
Anaphor 194
Answer Ellipsis 30, 295
Answer Fragment 30, 295
Articles 9
Aspect 241
Aspect Phrase 241
Attributes 11
Auxiliaries 44

Base Representation 107
Beneficiary 137
Branches 54
Burizio's Generalization 192, 294

Case Filter 182, 294
Category Feature 254
Classifier Phrase 232
Classifiers 232
Clefting 32
Closed class 7
Common nouns 8
Complementation 24
Complex Noun Phrase Island 169, 294
Conjunctions 9
Constituent 29
Controller 212
Coordinate Constituent Constraint 33
Coordinate Structure Island 168, 294
Coordination Test 33, 294
Copy 279

Daughters 53
Deep Structure 104
Degree words 9
Demonstrative Phrase 231
Demonstratives 9
Derivational 12
Displacement Test 32, 294
Ditransitive 8
Do-Insertion 106
Do-Support 106
Dominance 55

Early Modern English 115
Empty category 213
Exceptional Case Marking 184
Experiencer 136
Extended Projection Principle 146
Extension Condition 279, 294
External Merge 279

Finite Clauses 94
Finite Phrase 242
Flat Tree Structure 75
Focus Phrase 242
Force-Finiteness System 242
Force Phrase 242
Full Interpretation 248
Functional Categories 7

Gender 268
Generative Syntax 37
Goal 249
Government And Binding Theory 175
Grammar 4
Grammaticality 5

Head Movement Constraint 162
Hierarchical Tree Structure 75

Inclusiveness Principle 111
Inflectional 12
Instrument 137
Internal Merge 279
Intransitive 8
Iterativity 27

Label 54
Language 3
Left Branch Island 167, 294
Lexical Array 247
Lexical Categories 7
Lexicon 7
Logical Form 107

Main Clauses. 46
Measure Words 232
Minimal Distance Principle 217
Minimalist Program 247
Modals 44
Modifiers 22
Mood 241
Mood Phrase 241
Morphemes 4
Morphological case 183
Morphological Merger 161
Morphological Rules 4
Morphology 3
Morphosyntactic Features 248
Mother 53
Move 279
Movement Test 32, 294

Native speakers 5
Negation Projection 113
Neologism 7
No Crossing Constraint 56
No Extraction Constraint 162
Node 54
Non-Finite Clauses 94
Non-Obligatory Control 219

Non-standard   5
Non-terminal node   54
Number   268
Number Phrase   231
Numerals   9
Numeration   247

Object Control   216
Obligatory Control   219
One-Replacement Test   72
Open class   7
Ordering   27
Ordinary Coordination   33

Parts of speech   4
Past   44
Person   268
Phase Impenetrability Condition   274, 294
Phi-Features   239
Phonetic Form   107
Phonetics   3
Phonology   3
Phrase Structure Rules   37
Possessive Pron   9
Pragmatic   3
Precedence   56
Predicate   136
Predicate-Argument Structure   136
Preposing   32
Present   44
Principle-And-Parameter   79
Principle Of Lexical Satisfaction   110
Principles Of Theta Role Assignment   140
Pro-Form   31
Probe   249
Projection Principle   110
Pronoun Phrase   92
Proper Binding Condition   159
Proper nouns   8
Property   11
Pseudoclefting   32

Quantifier Float   237
Quantifier Phrase   230
Quantifiers   9
Question Phrase   102

R-expressions   199
Recipient   136

Recoverability Principle   112, 295
Reduction Chain Principle   276
Reflex Feature Checking   270
Replacement Test   31, 295
Right Node Raising   33
Root node   54

Selection   27
Semantics   3
Semantics   7
Shared Coordination   33
Sister   53
Sisterhood   250
Stand-Alone Test   30, 295
Standard   5
Structure Preservation Principle   108
Subcategorization Features   255
Subjacency   164
Subject Control   216
Subject Island Constraint   165
Subject-To-Subject Raising   207
Subject-Verb Agreement   268
Subordinate Clauses   46
Substitution Test   31, 295
Suppletion   13
Surface Structure   104
Syntactic categories   7
Syntactic Frame   15
Syntactic Rules   4
Syntax   3

Tense Words   44
Terminal node   54
Thematic Relations   135
Topicalization   32
Trace   105
Trace Thoery   105
Transformational Grammar   104
Transitive   8

Unaccusative Advancement   191
Universal Grammar   71

vP-Internal Subject Hypothesis   236

Wh-questions   121

Yes/no questions   121

Printed in the United States
By Bookmasters